A DAZZLING DARKNESS

An Anthology of
Western Mysticism

Patrick Grant

GRAND RAPIDS, MICHIGAN
WILLIAM B. EERDMANS PUBLISHING COMPANY

Introductions copyright © Patrick Grant 1985
First published in Great Britain by Fount Paperbacks, London, 1985

This edition published through special arrangement with William Collins
and Sons, Ltd. by Wm. B. Eerdmans Publishing Company, 255 Jefferson S.E.,
Grand Rapids, Mich. 49503

Library of Congress Cataloging in Publication Data
Main entry under title:

A Dazzling darkness.

Bibliography: p. 345
1. Mysticism—Addresses, essays, lectures.
I. Grant, Patrick.
BL625.D35 1985   248.2'2   85-16116

ISBN 0-8028-0088-2 (pbk.)

For
Terence Grant

There is in God (some say)
A deep, but dazzling darkness

Henry Vaughan, *The Night*

Contents

Preface

The excerpts which make up this anthology are the result of twenty-five years of reading, guided by certain problems and concerns described in the Introduction. I do not intend the collection to be scholarly, and I do not quote the latest, standard editions, but those which I happen to have read, and which I value. In general, though not exclusively, I have excerpted from works by writers who are mystics first, and then authors, rather than from the works of literary artists who happen to deal with mysticism. The brief commentary between sections is meant to outline one limited approach to the mystical way, and numbers appearing in the commentary refer to excerpts within the ensuing section. I have modernized the spelling in older texts, and have occasionally altered a word in older translations to avoid unnecessary archaism or to clarify a point.

Introduction

In an early discussion of what this introduction might contain, my editor suggested that I include something about how I became involved with mysticism in the first place. The good sense of this suggestion did not strike me straight away, but was soon evident on reflection that mysticism especially is a subject which cannot be well discussed separately from a framework of belief and personal involvement. My believing *that* is of course already a judgement which colours my attitude, but I do believe it, and consequently think myself well advised to declare something further of a conviction which thus constitutes the very meaning of my subject matter.

On the personal side, my interest in Western mysticism grows directly out of my birth and upbringing in Northern Ireland, as the child of Presbyterian and Roman Catholic parents. I was educated in a government ("Protestant") school, and in two Catholic schools. In all three, religious prejudice was rife, though this would have been explicitly denied because the problem was almost helplessly beyond the control of the generally well-intentioned adults in charge, who were its victims by a kind of habituation which they had ceased to recognize.

The lessons of this early education were, and they remain, simple. I knew something was profoundly (not just obviously) wrong because I knew both sides, and through intimate knowledge crossed the borders between them. I recognized how both dealt in suspicion and hostility out of scarcely definable fear, and that the habit of fear expressed as prejudice could soon justify violence, even in God's name. Such behaviour seemed then, as it does still to much of the world, the opposite of anything "Christ" could mean. And yet, it is always easier to observe prejudice in others than to recognize it in oneself, and the heart of the matter was less in blatantly pronounced religious bigotries than in secretly harboured, intimate aggressions and in attitudes of contempt permeating a whole universe of discourse. In short, the spectacle of ordinary, generous, well-intentioned people helplessly victimized by distortions of their own anxiety, whether within families, within schools, or within communities, was at once amazing and frightening. The human roots of such fear seemed scarcely expressible, but it was almost obsessively misrepresented when forced directly into popular religious thought by one side or the other. In this predicament, institutional religion seemed not only powerless to help, but to a considerable degree made things worse.

Against such a background, I developed, while at the Queen's University of Belfast, an interest in English literature of the seventeenth century, the period of great devotional poetry in which problems of religious toleration were being wrestled out in terms very similar to those still at the heart of much sectarian conflict in Northern Ireland. The Renaissance and Reformation remained central to my academic career, and my initial interest in the development of toleration soon came to include a concern for the rise of modern science and secularism. The complex relationships between science, secularism, and religion remain central to the interpretation of mysticism in the present anthology.

But to backtrack briefly: when I began to study devotional poetry of the English Renaissance and Reformation in 1961, scholarly debate was much taken up with the fact that the poets used devotional handbooks and treatises on meditation, largely of European origin. This debate still continues, and by becoming involved in it, I found myself reading large numbers of these treatises. The main problem lay with defining a relationship between poetry and the ideas on prayer which the handbooks offered. Briefly, it seemed to me that great devotional literature provided the fullest possible verbal expression of an individual's personal experience of a religious problem. Such literature seemed always profounder, subtler, and closer to authentic human experience than the theological ideas which were its ostensible subject. Literature thus became, in a special sense, a test of the ideas, where they were exposed to their own deficiency by comparison with larger realities of love and suffering, yearning and fear. Further reflection on this kind of issue led, inevitably, to the history of toleration and the rise of a modern secular and scientific society, a series of connected issues which subsequently became the subject of a number of academic studies.

An obvious question then occurred to me. It was commonplace in literary circles to view the devotional handbooks as a background to poetry, but what was one to make of the fact that the handbooks were themselves often poetic? Admittedly, they were often dull too, but they frequently achieved the distinction of literature, and this simple recognition led to my first full-length study of mysticism, where I was interested not in how poets used mystical treatises, but how mystics deployed poetry. My conclusions are contained in *Literature of Mysticism in Western Tradition* (1983), where I suggest that Western mystics treat the spiritual life itself as a kind of poetry of religion: they demand of life addressed supernaturally to God, a creative energy, tact, judgement, beauty and form analogous to literature with its profound testing of ideas in the crucible of personal experience.

Such a consideration of mysticism as the "poetry of religion" brings me directly to the present anthology, in which I have tried to choose excerpts striking in a literary way, whether as metaphor, or as pithy saying, or as compact wisdom, contributing to a vision of the world characterized by a creatively humanizing and redeeming energy. The whole enquiry I believe thus returns to its first impulse, in the conviction that something must be wrong with a religion engendering hatred. Unless that religion can offer some vision from within itself – a vision poised at the boundaries between orthodoxy and everything orthodoxy rejects or distorts, a vision sufficiently clear, powerful and complex to counteract its own corruptions – then that religion too must be wrong. Such a vision I think I have found among the Western mystics, and I attempt here to set some of it out.

I am at last in a position to say what I think mysticism is. As I have already suggested, it is the poetry of religion, and therefore it is the creative spirit of Christianity. But in a larger sense, mysticism is an experience of God's presence beyond the boundaries of culture and language, which the mystic none the less undertakes to communicate for humanity at large. The mystics thus claim that there is a supreme Reality to which human beings can attain, and they explain the consequences of this claim and conditions for realizing the experience. They insist on non-violence, on the surrender of self-will, and on toleration. The fruits of progress in prayer, they insist, are evident in the improvement of character, and the love of one's neighbour even in adversity. They would produce through prayer a poetry of conduct calling for tact, discernment and loving attention to detail. They find anger inadmissible, and preach instead relinquishment of power over others. Their goal is by way of sanity, or personal wholeness, through faith and a mature acceptance of suffering without recrimination. Their method is prayer, their promise is vision, and their warning is that a culture which forgets its relationship to the creator, guarantor of meaning itself, is a culture governed by human self-will, the root of evil.

In a special sense, we can expect mystics of the Latin West also to address our post-scientific culture in its own terms, in so far as its immediate spiritual roots are theirs too.

Certainly, the mystics would have us know that "natural philosophy" must serve either to alleviate human suffering in God's name, or to destroy man himself to the extent that he harnesses nature's power for selfish ends. The mystics thus offer a challenge which is no matter of antiquarian or occult interest, but of certain relevance, as surely as questions of non-violence and arms control, of secularism and toleration, of suffering and prejudice are relevant. They will speak imperatively, that is, as long as children take in with their first knowledge the structures of fear and hatred with which their elders surround themselves to defend what they call their good, and which, by a travesty worse than tragic, they may even insist on calling their God.

Chapter I

Creation and Fall

This chapter deals with two large and fundamental matters: the existence of God, and the catastrophic fall of creation from its primal integrity. These ideas are part of the basic mythology of Western civilization, and by mythology I mean a set of stories which draw a boundary round a community, giving it identity and explaining its relationship to certain basic facts of experience. Cultures, it follows, always grow out of myths.

With respect to mythology, however, the mystics are almost outsiders, for they take their stand on that very boundary which the old stories draw around culture. In so doing, they remind us that the myths are, after all, just stories which must be kept open to an unutterable reality which precedes all myth-making, and from which myth-making and culture themselves derive. This ultimately real, unutterable source, we may call God.

I have said "almost outsiders" because, far from being deserters from culture, the mystics are makers of it. Their special adventures in experience beyond the boundary and towards Reality itself, they feel, must be communicated if that Reality is to be served. As Evelyn Underhill says, mystics are ambassadors to the Absolute, and to communicate its messages they need language. Characteristically, they turn to mythology to disclose their own, singular experience of an over riding truth which would otherwise remain incommunicable.

Such an interpretive, acculturizing process is at work throughout the materials selected for this chapter, dealing with the stories of creation and fall. As always in mysticism, we should detect here a distinctive empirical strain. The myths, that is, are interpreted not only towards the supremely Real beyond the boundaries of language and culture, but towards our living experiences of what is most fundamental, actual, and pressing in the human predicament.

✠

i *Creator and Creature*

Belief in God is not deemed necessary to all experiences described as mystical. This is the case, for instance, with certain aspects of Buddhism, or nature mysticism. Western mystics, however, by and large believe in one God, and the authors with whom this book deals generally interpret mystical experience in terms of self-revelation by a supreme, self-subsistent creator. And yet the very abstractness of this way of putting it indicates how problematic is theological language for dealing with mysticism. Indeed, the mystics themselves rarely offer their own special experiences as proof of God's existence. Rather, they claim that within the darkness of faith God's presence becomes our personal knowledge, and in the life of prayer such personal knowledge is pursued through obscurity, discipline and intermittent glory to the end term itself, the Originating Principle encountered in an experience of union.

The following excerpts were initially written, therefore, out of belief, and in full self-consciousness of how language falls short of experience. Yet this deficiency does not mean the statements are useless: a deaf person, after all, could be well qualified to teach music theory, and might even write original compositions. Just so, language which addresses us in our incapacity fully to know God, might still tell us something about him.

By declaring, for instance, that our names for God are inadequate (1–7), mystics indicate how the Supreme Good is beyond being, and separate from creation. Yet we also learn that God is within (8–11); the creation is good, and human beings should live in mutual respect because they are in God's image. As John of Ruysbroeck points out (16), all is not right with human nature if it affirms God's transcendence without his immanence. A totally transcendent God, we may conjecture, is remote from compassion and love, whereas a totally immanent God becomes so humanized as to breed self-centred egotism and world-denying introversion.

Closely connected to the paradox of God's transcendence and immanence is the sense of God as sustainer (12–17). Most people at one time or another have experienced the peculiar, shocking sense that they need not have come into existence at all, and that they may well be snuffed out of it at any moment. We are, as philosophers say, contingent beings. But so are all other beings: the moon, for instance, need not be there, nor Africa, nor our dog. The very peculiarity of the world in conjunction with a sense of God's creative power leads us, in short, to reflect upon his perpetually sustaining energy. The very things we take most for granted are on the edge of an abyss, for a beneficence holds them in being.

We should also notice, however, the closely allied but less startling intuition that all creation contains traces of its maker (18–21). During the Middle Ages, spiritual writers – such as St Bonaventure – described God's creative patterning with a good deal of fanciful confidence, but the sense is perennial that nature's beauty and complexity betoken a wonderful, designing intelligence. Indeed, one privilege of human reason is to detect the forms of the creator's handiwork, whereby we are led through a multitude of fugitive glories towards the originating source (22–30).

The world we live in none the less is cruelly imperfect, and in so far as it is evil we must struggle against it. We should not romanticize nature's beauty (31–35), even though we are to stop short of concluding that God creates evil (36–41). We thus return to a radical obscurity of faith, that, despite incomprehensible suffering in the world, there is a good God. The mystics tend not to argue this, but assert simply that they know the answer. God is good, and he is the supreme Reality which they have come to know directly.

The spiritual writers therefore leave us with a series of paradoxes which must be held in suspension, perhaps as much to confound our simplicities as to urge on our adventure beyond the categories of myth, culture and language. God is separate from his creation, and present within it; we may discover him in his creatures but should not dwell upon the creatures, for they are imperfect; he allows evil, but he did not create it. And if such opposites are not simultaneously true, it seems that the integrity of mystical experience itself is jeopardized, for the mystics themselves assure us that human beings become less holy – less whole – in reverencing a God who cannot be validly experienced at least in these ways.

1. Some are atheists by neglect, others are so by affectation; they that think there is no God at some times, do not think so at all times.

    Benjamin Whichcote (1609–83),
    Select Aphorisms, 1

2. Nor is he virtue, nor light, nor he liveth, nor he is life, nor he is substance, nor age, nor time, nor there is any understandable touching of him, nor he is knowledge, nor truth, nor kingdom, nor wisdom, nor one, nor unity, nor Godhead or goodness; nor is he spirit, as we understand spirit; nor sonhood, nor fatherhood, nor any other

thing known by us or by any that be; nor he is anything of not-being things, nor anything of being things; nor any of those things that be, know him as he is, nor he knoweth those things that be as they be in themselves, but as they be in him.

Denis Hid Divinity (late 14th Century), Ch. 5

3. But nothing true can be spoken of God, because there is nothing above him. That the soul expresses God does not in anywise affect his real intrinsic being: no one can express what he actually is. Sometimes we say one thing is like another. We can say nothing of God because nothing is like him. Creatures enclose a mere nothing of God wherefore they cannot disclose him. The painter who has painted a good portrait therein shows his art: it is not himself that it reveals to us. Creatures can no more give out God than they can take in exactly what he is.

Meister Eckhart (1260–1327),
Sermons and Collations, XXXII

4. The things which are in part can be apprehended, known, and expressed; but the Perfect cannot be apprehended, known, or expressed by any creature as creature. Therefore we do not give a name to the Perfect, for it is none of these. The creature as creature cannot know nor apprehend it, name nor conceive it.

Theologia Germanica (c. 1350), Ch. I

5. Is it not true that I always retain in My hand a greater power than I bestow upon My creatures? Hast thou not seen how the sun by the power of its heat draws out the spots and stains from the white linen that it bleaches, and makes it whiter than it was before? How much more can I, the creator of the sun, keep in stainless whiteness

the soul upon whom I have had mercy, pouring forth upon it the warmth of My burning love?

> Nun Gertrude (?–1291),
> *Insinuationes divinae pietatis*, p. 146

6. And thus I saw that God rejoiceth that he is our Father, and God rejoiceth that he is our Mother, and God rejoiceth that he is our very spouse and our soul is his loved wife.

> Julian of Norwich (c. 1342–1420),
> *Revelations of Divine Love*, Ch. LII

7. God, almighty, is our nature's Father; and God, all-wisdom, is our nature's Mother; with the love and the goodness of the Holy Ghost: which is all one God, one Lord. And in the knitting and the oneing he is our very, true spouse, and we his loved wife, his fair maiden: with which wife he is never displeased. For he saith: I love thee and thou lovest me, and our love shall never be disparted in two.

> Julian of Norwich (c. 1342–1420),
> *Revelations of Divine Love*, Ch. LVIII

8. When God made man the innermost heart of the Godhead was put into man.

> Meister Eckhart (1260–1327),
> *Sayings*, 61

9. There is one power in the soul and that not merely power but being; and not merely being: it radiates life, and is so pure, so high and so innately noble that creatures cannot live in it; none but God can abide therein. Nay, even God himself is forbidden there so far as he is subject to condition. God cannot enter there in any guise: God is only there in his absolute divinity.

> Meister Eckhart (1260–1327),
> *Sermons and Collations*, LXXX

10. For Thou, most high, and most near; most secret, and most present; who hast not limbs some larger, some smaller, but art wholly every where, and no where in space, art not of such corporeal shape, yet hast Thou made man after Thine own image; and behold, from head to foot is he contained in space.

> Augustine of Hippo (345–430),
> *Confessions*, VI, 4

11. But if thou in the Spirit breakest through the death of the flesh, then thou seest the hidden God. For as the marrow in the bones penetrates, presses or breaks through, and gives virtue, power and strength to the flesh, and yet the flesh cannot comprehend or apprehend the marrow, but only the power and virtue thereof, no more canst thou see the hidden deity in thy flesh, but thou receivest its power, and understandest therein that God dwells in thee.

> Jacob Boehme (1575–1624),
> *Aurora*, "Of the Third Day", Ch. 21

12. He it is who gave you being, and who still continues the same to you. So that you depend now as much upon his power for the preserving of it, as you did before he gave it you.

> Luis de Granada (1504–88),
> *The Sinners Guide*, Book I, Part I, Ch. III

13. God everywhere beholds thee, and perfectly knows thy most secret inclinations and affections. He is so present to thee, he is so within thee, that without him thou canst not even move a finger.

> Louis de Blois (1506–65),
> *The Rule of the Spiritual Life*, Ch. XXIII

14. "O Love," said the Lover, "has the Beloved operation in the world?" "O Lover," answered Love, "if the Beloved

had not operation in the world, then could the world no longer sustain itself, but would return to nothingness; for even as through the action of the Beloved the world has come into being, even so, through his action, is it sustained in being."

Ramon Lull (c. 1232–1315),
The Tree of Love, Part III, Ch. III, 10

15. Can a creature be happy without God, who cannot *be* at all, without him?

Benjamin Whichcote (1609–83),
Select Aphorisms, 174

16. Though I have said before that we are one with God, and this is taught us by Holy Writ, yet now I will say that we must eternally remain other than God, and distinct from him, and this too is taught us by Holy Writ. And we must understand and feel both within us, if all is to be right with us.

John of Ruysbroeck (1293–1381),
The Sparkling Stone, Ch. X

17. We must beg God constantly in our prayers to uphold us by his hand; we should keep ever in our minds the truth that if he leaves us, most certainly we shall fall at once into the abyss, for we must never be so foolish as to trust in ourselves.

Teresa of Avila (1515–82),
The Interior Castle, Fifth Mansions, Ch. IV, 8

18. For the whole universe is, as it were, a book written by the finger of God, in which each creature forms a letter. But as one who has not learnt to read, when he looks into an open book, sees indeed the characters of the letters, but understands not their significance and force; in like manner, he who perceives not the things of God,

beholds the external aspect of creatures, but comprehends not their interior meaning.

Louis de Blois (1506–65),
The Rule of the Spiritual Life, Ch. XXVIII

19. If thy heart were right, then every creature would be a mirror of life and a book of holy doctrine. There is no creature so small and abject but it reflects the goodness of God.

Thomas à Kempis (c. 1379–1471),
Of the Imitation of Christ, Book II, Ch. IV

20. Dost thou now see this sun, O My spouse, these stars, this sky, this earth, these rocks? they are so many ways and roads to find Me; they did not make themselves; they are not without some principle which made them, and which is their last end, which preserves them, which guards them. And who is this principle and this end? It is God: the mothers of all things are the ideas which are in Me, in My power and goodness.

François de Sales (1567–1622),
Mystical Explanation of the Canticles, Discourse I

21. Perhaps we may not be philosophically acquainted with the relation which subsists between created things and their creator; yet we may easily find every creature pointing up to that Being whose image and super-scription it bears; and thus viewing the "invisible things of God, in the things that are made", may find God secretly flowing into our souls, and gently heading us from the outer court of the temple into the Holy of Holies.

John Smith (1618–52),
Select Discourses, VII

22. And herein lies the fruit, effect, and end of all things,

namely, that the soul may be led back to its own first original principle, which is God himself.

> Gerlac Petersen (1378–1411),
> *The Fiery Soliloquy with God*, Ch. V

23. True religion derives its pedigree from heaven; it descends from thence, and tends thither again. God is the first truth, the primitive goodness; and true religion is a vigorous efflux and emanation of this truth and goodness on the hearts of men, and therefore those who possess it, are called "partakers of the Divine nature".

> John Smith (1618–52),
> *Select Discourses*, VII

24. Religion is life and spirit, flowing from the living and life-giving God, and returning upwards to him from whom it came.

> John Smith (1618–52),
> *Select Discourses*, VII

25. And in all the other books our description descended from the highest things to the lowest; and, according to the quantity of descending, it spread out to a great multitude. But now it ascendeth in this book from the lowest things to the highest; and according to the measure of the ascension – the which is sometime suddener than other – it is made strait. And after all such ascension it shall be without voice, and all shall be knitted to a thing that is unspeakable.

> *Denis Hid Divinity* (late 14th Century), Ch. 3

26. Refer therefore all things to Me as their author: for I am He who gave them all. Think of them one by one as flowing from the highest good: and therefore unto Me as their source must all be traced.

> Thomas à Kempis (c. 1379–1471),
> *Of the Imitation of Christ*, Book IV, Ch. IX

27. A constant return to thy origin means, that the presence of all things, in which thou canst not find God, will seem like a wound to thee.

John Tauler (c. 1300–61),
The Inner Way, Sermon XIII

28. From the Father of Lights there goes forth and spreads through all creation a bright and spiritual light, recalling all things to itself, so far as their several natures permit; that everything may be established in its own order and degree, and, according to the capacity of its nature, may be perfected in God. That light is one and entirely the same through all things, not changed by the change of objects, but rather, so far as is possible, drawing what is various and diverse to a likeness and unity with itself.

Dean Colet on Dionysius the Areopagite (c. 500),
The Celestial Hierarchy, Ch. I

29. Everything in the Godhead is one, and of that there is nothing to be said. God works, the Godhead does no work, there is nothing to do; in it is no activity. It never envisaged any work. God and Godhead are as different as active and inactive. On my return to God, where I am formless, my breaking through will be far nobler than my emanation. I alone take all creatures out of their sense into my mind and make them one in me. When I go back into the ground, into the depths, into the well-spring of the Godhead, no one will ask me whence I came or whither I went. No one missed me: God passes away.

Meister Eckhart (1260–1327),
Sermons and Collations, LVI

30. I love because I love, and I love for the sake of loving. A great thing, my brethren, is love, if yet it returns to its Principle, if it is restored to its Origin, if it finds its way

back again to its Fountain-Head, so that it may be thus
enabled to continue flowing with an unfailing current.
Amongst all the emotions, sentiments, and feelings of the
soul, love stands distinguished in this respect, that in the
case of it alone has the creature the power to correspond
and to make a return to the Creator in kind, though not
in equality.

> Bernard of Clairvaux (1090–1153),
> *Sermons*, LXXXIII

31. Grant that all creatures may be of no esteem in my eyes,
    and be Thou alone the charm of my heart.

> Gertrude the Great (1256–1301),
> *Select Devotions on the Passion*, IX

32. The world is full of untruth, falsehood, and inconstancy;
    when profit is at an end, friendship is at an end, and to speak
    shortly, neither true love, nor entire joy, nor constant peace
    of mind, was ever obtained by any heart from creatures.

> Henry Suso (c. 1295–1366),
> *The Little Book of Eternal Wisdom*, Ch. VI

33. Thus likewise all knowledge of the parts is swallowed up
    when the whole is known; and where that Good is
    known, it cannot but be longed for and loved so greatly,
    that all other love wherewith the man hath loved himself
    and other things, fadeth away. And that inward sight
    likewise perceiveth what is best and noblest in all things,
    and loveth it in the one true Good, and only for the sake
    of that true Good.

> *Theologia Germanica* (c. 1350), Ch. XVIII

34. For in what measure we put off the creature, in the same
    measure are we able to put on the Creator; neither more
    nor less.

> *Theologia Germanica* (c. 1350), Ch. I

35. If thou wilt be like all things, thou must forsake all things; thou must turn thy desire away from them all, and not desire or hanker after any of them; thou must not extend thy will to possess that for thy own, or as thine own, which is something, whatsoever that something be. For as soon as ever thou takest something into thy desire, and receivest it into thee for thine own, or in propriety, then this very something (of what nature soever it is) is the same with thyself; and this worketh with thee in thy will, and thou art thence bound to protect it, and to take care of it, even as of thy own being. But if thou dost receive no thing into thy desire, then thou art free from all things, and rulest over all things at once, as a prince of God.

> Jacob Boehme (1575–1624),
> *The Way to Christ*, "Of the Supersensual Life"

36. God forbid that we should admit that God has created anything which is substantially evil, as Scripture says "everything that God had made was very good". For if they were created by God such as they are now, or made for this purpose; viz., to occupy these positions of malice, and ever to be ready for the deception and ruin of men, we should in opposition to the view of the above quoted Scripture slander God as the creator and author of evil.

> John Cassian (c. 360–434),
> *Second Conference of Abbot Serenus*, Ch. VI

37. How worthy is it of admiration that God should have created out of nothing the heavens, and the earth, and all that they contain; and that he is able to create more, since he is an infinite ocean of substance! He made all things (sin alone he did not make; and, indeed, sin ought not to be called a created substance); he also preserves all things. For, if he did not by his power preserve what he

has created, all things would instantly return to nothingness; because, in themselves, they are nothing, and depend entirely on God, by whom they were made.

Louis de Blois (1506–65),
The Rule of the Spiritual Life, Ch. XXVIII

38. Consider only the fates which overtake the little children. Human suffering is so great, so endless, so awful that I can hardly write of it. I could not go into hospitals and face it, as some do, lest my mind should be temporarily overcome. The whole and the worst the worst pessimist can say is far beneath the least particle of the truth, so immense is the misery of man. It is the duty of all rational beings to acknowledge the truth. There is not the least trace of directing intelligence in human affairs. This is a foundation of hope, because, if the present condition of things were ordered by a superior power, there would be no possibility of improving it for the better in the spite of that power.

Richard Jefferies (1848–87),
The Story of My Heart, Ch. IX

39. We find ourselves incapable of thinking any otherwise of God, than as the one only Good, or as you express it, an eternal immutable Will to all Goodness, which can will nothing else to all eternity, but to communicate good, and blessing, and happiness, and perfection to every life, according to its capacity to receive it.

William Law (1686–1761),
The Spirit of Love, p. 38

40. And he is in himself not so much good, as that essential good by which anything is good which is in any way good. In relation to all his creation he is the supreme good, and is so very good that nothing better can be

thought of; and he is the source of well-being for whatever is prosperous.

William of St Thierry (c. 1085–1148),
The Enigma of Faith, 52

41. O ever blooming, ever refulgent beauty of the majesty
above, thou brightest beam of everlasting light, thou life
by whose genial influence every living creature lives;
thou light from whose reflection every thing shines, and
by the communication of whose rays it is, that thousands
of millions of thousands of glorious spirits preserve the
resplendent brightness shed by thee upon them, and all
the glittering hosts of heaven stand round about the
throne of thy glory, ever since time was. O eternal and
everlasting, O pure and clear stream, issuing from that
fountain which no human eyes can discover; a fountain
without any first rise, a current without any bottom,
whose waters no banks circumscribe, no soil pollutes or
troubles. The mind of the most high God produced thee
out of the unfathomable depth of his own infinite
capacity.

Anselm (1033–1109),
Meditations, Ch. XIX

ii *The Fall and its Limits*

We have seen that the God whom mystics affirm by faith and
encounter in experience does not create evil. But the world is
full of evil: no fact could be plainer, and none more urgently
needs our attention.

As a means of approaching this problem, Christian
theology has traditionally looked to the ancient stories of
angelic rebellion and the fall of man from paradise. Yet these
stories and the theology which develops from them do not

give a satisfactory explanation of, say, mass famine, or cholera, or death by drowning. Part of the problem of original sin perhaps is that no explanation can save us from suffering its consequences, one of which is our lack of a fully satisfactory explanation.

For the mystics, however, the roots of incomprehensible evil to which the old stories point can be reduced quite simply to self-will, the creature's pride in appropriating creation for his own glory. This theory does not make us any more content with meningitis or famine, but it does offer one, searing imperative on how we ought to address our fallen predicament now that we are in it. Self-will, that is, constitutes the fundamental obstacle between ourselves and God, and when we battle self-will, we are battling the foundations of evil itself. Otherwise, we perpetuate the original sin of pride in every act of our misdirected love, from which enmity and wrath, separation and fear are the natural, inevitable results (1–8). Further, because we suffer essentially by separation, we are plunged by original sin into the material world itself in so far as it is inert and multiple, the condition of our dissolution and death. Though originally good, matter has become a circumstance and result of our alienation from God (9–16).

None the less, the fact remains that even the most exemplary human selflessness does not free us from the negative aspects of matter, such as death and the liabilities of the body: it does not prevent even the common cold, let alone an earthquake. Consequently, in accord with tradition, mystics allow themselves the participants in a primal catastrophe beyond time and name, of which mythology provides hints in the story of the fallen angels.

The myths therefore do not so much explain evil as indicate for the mystics how we might struggle against it (17–19). Victory would consist, ultimately, in redeeming matter itself, which would be experienced once more as energy, active in the service of God. In this context we might reflect on the striking modern advances of science towards rediscovering matter as energy, advances which may be interpreted in mystical language as redemptive. But the balance is precarious, for the mystics remind us that the first child of pride is wrath. And in so far as the power of science is deployed selfishly, it will be released as wrath, not redemptive love (21–25).

The old story of Adam and Eve (26–31) directs us to such truths in so far as it also shows the closely-forged links between self-will, fear, hatred and alienation. When we participate in redemption, the mystics tell us, we strike not only at the roots of our own hatred and alienation, but, in however small a way, at the roots of all such suffering.

1. Now that which first produced a divorce between God and his creation was that diabolical arrogancy and self-will which crept and wound itself, serpent-like, into the human mind. The greatest excellency of religion appears in its power to subdue this impetuous enemy. Then does religion perform its greatest conquests; then does it display its greatest strength, when it overcomes this domineering tyrant, which is so firmly seated in the centre of the soul.

John Smith (1618–52),
Select Discourses, VII

2. As all things are God's, so all things are to be used and regarded as the things of God. For men to abuse things on earth, and live to themselves, is the same rebellion against God, as for angels to abuse things in heaven; because God is just the same Lord of all on earth, as he is the Lord of all in heaven.

William Law (1686–1761),
A Serious Call, Ch. IV

3. Certain it is that pride can only exist in those who do possess something, or who believe themselves to have something. For this reason, because they did believe themselves to be possessed of something, came the pride and the fall of the first man and the angel; neither the angel nor the man did possess anything in themselves of themselves, for God alone hath this, and humility is found alone in those who are poor and who are persuaded that they do possess nothing.

Angela of Foligno (c. 1248–1309),
The Divine Consolation, Ch. II

4. It hath been said, that there is of nothing so much in hell as of self-will. The which is true, for there is nothing else there than self-will, and if there were no self-will there would be no Devil and no hell. When it is said that Lucifer fell from heaven, and turned away from God and the like, it meaneth nothing else than that he would have his own will.

Theologia Germanica (c. 1350), Ch. XLIX

5. The powers of darkness are the workings of nature or self: for nature, darkness, and self, are but three different expressions for one and the same thing.

William Law (1686–1761),
The Spirit of Love, Third Dialogue

6. This weakness I understand causeth fear: for where self-love is, there is always fear.

Juan de Valdes (1490–1541),
The Divine Considerations, LXXVIII

7. In the estate of innocency the love of man seemed nothing but the beams of love reverted upon another, for they loved no person but of whom he was beloved. All that he loved was good, and nothing evil. His love

seemed the goodness of a being expressed in the soul, or apprehended in the lover, and returned upon itself. But in the estate of misery (or rather grace) a soul loves freely and purely of its own self, with God's love, things that seem uncapable of love, naught and evil.

Thomas Traherne (c. 1636–74),
Centuries of Meditation, IV, 87

8. For one eats of the tree of knowledge of good who appropriates to himself his own will and prides himself upon the goods which the Lord publishes and works in him.

Francis of Assisi (1182–1226),
Admonitions, 2

9. Sin, that brought in sorrow and death, which could no way be cured but as the fountain of love opened itself in that spark of God which was yet left alive in him [mankind], springing up with oily healing, coagulating with that fire-life that did lie as smothered under the earthly part. Which, through a warm breathing thereupon from the tri-une being, gave a new existency to a divine and spiritual life, which gradually put forth into every part appertaining to the soul, with its bodily members, which is the true and full regeneration that perfecteth and bringeth forth the new creation, so that the mortality sinks away into its own abyss, from whence by the serpent's guile it was stirred up and awakened.

Jane Lead (1623–1704),
The Ascent to the Mount of Vision, XLIII

10. Sin, by its deadly infusion into the soul, wastes and eats out its innate vigour, and casts it into so deep a lethargy that it cannot recover itself.

John Smith (1618–52),
Select Discourses, VII

11. When man sinned, he went astray, rejecting the most mighty, wise, and benevolent Principle. As a result, he fell headlong into weakness, ignorance, and malice. From having been spiritual, he became carnal, animal, and sensual. He could no longer imitate divine power, behold divine light, or love divine goodness. The most perfect way for man to be raised out of this misery was for the first Principle to come down to man's level, offering Himself to him as an accessible object of knowledge, love, and imitation.

Bonaventure (1221–74),
The Breviloquium, IV, 1, 3

12. In fine, good cometh from the one universal cause; and evil from many partial deficiencies. God knows evil under the form of good, and with him the causes of evil things are faculties productive of good.

Dionysius the Areopagite (c. 500),
The Divine Names, Ch. IV, 30

13. But as you have justly removed all controversy about doctrines from the merits of the cause, and shown that it all lies in this one short, plain, and decisive point, namely the Fall of Man; a Fall proved and demonstrated to all my senses and reason, by every height and depth of nature, by every kind of misery, evil, and sin in the world, by everything we know of God, ourselves, and the world we live in; the ground and foundation of Christianity is undeniable, and no one can be too speedy a convert to the belief of it.

William Law (1686–1761),
The Way to Divine Knowledge

14. Without you, without your onslaughts, without your uprootings of us, we should remain all our lives inert, stagnant, puerile, ignorant both of ourselves and of God.

You who batter us and then dress our wounds, you who resist us and yield to us, you who wreck and build, you who shackle and liberate, the sap of our souls, the hand of God, the flesh of Christ: it is you, matter, that I bless.

Pierre Teilhard de Chardin (1881–1955),
Hymn of the Universe, "Hymn to Matter"

15. There is a latent principle of energy in the soul, which then begins to discover itself when the divine spirit sheds forth his influences upon it. Every thing, the more spiritual it is, the more active and energetic it is; so also, the more any thing sinks into matter, the more sluggish and unwieldy it becomes.

John Smith (1618–52),
Select Discourses, VII

16. God laid no foundation of wickedness in the principles of his creation: it is an unnatural superstructure of our own, without a foundation.

Benjamin Whichcote (1609–83),
Select Aphorisms, 153

17. There is no man that is altogether safe from temptations whilst he lives; for in ourselves is the root thereof, since we were born in concupiscence. As one temptation or tribulation goes away another comes in its place; and we shall ever have something to suffer, because we have lost the blessing of our felicity.

Thomas à Kempis (c. 1379–1471),
Of the Imitation of Christ, Book I, Ch. XIII

18. I say not that thou mayest here living recover so whole nor so perfect cleanness and innocence, knowing and loving of God, as thou haddest first, nor as thou shalt have; nor that thou mayest escape all the wretchedness and

pains of sin; nor that thou, living in deadly flesh, mayest destroy and quench all wholly the false vain love in thyself, nor flee all venial sins so that they will not – unless they be stopped by great fervour of charity – spring out of thine heart as water doth from a stinking well. But I would that, if thou mayest not fully quench it, thou mayest somewhat slake it and come to the cleanness of soul as near as thou mayest.

Walter Hilton (1300–96),
The Scale of Perfection, Book I, Ch. XLVI

19. The man said: "O Beloved, I am surprised that the evil spirit dares to go among these great men who live on the ninth rock." The *answer* came: "Do not be surprised; God himself was tempted by the evil spirit. The evil spirit is afraid of the men who have looked in the origin, and therefore he does all he can to trap them." The man said: "O Beloved, I see now that no one may assume he is free from the evil spirit." The *answer* came: "That is true; as long as soul and body are together he does not give up."

Rulman Merswin (c. 1307–82),
The Book of the Nine Rocks,
Discourse concerning the Ninth Rock

20. The Love that brought forth the existence of all things, changes not through the Fall of its creatures, but is continually at work, to bring back all fallen nature and creature to their first state of goodness. All that passes for a time between God and his fallen creature, is but one and the same thing, working for one and the same end; and though this is called wrath, that called punishment, curse, and death, it is all from the beginning to the end, nothing but the work of the first creating Love, and means nothing else, does nothing else, but those works of purifying fire, which must, and alone can burn away

all that dark evil, which separates the creature from its first created union with God.

William Law (1686–1761),
Address to the Clergy

21. For when Lucifer with his hateful and odious envy could not fill his pride and covetousness, then he kindled the wrath-fire in himself, and roared therewith into God's nature, as a fierce lion, and from whence then arose the wrath of God and all evil.

Jacob Boehme (1575–1624),
Aurora, Ch. 16

22. For when Adam and Eve were eating the fruit, evil and good, into the body, then the imagination of the body received vanity in the fruit, and then vanity awaked in the flesh, and the dark world got the upper hand and dominion in the vanity of the earthliness; upon which the fair image of heaven, that proceeded out of the heavenly divine world, instantly disappeared.

Here Adam and Eve died to the kingdom of heaven, and awaked to the outward world, and then the fair soul as it stood in the love of God, disappeared as to the holy power, virtue, and property; and instead thereof, the wrathful anger, viz. the dark fire world awoke in it, and so the soul became in one part, viz. in the inward nature, a half devil, and in the outward part as related to the outward world, a beast.

Jacob Boehme (1575–1624),
The Way to Christ, III "Of Regeneration", Ch. 2

23. O beautiful love, I have broken my faith with thee in my father Adam, and with my fiery strength have turned myself to the pleasure and vanity of the outward world. I have fallen in love with a stranger, and had been constrained to walk in the valley of darkness in this strange

love, if thou hadst not come into the house of my misery, in thy great faithfulness, by thy piercing through and destroying God's anger, hell, and dark death, and restored thy meekness and love to my fiery life.

> Jacob Boehme (1575–1624),
> *The Way to Christ*, I "Of True Repentance", II

24. This, I presume, is enough to show you, that the Atonement made by Christ is itself the greatest of all proofs, that it was not to atone or extinguish any wrath in the Deity itself; nor, indeed, any way to affect or alter any quality, or temper in the Divine Mind, but purely and solely to overcome and remove all that death and hell, and wrath, and darkness, that had opened itself in the nature, birth, and life of fallen man.

> William Law (1686–1761),
> *The Spirit of Love*, Second Dialogue

25. I said the serpents of covetousness, envy, pride, and wrath, because they are alone the real, dreadful, original serpents; and all earthly serpents are but transitory, partial, and weak out-births of them. All evil earthly beasts, are but short-lived images, or creaturely eruptions of that hellish disorder, that is broken out from the fallen spiritual world; and by their manifold variety, they show us that multiplicity of evil, that lies in the womb of that abyss of dark rage, which (N.B.) has no maker, but the three first properties of nature, fallen from God, and working in their own darkness.

> William Law (1686–1761),
> *The Spirit of Love*, Third Dialogue

26. For whenever we speak of the Adam, and disobedience, and of the old man, of self-seeking, self-will, and self-serving, of the I, the Me, and the Mine, nature, falsehood, the Devil, sin; it is all one and the same thing.

These are all contrary to God, and remain without God.
Theologia Germanica (c. 1350), Ch. XLIII

27. It is said, it was because Adam ate the apple that he was
lost, or fell. I say, it was because of his claiming something for his own, and because of his I, Mine, Me, and
the like. Had he eaten seven apples, and yet never
claimed anything for his own, he would not have fallen.
Theologia Germanica (c. 1350), Ch. III

28. The air is better, being a living miracle as it now is, than
if it were crammed and filled with crowns and sceptres.
The mountains are better than solid diamonds, and those
things which scarcity maketh jewels (when you enjoy
these) are yours in their places. Why should you not
render thanks to God for them all? You are the Adam, or
the Eve that enjoy them. Why should you not exult and
triumph in his love who hath done so great things for
you? Why should you not rejoice and sing his praises?
Learn to enjoy what you have first, and covet more if
you can afterwards.
Thomas Traherne (c. 1636–74),
Centuries of Meditation, II, 12

29. It may be that vice, depravity, and crime are nearly
always, or even perhaps always, in their essence,
attempts to eat beauty, to eat what we should only look
at. Eve began it. If she caused humanity to be lost by
eating the fruit, the opposite attitude, looking at the fruit
without eating it, should be what is required to save it.
"Two winged companions," says an Upanishad, "two
birds are on the branch of a tree. One eats the fruit, the
other looks at it." These two birds are the two parts of
our soul.
Simone Weil (1909–43),
Waiting on God, "Forms of the Implicit Love of God"

30. This fall of the rebellious angels caused a great void in the celestial choir, and God, not being willing to create other angels, appointed to their places other creatures. For this purpose he created man, and gave him a body and soul to the end that he might, if he chose, one day attain to the eminent dignity of which the rebel angels had rendered themselves unworthy.

Bridget of Sweden (1303–73),
Select Revelations, Ch. IV

31. There followed, as we know, the chosen catastrophe which we call the Fall. Whether in that state in which mankind was, the Fall was a single act of a single soul, or the simultaneous act of all souls, this is not the place to discuss. It is, I suppose, possible (since it is to be believed that every human creature sins) that in some way every human nature sinned at once; that the whole web was at once and everywhere ruined. That is irrelevant to the fact that, however it happened, it certainly happened. The will of man sinned. But the will of man was a spiritual quality; it was in his soul. It was that power in him which we call the soul that sinned. It was not the power which we call the flesh. It was therefore the "supernatural" which sinned. The "natural", as we now call it, did not. They cannot, of course, be separated. But if, in terminology, they can be, then it is the matter of our substance which has remained faithful, and the immaterial which has not.

Charles Williams (1886–1945),
The Image of the City, "Natural Goodness"

iii *Spiritual Hierarchies*

The Fall of Man, as we now see, is a myth constructed to account for evil, and its theory has two poles. On the one hand, original sin is rooted in self-will; on the other, the reality and implications of natural evil are so incomprehensible and overwhelming that they seem to indicate some primal catastrophe beyond the bounds of our world. One way of approaching this disaster is through the story of the rebellious angels, with Lucifer at their head.

Angels are pure spirits, and we infer their existence partly on the grounds that, just as the beasts are below us in intelligence, so it is feasible that created beings are above us. This conclusion is by way of rational inference, but the heart also has its reasons, and, in this sense, angels are celestial powers answering our intuition that the universe is alive with intelligent organization, that it is cared for, that it has laws, and is a startlingly various, beautiful, terrible orchestration of directed energies. When we consider angels in this way, we are clearly open to the accusation of projecting our own desire for order upon the creation at large: angels, it may be argued, are figments of imagination. And so they are if we venture too far in the direction of concreteness. The issue must, rather, be left poised between a conviction that God is our transcendent creator, and that he is immanent in creation. As we shall see (VI, i), the doctrine of the Trinity especially safeguards this divine mystery, and in so far as men are created in God's image, they reflect the Trinitarian mystery. Analogously, there is a tradition – stemming largely from Dionysius the Areopagite – describing the angels also in terms of threefold hierarchies (1–7).

For the mystics, however, speculation on the existence of angelic hierarchies is less significant than the question of angelic knowledge. As human beings, we express ourselves discursively, laboriously, and indirectly, because our knowledge must proceed through the use of spatial images and sequences of words structured in time. But being free of our kind of material embodiment, the angels know by direct intuition. Among the scholastic philosophers – for instance, Thomas Aquinas – discussion of angelic knowledge by direct intuition becomes in fact a discussion of contemplation (see further, V, i), which the mystics claim to experience when they know in a purely spiritual manner (8–17).

Still, we are not angels and should not aspire to be, for human beings are created with special privileges. Only humans born into a material world can shape it through imagination and through love which requires physical separation as its opportunity. Only human beings can die, and in a sense this is also their privilege, for they are thereby free to discover experientially a love which defeats death. As Jacob Boehme says (24), man sees deeper than the angels (18–24).

Finally, angels act as God's messengers, which is their main biblical function (25–29). The reassurance that a multitude of intelligences is at work to assist mankind in a universe which appears vastly empty, suggests that the world is not altogether unfriendly. None the less, such spiritual powers are also in contention with one another, for the war in heaven does not cease until earth is redeemed.

1. None of the faithful question the fact that before the formation of this visible creation God made spiritual and celestial powers, in order that owing to the very fact that they knew that they had been formed out of nothing by the goodness of the creator for such glory and bliss, they might render to him continual thanks and ceaselessly continue to praise him.

John Cassian (c. 360–434),
Conference of Abbot Theodore, Ch. VII

2. Now, there are nine choirs of Angels, forming three hierarchies, in each of which there are three choirs. Now, these three hierarchies have each their own peculiar and different effect on the three parts of man. The first is the outer man, the second is his reason, and the third is his likeness to God: and yet all these three form one man. In all three the Angels have their work to do.

John Tauler (c. 1300–61),
The Inner Way, Sermon XXIV

3. God, who is One and Three, has arranged threefold hierarchies among the blessed Spirits, after the pattern of the order in his own being; and these are called by Dionysius at one time Functions, at another Distinctions, and at another, Hierarchies. God, who is the founder of all things and of every order, alone of a surety knows all things exactly; and he made known by his angels to the prophets (whom Dionysius also rightly calls Divine Teachers, since he is rightly and truly a divine teacher who speaks out what is revealed by God); – he made known to them in some measure, I say, what they in turn, so far as was allowed them, committed to writing.

Dean Colet on Dionysius the Areopagite (c. 500),
The Celestial Hierarchy, Ch. VI

4. Correspondingly, there is a threefold distinction between the highest hierarchies of heaven: that is, the Thrones, Cherubim, and Seraphim. Whoever wishes to attain beatitude through his merits must therefore conform himself to these three, as closely as is possible in this state of wayfaring, in order to obtain the tranquillity of peace, the splendour of truth, and the sweetness of love. For in these three the Lord Himself reposes, dwelling as in His own abode.

Bonaventure (1221–74),
The Triple Way, Ch. III, 1

5. The air, the sunlight, the night, all that surrounds me seems crowded with inexpressible powers, with the influence of Souls, or existences, so that I walk in the midst of immortal things. I myself am a living witness of it.

> Richard Jefferies (1848–87),
> *The Story of My Heart*, Ch. III

6. The angelical kingdoms are throughout formed according to the divine being, and they have no other form or condition than the divine being has in its Trinity. Only this is the difference; that their bodies are creatures, which have a beginning and end, and that the kingdom where their locality, habitation or court is, is not their corporeal propriety, or proper own, having it for their natural right, as they have their bodies for a natural right.

> Jacob Boehme (1575–1624), *Aurora*, Ch. 8

7. I believe and understand the ministration of angels, as clerks tell us: but it was not shewed me. For Himself is nearest and meekest, highest and lowest, and doeth all. And not only all that we need, but also He doeth all that is worshipful, to our joy in heaven.

> Julian of Norwich (c. 1342–1420),
> *Revelations of Divine Love*, Ch. LXXX

8. This is properly the exercise of angels: for their knowledge is not by discourse, but by one simple intuition all objects are represented to their view at once, with all their natures, qualities, relations, dependences and effects. But man that receives all his knowledge first from his senses, can only by effects and outward appearances with the labour of reasoning collect the nature of objects, and this but imperfectly. But his reasoning being ended, then he can at once contemplate all that is known to him in the object.

> Augustine Baker (1575–1641),
> *Sancta Sophia*, Treat. 3, Sec. 4, Ch. 1, Part 7

9. Now in holy scripture our chiefest happiness and perfection is said to consist in this, that we shall be like unto angels both in our knowledge and love, for we shall (as they) have a perfect view and contemplation of God as he is, not by any created forms and representations.

Augustine Baker (1575–1641),
Sancta Sophia, Treat. 3, Sec. 4, Ch. 1, Part 8

10. Those writers also use very largely the excellent nature of man, because this is most akin to us; and thus, by borrowing similitudes from all its parts, they make angels as it were men. Moreover, by means of many other objects of various kinds, such as are familiar to us, they signify to men the natures, powers, actions, properties, likeness, difference, simplicity, firmness, steadfastness, strength, obedience, order, beauty, light, wisdom, pleasantness, beneficence, vigour, swiftness, subtlety, freedom, chieftancy, potency, authority, equity, government, fertility, fruitfulness, quickening, sanctity, religion, worship of God, happiness, blessedness, reign, abundance, plenty, riches, glory, the contemplation, in fine, and the joy, of those blessed spirits. These objects of sense and metaphors were sought on all sides and from every quarter by the ancient divines, those great prophets, with wonderful sagacity and love; that by this way and method they might both teach feeble men what are the things of God, and might preserve the dignity of things divine.

Dean Colet on Dionysius the Areopagite (c. 500),
The Celestial Hierarchy, Ch. XV

11. If I had the tongue of an angel, and thou hadst an angelical understanding, we might very finely discourse of it. But the spirit only sees it, and the tongue cannot advance towards it. For I can use no other words than

the words of this world; but now the Holy Ghost being
in thee, thy soul will well apprehend it.

> Jacob Boehme (1575–1624),
> *Aurora*, Ch. 4

12. On the Angels, who are of clear and transparent natures,
the light is poured forth in naked simplicity; but for men,
according to the wonderful goodness of God, it is
administered with folds and coverings, so to speak; that
it may not by its excessive brightness dazzle and offend
the weak eyes of their mind; and that men may be more
conveniently drawn, through fit sensible signs, to the
truth signified.

> Dean Colet on Dionysius the Areopagite (c. 500),
> *The Celestial Hierarchy*, Ch. I

13. And there, amidst the blinding blissful impulsions of His
dazzling rays, we shall, in a diviner manner than at
present, be like unto the heavenly Intelligences. For, as
the infallible Scripture saith, we shall be equal to the
angels and shall be the Sons of God, being Sons of the
Resurrection. But at present we employ (so far as in us
lies), appropriate symbols for things divine; and then
from these we press on upwards according to our powers
to behold in simple unity the Truth perceived by spiritual
contemplations, and leaving behind us all human
notions of godlike things, we still the activities of our
minds, and reach (so far as this may be) into the Super-
Essential Ray.

> Dionysius the Areopagite (c. 500),
> *The Divine Names*, Ch. I, 4

14. What is an angel? Three doctors give three different
definitions of what an angel is. Dionysius says, An angel
is a mirror without flaw and passing clear containing the
reflection of God's light. Augustine says, An angel is nigh

unto God and matter is nigh unto him. John Damascene says, An angel is a reflection of God and through all that is his there is shining the image of God. The soul has this image in her summit whereon the light of God for ever shines. This is his first definition of an angel. Later on he calls him a dividing sword, aflame with divine desire, and, he adds, "angels are free and inimical to matter".

Meister Eckhart (1260–1327),
Sermons and Collations, XXVIII

15. Instance the lowest angel in his pure nature: the smallest spark or love-light that ever fell from him would light up the whole world with love and joy. See his innate perfection! Moreover, as I have explained at various times, the angels are numerous beyond number.

Meister Eckhart (1260–1327),
Sermons and Collations, V

16. In you my daughter, I work three marvellous designs. I cause you to see with the eyes of the spirit, to hear with the ears of the spirit, and make myself felt in the depth of your heart. What you see, however, is not exactly what you imagine it to be. If you could observe as it is in fact the spiritual beauty of the angels and glorified souls, the joy of your heart would be so great, that your body, unable to support it, would be broken as an earthen vessel. The sight of the demons such as they are would cause you sudden death, or, at least, excessive pain, so frightful are they to behold. For this reason, objects purely spiritual appear to you only in corporal forms: angels and blessed souls under those of living men, and demons under the forms of animals and other creatures.

Bridget of Sweden (1303–73),
Select Revelations, Ch. V

17. Who so then will hear angels' song, and not be deceived

by feigning of himself, nor by imagination, nor by the illusion of the enemy, him behoveth for to have perfect charity.

Walter Hilton (1300–96),
Of the Song of Angels

18. The sense of repentance is better assurance of pardon than the testimony of an angel.

Benjamin Whichcote (1609–83),
Select Aphorisms, 50

19. There are souls who in this life receive a more perfect illumination than the angels.

John of the Cross (1542–91),
Spiritual Maxims, 172

20. For the perfect lonely man hugely burns in God's love; and whiles in surpassing of mind he is rapt above himself by contemplation, he is lifted up joying unto that sweet sound and heavenly noise. And such a one, forsooth, is likened to the seraphim, burning within himself in charity without comparison and most steadfast, whose heart is figured to godly fire; and in full light and burning he is borne up into his love. And forsooth after this life he shall be suddenly taken up to the high seats of the heavenly citizens, that in the place of Lucifer he may full brightly be.

Richard Rolle (c. 1300–49),
The Fire of Love, Ch. XIII

21. As the seraphim in high heaven truly are they burnt, who sit in solitude of body, yet their minds walk among the angels to Christ their Beloved, whom they have desired: the which also most sweetly have sung this prayer of endless love, in Jesu joying.

Richard Rolle (c. 1300–49),
The Fire of Love, Ch. II

22. As we have remarked above, therefore, that material substance of this world, possessing a nature admitting of all possible transformations, is, when dragged down to beings of a lower order, moulded into the crasser and more solid condition of a body, so as to distinguish those visible and varying forms of the world; but when it becomes the servant of more perfect and more blessed beings, it shines in the splendour of celestial bodies, and adorns either the angels of God or the sons of the resurrection with the clothing of a spiritual body, out of all which will be filled up the diverse and varying state of the one world.

Origen (c. 185–253),
On First Principles, Book II, Ch. II

23. The holy soul of a man and the spirit of an angel is and has one and the same substance and being, and there is no difference therein, but only in the quality itself, or their corporeal government; that which qualifies outwardly or from without in man, by the air, has a corrupt earthly quality, yet on the other side it has also a divine and heavenly quality hidden from the creatures.

Jacob Boehme (1575–1624),
Aurora, Ch. 5

24. For the holy soul is one spirit with God; though indeed it is a creature, yet it is like to the angels. Also the soul of man sees much deeper than the angels; for the angels see only to the heavenly pomp, but the soul sees both the heavenly and the hellish, for it lives between both.

Jacob Boehme (1575–1624),
Aurora, Ch. 11

25. The divine wisdom which in heaven illumines the angels, and cleanses them of their ignorances, is the same which illumines men upon earth, and cleanses them of their

errors and imperfections; it flows from God through the first orders of the hierarchies down to the lowest, and thence to men.

John of the Cross (1542–91),
Spiritual Maxims, 170

26. The third spirit that speaketh to a man is the angel, and his speaking is for virtue, which leadeth the man to God. The highest angel draws his image from God; this image is multiplied in him, and he giveth it over to a second angel; this one again giveth it to the lowest angel, and this lowest angel at length giveth it to the soul, which obtains thereby the power of distinguishing how she has to seize and hold the truth, and how she shall practice each virtue in proper order and measure, and according to necessity. And this clear distinction which man obtains is given him by the angel, who also lets him see crime, that he may guard against it.

John Tauler (c. 1300–61),
The Following of Christ, Part I, 87

27. But during our life here angels are delegated, by the mercy of God, to the protection of mankind. For each one has his own angel as his guardian and preserver, and also as his constant monitor and instigator to what is good; otherwise weak man would neither be able to persist in the good, nor to oppose the evil.

Dean Colet on Dionysius the Areopagite (c. 500),
The Celestial Hierarchy, Ch. XVI

28. If we may say that the Lord, whose portion was Jacob and the lot of whose inheritance was Israel, is Himself to be understood as the Bridegroom; then His companions must be those angels, according to whose number the Most High, when He divided the nations and scattered the sons of Adam, appointed the nations' bounds

according to the number of the angels of God, as
Scripture says. So perhaps the flocks of the Bridegroom's
companions may be all those nations that are divided up
like herds under angel shepherds.

Origen (c. 185–253),
Commentary on the Song of Songs, Book II, 4

29. But the angels, in the spirit of liberty, are anxiously
    solicitous to exercise towards us the offices of piety, and
    show themselves to mortals as willing and eager minis-
    ters "of future goods", recognizing in us their predes-
    tined companions for eternity and the co-heirs of their
    own immortal felicity. The irrational spirits, therefore,
    serve us from necessity, the angelic out of love; and,
    doubtless, it is as a means of benefiting us that both have
    need of bodies.

Bernard of Clairvaux (1090–1153),
Sermons, V

iv *Separation and Self-Will*

There is a consistent opinion, then, among the mystics that
the root of evil is self-will, and the most serious consequence
of evil is our separation from God. The whole mystical enterprise can therefore be described as the search for union
with God through denial of self-will.

In this context, the mystics draw our attention to a
perennial human experience of alienation, seeing in it a divine
discontent which none but God can satisfy (1–9). But we
must also recall that through our encounter with material
things we become self-conscious, and, consequently, capable
of love, for we cannot love an object unless we are distinct
from it (10–19).

The narrow, material grasping of self-will is therefore the

opposite of love (20–30). As Catherine of Siena says (27), self-will poisons the whole world, and overcoming it is a gradual process (31–36), even a kind of purgatory in which improper attachment to creatures is burned away as we follow an arduous path towards re-union with God. In a sense, the rest of this book is an enquiry into the nature of this path.

1. There can be no greater hurt than by sin to be separated from God, the fountain of all goodness, and to be turned to most hurtful misery.

Juan Luis Vives (1492–1540),
Introduction to Wisdom, fvii

2. It is a deplorable thing that those who are near the fountain should die of thirst.

François Malaval (1627–1719),
A Simple Method of Raising the Soul to Contemplation,
Second Treatise, Dialogue XII

3. The pains of souls in hell consist in the knowledge of ever being separated from God – the reason they do not feel this separation here, is because the body which amuses itself with created objects procures a diversion and takes away the attention of the soul from its attraction to the centre, till the inquietude of its separation hinders it from finding any peaceable rest on earth.

Madame Guyon (1648–1717),
The Devout Christian, "Mortifications"

4. It might seem that the infinite disproportion and in-equality there is between thee and me, ought to keep me at a distance, out of respect: but thou permittest me, it is saying too little, thou commandest me to love thee.

François Fenelon (1651-1715),
Pious Reflections, The Thirty-First Day

5. And therefore think of God in thy work as thou dost on
   thyself, and on thyself as thou dost on God: that he is as
   he is and thou art as thou art; so that thy thought be not
   scattered nor separated, but oned in him that is all;
   evermore saving this difference betwixt thee and him,
   that he is thy being and thou not his.
       Epistle of Privy Counsel (late 14th Century), Ch. 1

6. The hindrance is the rust of sin; the fire consumes the
   rust, and thus the soul goes on laying itself open to the
   divine inflowing. It is as with a covered object. The
   object cannot respond to the rays of the sun, not because
   the sun ceases to shine – for it shines without intermission – but because the covering intervenes. Let the covering be destroyed, again the object will be exposed to the
   sun, and will answer to the rays which beat against it in
   proportion as the work of destruction advances.
                          Catherine of Genoa (1447–1510),
                              The Treatise on Purgatory, Ch. II

7. Thou purest Lover, thou Lord of all creation; O that I
   had the wings of true freedom that I might flee away and
   rest in thee.
                          Thomas à Kempis (c. 1379–1471),
                  Of the Imitation of Christ, Book IV, Ch. XXI

8. Nothing should alienate us from one another, but that
   which alienates us from God.
                          Benjamin Whichcote (1609–83),
                                     Select Aphorisms, 9

9. For nothing is sweeter to me than to love thee, my God;
   and nothing more bitter than to be held back from and
   kept a stranger to thy love by anything whatsoever.
                              John Tauler (c. 1300–61),
               Meditations on the Life and Passion, Ch. 27

10. All the time that love is with love, love does not know how dear love is; but when love separates from love, then only does love feel how dear love was.

Henry Suso (c. 1295–1366),
The Little Book of Eternal Wisdom, Ch. IX

11. When I was not, thou gavest me being. When I had separated from thee, thou didst not separate from me; when I wished to escape from thee, thou didst hold me sweetly captive. Yes, thou Eternal Wisdom, if my heart might embrace thee and consume all my days with thee in love and praise, such would be its desire; for truly that man is blest whom thou dost anticipate so lovingly that thou lettest him have nowhere true rest, till he seeks his rest in thee alone.

Henry Suso (c. 1295–1366),
The Little Book of Eternal Wisdom, Ch. I

12. Possibility of separation ariseth from the fact that a union is not of the closest, but, where a union is of the closest possible, there no intermediary can exist. Separation, then, can have no place where naught can mediate between the things united. But where that which is united subsisteth not in that which uniteth, the union is not the closest possible; for 'tis a closer union where the united subsisteth in the uniter than·where it subsisteth separately, separation being a withdrawal from perfect union.

Nicholas of Cusa (1401–64),
The Vision of God, Ch. XIX

13. It depends upon God, and it returns to God as to its Eternal Origin. And in this wise it has never been, nor ever shall be, separated from God; for this union is within us by our naked nature, and, were this nature to be separated from God, it would fall into pure

nothingness. And this union is above time and space, and is always and incessantly active according to the way of God.

John of Ruysbroeck (1293–1381),
Adornment of the Spiritual Marriage, Ch. LVII

14. And this is the life of love in its highest working, above reason and above understanding; for reason can here neither give nor take away from love, for our love is touched by the Divine love. And as I understand it, here there can never more be separation from God.

John of Ruysbroeck (1293–1381),
Adornment of the Spiritual Marriage, Ch. LIII

15. Too late loved I thee, O thou Beauty of ancient days, yet ever new! too late I loved thee! And behold, thou wert within, and I abroad, and there I searched for thee; deformed I, plunging amid those fair forms, which thou hadst made. Thou wert with me, but I was not with thee. Things held me far from thee, which, unless they were in thee, were not at all. Thou calledst, and shoutedst, and burstest, my deafness. Thou flashedst, shonest, and scatterdst my blindness. Thou breathedst odours, and I drew in breath and pant for thee. I tasted, and hunger and thirst. Thou touchedst me, and I burned for thy peace.

Augustine of Hippo (345–430),
Confessions, Book X, 38

16. Separation is not to be comprehended.

Richard Jefferies (1848–87),
The Story of My Heart, Ch. III

17. Further, God absorbs the soul, leaving no trace. This means that the soul ravished by God into the peace and quiet of his secret self makes little show save to her kind.

There the soul knows no separation, for he who has absorbed her has merged her in himself. She well knows that she is but knows not what she is.

Meister Eckhart (1260–1327),
Tractates, XIII

18. God is the denial of denials: the one which is exclusive of all otherness.

Meister Eckhart (1260–1327),
Sermons and Collations, XLIII

19. Death separates soul from body, but love separates all things from the soul; she will not tolerate at any cost what is not God nor God's.

Meister Eckhart (1260–1327),
Sermons and Collations, IV

20. What is it, that fallen man wants to be redeemed from, but pride and wrath, envy and covetousness? He can have no higher separation or apostasy from God, no fuller union with Satan and his angels, than he has of the spirit of these tempers: they constitute that, which whether you call it self, or Satan in him, the meaning is the same.

William Law (1686–1761),
Address to the Clergy

21. He that takes himself out of God's hands into his own, by-and-by will not know what to do with himself.

Benjamin Whichcote (1609–83),
Select Aphorisms, 172

22. So it is good and just and right to deem that if there were aught better than God, that must be loved better than God. And thus God loveth not himself as himself, but as Goodness. And if there were, and he knew, aught better

than God, he would love that and not himself. Thus the Self and the Me are wholly sundered from God, and belong to him only in so far as they are necessary for him to be a Person.

Theologia Germanica (c. 1350), Ch. XXXII

23. But could we renounce ourselves, and all selfhood in our works, we should, with our bare and imageless spirit, transcend all things: and, without intermediary, should be led of the Spirit of God into the Nudity. And then we should feel the certainty that we are indeed the sons of God.

John of Ruysbroeck (1293–1381),
The Sparkling Stone, Ch. VIII

24. If the soul turn all its vigour and force within itself, it is separated from the senses by this very action alone; and so employing its whole force and strength within, it leaves the senses without vigour; and the more it advances and approaches to God, the more it is disjoined from itself. This is the reason why those persons in whom the attractions of grace are strong, do find themselves wholly weakened in the outward man, so as many times to swoon or faint away.

Madame Guyon (1648–1717),
A Method of Prayer, Ch. X

25. Nothing is opposite to God so much as egotism; and all the malignity of man is in this egotism, it being the source of his malice; so that the more any soul loseth its egotism the more pure it becometh; and that which would be a defect in a soul living to itself is no longer so (by reason of the purity and innocence which it hath contracted), since it lost the egotism which caused the severance between God and the soul.

Madame Guyon (1648–1717),
A Method of Prayer, Ch. XXIV

26. God ties your hands and feet to be able to carry on his work
without interference; and you do nothing but struggle, and
make every effort, but in vain, to break these sacred bonds,
and to work yourself according to your own inclination.
What infidelity! God requires no other work of you but to
remain peacefully in your chains and weakness. As for your
duties, do outwardly as well as you can, and I will answer
for the interior, for God is there in an imperceptible manner
to draw you from all that can be perceived by the senses.

Jean-Pierre de Caussade (1675–1751),
Spiritual Counsels, Seventh Book,
"The Last Trials", Letter X

27. With this self-love they have poisoned the whole world,
for, just as the love of Me contains in itself every virtue
brought forth upon their neighbour, as I have shown thee,
so sensual self-love, since it proceeds from pride (and love
of Me proceeds from charity) contains in itself every evil;
and these evils they perform by means of creatures, being
separated and divided from love of their neighbour.

Catherine of Siena (1347–80),
The Dialogue, Ch. XVII

28. Because he is separated from My grace and the love of his
neighbour, and being, by sin, deprived of life, he turns to
that which is naught, because I am He that is. So that he
who is solitary, that is, who is alone in self-love, is not
mentioned by My truth and is not acceptable to Me.

Catherine of Siena (1347–80),
The Dialogue, Ch. LIV

29. In a word, Philothea, it is morally impossible for him
who dwells in the presence of God to lose himself.

François Malaval (1627–1719),
*A Simple Method of Raising the Soul to
Contemplation*, First Treatise

30. Oft times our enemy can wish no more hurt, than that we may have our own desires.

> Juan Luis Vives (1492–1540),
> *Introduction to Wisdom*, fvi

31. Raise me up then, matter, to those heights, through struggle and separation and death; raise me up until, at long last, it becomes possible for me in perfect chastity to embrace the universe.

> Pierre Teilhard de Chardin (1881–1955),
> *Hymn of the Universe*, "Hymn to Matter"

32. First Principle. Union with God, the source of all purity, can only be attained according to the degree in which the soul is detached from all things created, which are the source of continual corruption and impurity. Second Principle. This detachment, which, when it has attained perfection, is called mystical death, has two objects; the exterior, that is to say, creatures other than ourselves; and interior, that is to say, our own ideas, satisfactions, and interests – in one word – ourselves.

> Jean-Pierre de Caussade (1675–1751),
> *Spiritual Counsels*, Seventh Book,
> "The Last Things", Letter XV

33. I am the fire which purifies the soul, and the closer the soul is to Me, the purer she becomes, and the further she is from Me, the more does her purity leave her; which is the reason why men of the world fall into such iniquities, for they are separated from Me, while the soul, who, without any medium, unites herself directly to Me, participates in My purity.

> Catherine of Siena (1347–80),
> *The Dialogue*, Ch. C

34. And when the soul finds itself on its way back to that

first state, it is so enkindled with the desire of becoming one with God, that this desire becomes its purgatory; not that the soul can look at purgatory as such, but the instinct by which it is kindled, and the impediment by which it is hindered, constitute its purgatory. God performs this last act of love without the co-operation of man; for there are so many secret imperfections within the soul, that the sight of them would drive it to despair.

Catherine of Genoa (1447–1510),
The Treatise on Purgatory, Ch. XI

35. For then hast thou set a mean between thyself and God, when thou lovest aught that separateth thee from his love.

Angela of Foligno (c. 1248–1309),
The Way of the Cross, 6

36. Now he that willeth to love God perfectly must dispossess himself wholly of the love of every creature, for he may have no mean between himself and God. And so many such means are there as there be things which a man loves or may love apart from God.

Angela of Foligno (c. 1248–1309),
The Way of the Cross, 1

Chapter II

The Human Estate

This chapter draws attention to a set of familiar experiences especially valued by mystics. Human beings, for instance, often find refreshment in solitude, and all of us have wondered at the beauties of creation and the strangeness of ourselves. Likewise, most people have enjoyed the activities of imagination, and we are forever launching out on adventures of learning and enquiry without full guarantees or assurances that we will find what we seek.

Such commonplace events are the key to the four following sub-headings, for it is important to establish that the mystics do not direct us away from normal human experience, but, rather, the reverse: if the mystical life leads us to God it does so by means of our humanity and not in spite of it.

✠

i Solitude

The battle against self-will begins in solitude, which should not be confused with separation. As we have seen, separation is the basic condition of suffering and is therefore allied to self-will, the root of evil. Our bones, for example, sustain us and enable us to act, and while they do so we are unconscious of them. But when a bone is damaged it declares, as it were,

its separateness, as Aldous Huxley says, and the pain we
suffer prevents us from acting normally. Solitude is rather the
condition in which we can reflect on the surprising, unconscious harmony within ourselves which enables us to act
normally. For when we are in solitude we find that we are
beings with a capacity for reflection; we have an interior,
self-conscious life marked by genius for relationship, and
drawn to responsibility and compassion.

There is no special difficulty in re-discovering for ourselves
this basic evidence of our spirituality. A serene, self-reflective
detachment is all that is necessary, and "solitude" is a name
for whatever circumstances lead us to it (1–9). But as with so
many other topics associated with mysticism, solitude needs
to be distinguished carefully from its negative counterpart, in
this case, isolation. The isolationist merely thinks himself
above other men, and his act of physical separation from the
community is either cynical or escapist. Solitude, by contrast,
discovers to us in the surprising presence to ourselves the very
ground of compassion. Far from running away from the
world's problems, the solitary proclaims an active resistance
to all that would dehumanize his fellow men by reducing
them to unreflecting functionaries. The internal freedom
which true solitude discloses is thus the heritage of every
person and constitutes the human dignity of each (10–19).

It follows that we can preserve our solitude even in the
midst of a crowd, for solitude does not depend on our
sojourn in a place apart, but on our awareness of the still
centre wherein we are self-conscious. Admittedly, the actual,
physical detachment of one's self can be, for some, a means of
discovering and proclaiming their spirituality, but the bless-
ings of solitude might come to us anywhere – a moment in
the garden, a moment in the hall, as Richard of St Victor says
(25). In such moments we are glad and refreshed, for solitude
is recreative (20–28), and should not breed anxious self-
interrogation; it comes upon us rather as a "honey-sweetness
without heaviness" (23).

1. Now by the unanimous acknowledgement of all mystic writers, the only proper school of contemplation is solitude: that is, a condition of life both externally freed from the distractive encumbrances, tempting flatteries, and disquieting solicitudes of the world.

Augustine Baker (1575–1641),
Sancta Sophia, Treat. 1, Sec. 3, Ch. 1, Part 2

2. Unless a man takes himself sometimes *out of* the world by retirement and self-reflection, he will be in danger of losing himself *in* the world.

Benjamin Whichcote (1609–83),
Select Aphorisms, 150

3. Inner solitude consists in the forgetting of all creatures, in detachment, in a perfect abnegation of all purpose, desire, thought and will. This is the true solitude, wherein the soul reposes with a sweet and inward serenity, in the arms of the Highest Good. O what infinite room is there in a soul that has attained to this divine solitude.

Miguel de Molinos (1640–97),
A Spiritual Guide Which Disentangles the Soul,
Ch. XII, 119

4. Know, that the more the soul puts off her self, the more way she makes into this inner solitude, and becomes clothed with God.

Miguel de Molinos (1640–97),
A Spiritual Guide Which Disentangles the Soul,
Ch. XII, 124

5. Another help towards this is solitude, because it not only puts away from the heart and the senses the occasions of distraction, and the occasions of sin, but it also leads one to retire within oneself, and hold converse with God and

one's own self, when we feel the opportunity of our position excludes any other companionship.

Peter of Alcantara (1499–1562),
A Golden Treatise of Mental Prayer, Part II, Ch. II

6. In that solitude of the soul, its perfect detachment from all things, wherein it lives alone with God – there he guides it, moves it, and elevates it to divine things. He guides the intellect in the perception of divine things, because it is now detached from all contrary knowledge, and alone. He moves the will freely to love himself, because it is now alone, disencumbered from all other affections. He fills the memory with divine knowledge, because it also is now alone, emptied of all imaginations and fancies. For the instant the soul clears and empties its faculties of all earthly objects, and from attachments to higher things, keeping them in solitude, God immediately fills them with the invisible and divine; it being God himself who guides it in this solitude.

John of the Cross (1542–91),
A Spiritual Canticle Between the Soul and Christ,
St. XXXV

7. Is God the God of solitaries alone? Nay, but of all. For the Lord hath pity on all, and hateth nothing that he hath made. I would rather thou thoughtest it were everywhere light save with thee, and that thou shouldst judge worse of thyself than of any man.

William of St Thierry (c. 1085–1148),
The Golden Epistle, Ch. 2, 6

8. One great discouragement to felicity, or rather to great souls in the pursuit of felicity, is the solitariness of the way that leadeth to her temple. A man that studies happiness must sit alone like a sparrow upon the house top, and like a pelican in the wilderness. And the reason

is because all men praise happiness and despise it. Very few shall a man find in the way of wisdom: and few indeed that having given up their names to wisdom and felicity, that will persevere in seeking it.

Thomas Traherne (c. 1636–74),
Centuries of Meditation, IV, 13

9. We are not forced to take wings to find Him, but have only to seek solitude and to look within ourselves.

Teresa of Avila (1515–82),
The Way of Perfection, Ch. XXVIII

10. Now though this so necessary solitude be found both more perfectly and more permanently in a well-ordered religious state . . . yet is it not so confined to that state, but that in the world also, and in a secular course of life God hath raised and guided many souls in these perfect ways, affording them there as much solitude and as much internal freedom of spirit as he saw was necessary to bring them to a high degree of perfection.

Augustine Baker (1575–1641),
Sancta Sophia, Treat. 1, Sec. 3, Ch. 1, Part 3

11. The Lover went into solitude; and his heart was accompanied by thoughts, his eyes by tears, and his body by fasts and afflictions. But when the Lover returned to the companionship of men, these things went no longer with him, and the Lover remained quite alone in the company of many people.

Ramon Lull (c. 1232–1315),
The Book of the Lover and the Beloved, 228

12. The Lover longed for solitude, and went away to live alone, that he might gain the companionship of his Beloved, for amid many people he was lonely.

Ramon Lull (c. 1232–1315),
The Book of the Lover and the Beloved, 45

13. No man goes out securely: but he who loves to hide. No man speaks securely: but he who loves to hold his peace.

> Thomas à Kempis (c. 1379–1471),
> *Of the Imitation of Christ*, Book I, Ch. XX

14. And so we ought to know that if we retire to solitude or secret places, without our faults first being cured, their operation is but repressed, while the power of feeling them is not extinguished.

> John Cassian (c. 360–434),
> *Conference of Abbot John*, Ch. XII

15. For solitude, and prison, are names of wretchedness; whereas a cell must in no wise be the enclosure of necessity, but the dwelling-place of peace, a door that is closed; not a hiding place, but a secret place.

> William of St Thierry (c. 1085–1148),
> *The Golden Epistle*, Ch. 4, 9

16. Nothing better helps a religious to remain silent than flight from the company of others and the pursuit of a life of solitude. The man who has already risen above the contingencies of human existence has need of no other consoler or interlocutor than God. Hence, he should live in peace and solitude. Having God as a companion, he is not to be concerned with the company of men. Thus, it is said in the third book of Lamentations: *He shall sit solitary and hold his peace: because he hath taken it up upon himself.* He shall sit solitary by avoiding the company of men, he shall hold his peace by meditating upon the joys of heaven, and he has risen above his state by tasting celestial delights.

> Bonaventure (1221–74),
> *On the Perfection of Life*, Ch. IV, 3

17. There is no true solitude except interior solitude. And

interior solitude is not possible for anyone who does not accept his right place in relation to other men. There is no true peace possible for the man who still imagines that some accident of talent or grace or virtue segregates him from other men and places him above them. Solitude is not separation.

Thomas Merton (1915–68),
New Seeds of Contemplation, Ch. 8

18. True solitude is the home of the person, false solitude the refuge of the individualist. The person is constituted by a uniquely subsisting capacity to love – by a radical ability to care for all beings made by God and loved by Him. Such a capacity is destroyed by the loss of perspective. Without a certain element of solitude there can be no compassion because when a man is lost in the wheels of a social machine he is no longer aware of human needs as a matter of personal responsibility. One can escape from men by plunging into the midst of a crowd!

Thomas Merton (1915–68),
New Seeds of Contemplation, Ch. 8

19. This is not learnt by flight, by one who runs away from things, who turns his back upon the world and flees into the desert: he must learn to find the solitude within where or with whomsoever he may be. He must discover how to enter things and seizing God therein, get a clear impression firmly rooted in his mind, just as one learns to write. In order to acquire this art a man must practise hard and often however dull and troublesome it is and however much beyond him it may seem to be.

Meister Eckhart (1260–1327),
In Collationibus

20. For a true travail has gone forth, not by one only in singularity, but by many who have been carried into the

spiritual wilderness in abstraction and separation from all worldly conversation, ascending upon the eagle wing so high as to acquaint themselves with the high Throne Dominions in the heavenly places, that they might behold the patterns there that are to be imitated here below.

Jane Lead (1623–1704),
The Ascent to the Mount of Vision, XL

21. External silence is most necessary to cultivate the internal; and indeed 'tis impossible to become inward without loving silence and retirement.

Madame Guyon (1648–1717),
A Method of Prayer, Ch. XIV

22. The Father uttered one Word; that Word is his Son: and he utters him for ever in everlasting silence, and the soul to hear it must be silent.

John of the Cross (1542–91),
Spiritual Maxims, 284

23. Love forsooth dwells in the heart of the solitary if he seek nothing from vain lordship. Here he utterly burns and longs for light whiles he thus clearly savours things heavenly; and sings with honey-sweetness and without heaviness; as the seraphim – to whom he is like in loving mind – cries and says to his noble Lover: "Behold, loving, I burn; greedily desiring."

Richard Rolle (1300–49),
The Fire of Love, Ch. XIV

24. Later on I began to have daily pilgrimages to think these things. There was a feeling that I must go somewhere, and be alone. It was a necessity to have a few minutes of this separate life every day; my mind required to live its own life apart from other things. A great oak at a short

distance was one resort, and sitting on the grass at the roots, or leaning against the trunk and looking over the quiet meadows towards the bright southern sky, I could live my own life a little while.

Richard Jefferies (1848–87),
The Story of My Heart, Ch. V

25. But because a singular love loves solitude and seeks for a solitary place, it behooves us to throw out the entire crowd of such a sort, not only of thoughts but also even of affections, so that we may be at liberty to cling more freely and more joyfully to the embraces of our beloved one. How great, I ask, is the delay in such waiting? How often must one repeat: "Wait and wait again, a moment here and a moment there"? A moment in one place, a moment in another. A moment in the garden, a moment in the hall, a moment in the chamber until at last finally after much waiting and great weariness He enters the bedchamber and occupies the most intimate and secret place. A moment in the garden while the whole crowd of those making a disturbance is dispersed. A moment in the hall while the chamber is decorated. A moment in the chamber while the bridal bed is prepared. And the Beloved is forced to wait a moment and a moment in all of these places: a moment here and a moment there.

Richard of St Victor (c. 1123–75),
The Mystical Ark, Book IV, Ch. XV

26. But amongst the fruits of solitude, this is eminent, that one can therein more easily consider God as God; which makes the spouse use those two words "alone", "without", that is, apart from all creatures.

François de Sales (1562–1622),
Mystical Explanation of the Canticles, Discourse V

27. The goods of God, which are beyond all measure, can be
    contained only in an empty and solitary heart.

    John of the Cross (1542–91),
    Spiritual Maxims, 347

28. It appears to me, therefore, that it is into this solitude the
    Spouse has retired, and there, overpowered by the
    beauty of the place, has sweetly fallen asleep in the arms
    of her Beloved. In other words, she has been visited by
    the slumber of spiritual rapture, and this is the sleep out
    of which the young maidens are forbidden to awaken
    her, until she herself pleases.

    Bernard of Clairvaux (1090–1153),
    Sermons, LII

ii *The Mystical Seed*

The refreshment and self-discovery which accompany
solitude can vary in intensity, and mystics draw our attention
to certain fleeting experiences which may also mark the
awakening of our spiritual nature. These experiences are
often compared to a spark, a beam, a flash, or a "seed of
light" (24). The Latin words *synderesis* (a mis-transcription
of the Greek *syneidesis*, or "consciousness") and *apex* are
theological terms for describing this basic, illuminated core of
human consciousness which constitutes our inalienable spirituality, but detailed debate on the meaning of these terms
need not detain us here.

Excerpts 1–14 use a variety of metaphors to describe
synderesis, in each case indicating a sudden, fleeting
awareness of high spiritual energy. It should be pointed out
that the claims here are not extravagant, and we are not
invited, for instance, to work at stimulating some kind of
sparkling light. We are, instead, assured that the normal

fruits of solitude (a discovery in ourselves of divine longing [1], a sense of beneficence [2], a simple reflection on faith [12]), can trigger a glancing, appreciative awareness of creative power for good within ourselves.

The spark or seed of light, however, is not confined to human self-consciousness. The whole of creation in varying degrees can shoot forth bright rays, surprising evidences of the gratuitous glory of things bearing traces of their creator, traces on which the human intelligence can seize in a kaleidoscopic variety of momentary illuminations whereby the inner being of things and the inner human self are grasped as a unity. Great poetry and art are full of such moments, so that the mystic and the poet, to this extent, point us to the same end. The seed of light therefore puts us in contact with things, and another way of describing it is in terms of touch, for it can be a searing spark (15) and the touch of a lover (15–20).

At this point we might reflect that the term "seed" implies not only energy, but also a process of cultivation and organic growth; if we are to receive the seed of light as a gift, we must be prepared to develop the plant which grows from it. Excerpts 21–39 deal with the idea of spiritual cultivation, deploying metaphors of light and energy to remind us that growth is laborious and careful, and not only a matter of sparkling moments. These, however beautiful, remain aesthetic, like the flowers of courtship. They bear as much relationship to the final fruition of mystical experience as such flowers bear to a fruitful marriage.

1. How do we detect this spark within us? I imagine that it is different in each person, which would not be surprising since every person is unique. I think it has something to do with a longing deep down within us. We long to know and possess the good, or the good that we see in a great number of persons and objects which fall within our experience. In the end we discover that the pursuit of

truth and goodness leads us to long for truth and
goodness in their absolute form. This absolute truth and
this absolute goodness we call God.

Basil Hume (1923–),
To Be a Pilgrim, "Spiritual Health"

2. Lastly, to man is given a spark of the Divine Mind,
which stimulates him, without any hope of reward, and
of his own free will to do good to all: for of God, this is
the most natural and appropriate attribute, to consult
the good of all by disinterested beneficence.

Desiderius Erasmus (1466?–1536),
Antipolemus

3. Religion, where it dwells in truth and power, renews the
very spirit of our minds, and teaches us to view the
various perfections which may be discovered in the
creature, not so much as the perfection of this or that
individual object, but as so many rays issuing from Him,
who is the First and Essential Perfection. Every particular good is a blossom of the first goodness, every created
excellence a beam of uncreated glory, and should we
separate these from God, all affection lavished upon
them would only be so much idolatry.

John Smith (1618–52),
Select Discourses, VII

4. Under the direction of this ray of divine light, will I every
moment do, without anxiety, according to the best of my
abilities, whatever thy providence shall put me in the
way of doing.

François Fenelon (1651–1715),
Pious Reflections, The Thirteenth Day

5. "What is the being of thy Beloved?" He answered: "It is
a bright ray throughout all things, even as the sun which

shines over all the world. For if it withdraw its brightness, it leaves all things in darkness; and when it shines forth it brings the day. Even more so is my Beloved."

Ramon Lull (c. 1232–1315),
The Book of the Lover and the Beloved, 294

6. And therefore take heed to this work and to the marvellous manner of it within thy soul. For if it be truly conceived, it is but a sudden stirring, and as it were unadvised, speedily springing unto God as a sparkle from the coal. And it is marvellous to number the stirrings that may be in one hour wrought in a soul that is disposed to this work. And yet, in one stirring of all these, it may have suddenly and perfectly forgotten all created things. But fast after each stirring, through the corruption of the flesh, it falleth down again to some thought, or to some done or undone deed. But what matter? For fast after, it riseth again as suddenly as it did before.

The Cloud of Unknowing (late 14th Century), Ch. 4

7. For the small power which remains is as it were a spark buried in the ashes. This is that natural reason encompassed about with great darkness, yet still having judgement of good and evil, and discrimination between true and false, although it be powerless to fulfil all that it approves, and enjoys no longer the full light of truth nor soundness in its own affections.

Thomas à Kempis (c. 1379–1471),
Of the Imitation of Christ, Book IV, Ch. LV

8. My dear friends, dwell in the everlasting seed of God, in which ye all will feel life eternal, that never hath an end.

George Fox (1624–91),
Epistles, CXX

9. The heavenly and truly divine love comes to men thus, when in the soul itself the spark of true goodness, kindled in the soul by the Divine Word, is able to burst forth into flame; and, what is of the highest importance, salvation runs parallel with sincere willingness – choice and life being, so to speak, yoked together.

Clement of Alexandria (c. 150–215),
Exhortation to the Heathen, Ch. XI

10. For, by the unceasing and absolute renunciation of thyself and all things, thou shalt in pureness cast all things aside, and be released from all, and so shalt be led upwards to the Ray of that divine Darkness which exceedeth all existence.

Dionysius the Areopagite (c. 500),
The Mystical Theology, Ch. I

11. For the Holy Ghost will not be caught, held, or retained in the sinful flesh, but rises up like a flash of lightning, as fire flashes and sparkles out of a stone, when a man strikes fire upon it.

Jacob Boehme (1575–1624),
Aurora, Ch. 11

12. Your great attraction towards simplicity is a grace that can have no other effect than to unite you more closely with God, for simplicity tends to unity, and this can be obtained, first, by a simple and loving interior looking to God in pure faith, whether this interior looking is perceptible by its sweetness, as at present, or becomes almost unknown to the senses by being in the depths of the soul, or in the apex, or point of the spirit.

Jean-Pierre de Caussade (1675–1751),
Spiritual Counsels, Letter XVI

13. Also the highest power of the spirit, which is called

synteresis – the understanding faculty – is brought back to its first nobility by the passion of Christ. The faculty is created immediately for God without mediums, but it was brought under a medium by the fall of Adam, and this medium must be destroyed in Christ, so that the spirit may be entirely stripped of all mediums.

John Tauler (c. 1300–61),
The Following of Christ, II, 52

14. It is called sinderesis, and is all one with the soul's nature, a spark of the divine nature. It cannot abide what is not good. It is without stain; perfectly pure and wholly superior to temporal things it dwells in unchanging stability, like eternity. Anything that enters here must first be freed from multiplicity and sensible affections. The powers of the soul, outer and inner, are all summed up in this, and whatever gets into this highest power it passes on to all the rest, an act eternal in its nature: it is so quick it is practically timeless.

Meister Eckhart (1260–1327),
Sermons and Collations, IX

15. The contact of the fire is that most delicate touch of the Beloved which the soul feels at times, even when least expecting it, and which is so penetrating that the heart is set on fire with love. It seems to be but a spark of fire leaping up and burning.

John of the Cross (1542–91),
A Spiritual Canticle Between the Soul and Christ,
St. XXV

16. The third kind of pain is like dying; it is as if the whole soul were festering because of its wound. It is dying a living death until love, having slain it, shall make it live the life of love, transforming it in love. Thy dying of love is effected by a single touch of the knowledge of the

Divinity. This is the "I know not what", of which the creatures can but babble. This touch is not continuous nor protracted, but quick in its course, for otherwise soul and body would part.

John of the Cross (1542–91),
A Spiritual Canticle Between the Soul and Christ, St. VII

17. And above this touch, in the still being of the spirit, there broods an incomprehensible Brightness. And that is the most high Trinity whence this touch proceeds. There God lives and reigns in the spirit, and the spirit in God.

John of Ruysbroeck (1293–1381),
Adornment of the Spiritual Marriage, Ch. LI

18. And this is the touch which I mean. And the creature passively endures this touch. For here there is a union of the higher powers within the unity of the spirit, above the multiplicity of all the virtues, and here no one works save God alone, in untrammelled goodness; which is the cause of all our virtues and of all blessedness.

John of Ruysbroeck (1293–1381),
Adornment of the Spiritual Marriage, Ch. LI

19. I have been thinking that God might be likened to a burning furnace from which a small spark flies into the soul that feels the heat of this great fire, which, however, is insufficient to consume it. The sensation is so delightful that the spirit lingers in the pain produced by its contact. This seems to me the best comparison I can find, for the pain is delicious and is not really pain at all, nor does it always continue in the same degree; sometimes it lasts for a long time; on other occasions it passes quickly. This is as God chooses, for no human means can obtain it; and though felt at times for a long while, yet it is intermittent.

Teresa of Avila (1515–82),
The Interior Castle, Sixth Mansions, Ch. II, 6

20. It is a remote touch of divine love, like the ends of the sunbeams reflected in a burning-glass, which maketh the pleasantness and pleasant properties of all plants; the lustre, gracefulness, virtue of all precious stones and pearls; the joy of all relations.

Peter Sterry (c. 1614–72),
*The Rise, Race, and Royalty of the Kingdom of God
in the Soul of Man*, p. 396

21. O you who are coming out of the sepulchre! you feel within yourselves a germ of life springing up little by little: you are quite astonished to find a secret strength taking possession of you: your ashes are reanimated: you feel yourselves to be in a new country. The poor soul, which only expected to remain at rest in its grave, receives an agreeable surprise. It does not know what to think: it supposes that the sun must have shed upon it a few scattered rays through some opening or chink, whose brightness will only last for a moment. It is still more astonished when it feels this secret vigour permeating its entire being, and finds that it gradually receives a new life, to lose it no more for ever, unless it be by the most flagrant unfaithfulness.

Madame Guyon (1648–1717),
Spiritual Torrents, Ch. IX

22. As a careful cultivator of his own land first turns the soil, and cleanses it from weeds and thistles, and afterwards casts in the seed; so, he who expects to receive from God the seed of his grace, must first cleanse the soil of his heart, that the seed of the Spirit falling therein may bring forth perfect and abundant fruit.

Macarius (c. 300–90),
Institutes of Christian Perfection, Book VII, Ch. VI

23. Men scatter the seed of heaven at large so that he who

will may take it. But God, when he sows, never sows wastefully. He even makes the earth hungry to receive the seed, and even when it is not prepared for it. I say also that God will speak to you more intelligibly because he knows best how to temper the lights to your capacity, and more than that, he will strengthen your eyes, so that you will be able to bear a greater clearness.

François Malaval (1627–1719),
*A Simple Method of Raising the Soul to
Contemplation*, First Treatise

24. The soft springing Word replied that there was already a seed of light sown, and an united golden grain of faith, which would assuredly put forth their heads, that the time of the lily may be known.

Jane Lead (1623–1704),
The Ascent to the Mount of Vision, XXIII

25. He tempered the poisonous fire kindled in our flesh by the serpent which incited us to sin: he restrained it then and is to kill it finally. At the same time he inserted a germ – a seed, we might call it – of his spirit and grace, which, enclosed within our soul and cultivated as it should be, might afterwards sprout at its appointed time, increase in strength, and grow to the measure of the "perfect man" as St Paul terms it.

Luis de Leon (1528–91),
The Names of Christ, 55

26. This means that Christ is the fruit, so called by Holy Scripture to show that he is the end to which all things are directed, for whose blessed birth all things were created and planned. As, in the tree, root, trunk, branches, leaves, and flower exist for the sake of the fruit, so the vast heavens we see; their twinkling stars; the source of light, orbed and beautiful, which illumines

all; the earth, painted with flowers; the waters with their fish; men, animals and all this immense, splendid universe, were formed by God that his Son might be made man and to produce this one divine fruit which is Christ, whom we might call the universal offspring of all things.

Luis de Leon (1528–91),
The Names of Christ, 51

27. Now God is One. Christ is the Seed.

Peter Sterry (c. 1614–72),
The Rise, Race, and Royalty of the Kingdom of God in the Soul of Man, p. 356

28. God is the person, the subsistency, the root, out of which the whole tree with all its arms and branches of both natures, human and divine, springeth; in which it subsisteth; from which all operations, and fruits proceed; to which all denominations belong, which is the name to be named in all, and to which every name belongeth. This is Christ. The one seed, the one spirit in all the saints, in all the graces, and comforts of the Gospel is this Christ, that one person, which is the only true God. Thus God is one in all.

Peter Sterry (c. 1614–72),
The Rise, Race, and Royalty of the Kingdom of God in the Soul of Man, p. 356

29. Stay till the grain of mustard seed itself breaks forth from among the clods which buried it, and till through the descent of the dew of heaven it springs up and shows itself openly. This holy assurance is the budding and blossoming of felicity in our own souls; it is the inward sense and feeling of the true life and spirit, sweetness and beauty of grace powerfully displaying its own energy within us.

John Smith (1618–52),
Select Discourses, VII

30. The Beloved planted many seeds in the heart of his
    Lover, but one of them only took life and put forth leaf
    and gave flower and fruit. Think you that from this
    single fruit may come many seeds?

    Ramon Lull (c. 1232–1315),
    The Book of the Lover and the Beloved, 248

31. From a pure heart comes the fruit of a good life.

    Thomas à Kempis (c. 1379–1471),
    Of the Imitation of Christ, Book IV, Ch. XXXI

32. It is not to no purpose, to speak things that are not
    presently understood. Seed, though it lies in the ground
    awhile unseen, is not lost or thrown away, but will bring
    forth fruit.

    Benjamin Whichcote (1609–83),
    Select Aphorisms, 66

33. Thus must the noble grain of wheat lie hidden for a little
    while in the earth, and be worn away by divers storms,
    and die in itself, if it is to bring forth fruit.

    John Tauler (c. 1300–61),
    Meditations on the Life and Passion
    Ch. 39

34. Christ hung not on the cross, a small, dry, and barren
    wood, but like the grape upon the vine, or the flower
    upon the stem, since he is himself the most noble flower
    of the rod of Jesse, whereon the Holy Ghost hath rested.

    John Tauler (c. 1300–61),
    Meditations on the Life and Passion
    Ch. 38

35. The light of Divine grace is a fruit-bearing shoot, com-
    ing forth from the living paradise of the eternal
    kingdom; and no deed can bring refreshment or profit to

man if it be not born of this shoot. This shoot of Divine grace, which makes man pleasing to God, and through which he merits eternal life, is offered to all men. But it is not grafted into all, because some will not cut away the wild branches of their trees; that is, unbelief, and a perverse and disobedient will opposed to the commandments of God.

John of Ruysbroeck (1293–1381),
Adornment of the Spiritual Marriage, Ch. I

36. Not just the teaching Church, now, but the living Church: the seed of super-vitalization planted at the heart of the noosphere by the appearance in history of Jesus Christ: not a parasitic organism, duplicating or distorting the evolutionary cone of man, but an even more interior cone, impregnating, taking possession of, and gradually uplifting the rising mass of the world, and converging concentrically towards the same apex.

Pierre Teilhard de Chardin (1881–1955),
Activation of Energy,
"Outline of a Dialectic of Spirit", IV

37. It was to me a great joy to consider my soul as a garden, and our Lord as walking in it. I used to beseech him to increase the fragrance of the little flowers of virtues – which were beginning, as it seemed, to bud – and preserve them, that they might be to his glory; for I desired nothing for myself. I prayed him to cut those he liked, because I already knew that they would grow the better.

Teresa of Avila (1515–82),
Life, Ch. XIV, 13

38. God infused the seeds of every kind of life into man. Whatever seeds every one chooseth those spring up within him, and the fruits of those shall he bear and enjoy. If sensual things are chosen by him he shall be-

come a beast, if reasonable a celestial creature; if intellectual an angel and a son of God; and if being content with the lot of no creatures, he withdraws himself into the centre of his own unity, he shall be one spirit with God, and dwell above all in the solitary darkness of his eternal Father.

Thomas Traherne (c. 1636–74),
Centuries of Meditation, IV, 77

39. Let us now endeavour, under the guidance of the Spirit of truth, to extract the mystical meaning which lies underneath the rind of the letter. If we suppose the speaker in this place to be the universal Church of the saints, the flowers and the fruits must be understood as representing ourselves, and not us only, but all others, equally, throughout the whole earth, who have been converted from a worldly life. By the flowers are designated the young and tender virtues of those who are still in their spiritual beginnings, whilst the fruit is meant to symbolize the strength and maturity of the perfect.

Bernard of Clairvaux (1090–1153),
Sermons, LI

iii *Incarnation and Imagination*

Incarnation can be described, in terms of the previous section, as cultivating seeds of spirit in the world. Our moments of beauty, beneficence and loving relationship are incarnational in so far as they promote the overcoming of evil and separateness, and tend to the re-unification, or at-onement, of creation with God. It follows that incarnation is world-affirming, and we are to deny the world only in so far as it is ungodly. Of course the world is ungodly enough, as Christianity teaches, for it crucified its own maker, who, for love of it, did not disdain to enter it in human form. And here we encounter the incarnation specifically in relation to Jesus Christ.

On the one hand the Christ-impulse is made incarnate in every act of love and beauty which counteracts evil and spiritualizes nature. On the other hand, Christians hold that this impulse received a special and unique expression in Jesus of Nazareth. The meaning, that is, of incarnation and redemption is made uniquely clear by that singular life, and one way of testing this claim is by its comprehensiveness and relevance to human beings in the world, called alike to a supernatural destiny beyond it, and a natural responsibility within it.

As excerpts 1–15 suggest, incarnation stresses redemption through persons meeting in the world. We are, admittedly, to pass beyond incarnational process (5), but we must do so by passing through our own state of humanity, serving the Christ-impulse in whatever sparks and touches would bring order and harmony out of our chaos of fear, enmity and suffering. Christ, we are told, is the very principle of restorative balance (16–19), and redemption entails the vigilant cherishing, continual offering and willing disposition to cultivate patiently the seeds of light in the world around us (20–24).

At this point, certain affinities between incarnation and imagination become clear, because imagination is a source of insight and beauty discovering the sparks and beams of our spiritual relationship with things. Imagination's drawing us to God can thus be described as truly incarnational.

Mystics, however, tend to warn us more firmly about the limitations of imagination than they do about incarnation. The end to which we aspire, they tell us, is beyond images: it is ineffable, nameless and unmediated (23–31). None of this is inconsistent with the teaching on incarnation (for we are to pass beyond the incarnational, as Jesus did), and there is, not surprisingly, a consistent witness to the contrary fact that we cannot really deal with the world without recourse to images (32–37).

None the less, the so-called "affirmative way" (stressing the positive function of images) tends to carry less weight among Western mystics in general than the "negative way" (stressing that images fall short of truth [35]). We may conjecture that this is so partly because authors are bound to images in the act of writing, and there is a healthy, corrective tendency in calling attention to the limitations of the very words they are using. The opposite tendency prevails with the incarnation of Jesus, who was denied by the world, and crucified. The world must therefore be urged to discover the positive meaning of the thing it so violently rejected.

Beauty, then, does indeed draw us to God (38–40), but imagination must become self-consciously incarnational to avoid enchantment by mere aestheticism. To an equivalent and opposite degree, incarnation must continuously seek imaginative expression if we are to know its engendering, redemptive process.

1. *Eternal Wisdom.* The highest emanation of all beings, taken in their natural order, is through the noblest beings to the lowest, but their refluence to their origin is through the lowest to the highest. Therefore, if thou art wishful to behold Me in My uncreated Divinity thou must learn how to know and love Me here in My suffering humanity for this is the speediest way to eternal salvation.

Henry Suso (c. 1295–1366),
The Little Book of Eternal Wisdom, Ch. I

2. The Lover lifted up the powers of his soul, and mounted the ladder of humanity to glory in the Divine Nature; and from the Divine Nature the powers of his soul descended, to glory in the human nature of his Beloved.

Ramon Lull (c. 1232–1315),
The Book of the Lover and the Beloved, 314

3. But here the mind of Christ is the mind of the soul, natural and habitual to it, as something no longer distinct from itself, but as its own being and its own life; Christ exercising it without going out of the soul, and the soul exercising it with him, in him, without going out of him; not like something distinct, which it knows, sees, attempts, practises, but as that which is natural to it.

Madame Guyon (1648–1717),
Spiritual Torrents, Ch. IX

4. God therefore cometh unto us mediately, that is to say, through grace, that is, through wisdom, truth, justice and the rest.

Gerlac Petersen (1378–1411),
The Fiery Soliloquy with God, Ch. XXVI

5. For as long as He was with them they loved Him much, but it was fleshly in His manhood; and therefore it was profitable to them that He should withdraw the bodily form from their sight, that the Holy Ghost might come to them and teach them to love Him and know Him more spiritually, as He did on the day of Pentecost. Right so is it profitable to some that our Lord withdraw a little the bodily and the fleshly likeness from the eye of the soul, that the heart might be set and fixed more busily in ghostly desire and seeking of His godhead.

Walter Hilton (1300–96),
The Scale of Perfection, Book I, Ch. XXXVI

6. For Thou art alike the way unto truth, and the truth itself; Thou art alike the way unto the life of the intellect and that life itself; Thou art alike the fragrance of the food of joy and the taste that maketh joyful. Be Thou, then, most sweet Jesu, blessed for ever!

Nicholas of Cusa (1401–64),
The Vision of God, Ch. XX

7. You know that every meeting is a coming together of two persons, who come from different places, which are separated from, and opposite to, each other. Now Christ comes from above as a Lord and generous giver, who can do all things. And we come from below as the poor servants, who can do nothing of ourselves, but have need of everything. The coming of Christ to us is from within outwards, and we go towards him from without inwards; and this is why a spiritual meeting must here take place. And this coming and this meeting of ourselves and Christ takes place in two ways, to wit, with means and without means.

John of Ruysbroeck (1293–1381),
Adornment of the Spiritual Marriage, Ch. LVI

8. For since we are neither all soul, nor all body; seeing none of our actions are either separately of the soul, or separately of the body; seeing we have no habits but such as are produced by the actions both of our souls and bodies; it is certain that if we would arrive at habits of devotion, or delight in God, we must not only meditate and exercise our souls, but we must practise and exercise our bodies to all such outward actions as are conformable to these inward tempers.

William Law (1686–1761),
A Serious Call, Ch. XV

9. But the true Mediator, whom in Thy secret mercy Thou hast shewed to the humble, and sentest, that by his example also they might learn that same humility, that Mediator between God and man, the man Christ Jesus, appeared betwixt mortal sinners and the immortal Just One; mortal with me, just with God.

Augustine of Hippo (345–430),
Confessions, Book X, 68

10. Since, then, we see in Him some things so human that they appear to differ in no respect from the common frailty of mortals, and some things so divine that they can appropriately belong to nothing else than to the primal and ineffable nature of Deity, the narrowness of human understanding can find no outlet; but, overcome with the amazement of a mighty admiration, knows not whither to withdraw, or what to take hold of, or whither to turn.

Origen (c. 185–253),
On First Principles, Book II, Ch. VI

11. And thus is Jesus our very mother in nature [by virtue] of our first making; and he is our very mother in grace, by taking our nature made.

Julian of Norwich (c. 1342–1420),
Revelations of Divine Love, Ch. LIX

12. Thus Jesus Christ that doeth good against evil is our very mother: we have our being of him – where the ground of motherhood beginneth – with all the sweet keeping of love that endlessly followeth. As verily as God is our father, so verily God is our mother; and that shewed he in all, and especially in these sweet words where he saith: *I it am.*

Julian of Norwich (c. 1342–1420),
Revelations of Divine Love, Ch. LIX

13. Now God in eternity is without contradiction, suffering and grief, and nothing can hurt or vex him of all that is or befalleth. But with God, when he is made man, it is otherwise.

Theologia Germanica (c. 1350), Ch. XL

14. It is evident, then, that this holy kiss is a necessary condescension to the world, for two reasons: firstly, in

order to fortify the faith of the weak; secondly, in order to gratify the desires of the perfect. It is also plain, I hope, that this mystical kiss is nothing else than the mediator between God and men, the man Christ Jesus, who, with the Father and the Holy Ghost, liveth and reigneth for ever and ever. Amen.

Bernard of Clairvaux (1090–1153),
Sermons, II

15. Behold the mystery of the earth; as that generates or brings forth, so must thou generate or bring forth. The earth is not that body, which grows or sprouts forth, but is the mother of that body; as also thy flesh is not the spirit, but the flesh is the mother of the spirit. But now in both of them, viz. in the earth and in thy flesh, there is the light of the clear deity hidden, and it breaks through, and generates to itself a body according to the kind of each body; for man according to his body, and for the earth, according to its body; for as the mother is, so also is the child.

Jacob Boehme (1575–1624),
Aurora, Ch. 21

16. In this season of the year the sun of heaven enters the sign of *Libra*, which means the Scales; for day and night are evenly balanced, and the sun divides the light from the darkness in equal parts. So likewise Christ stands in the sign of the Balance for the resigned man.

John of Ruysbroeck (1293–1381),
Adornment of the Spiritual Marriage, Ch. XXIX

17. For in this time the working of creatures was not shewed, but [the working] of our Lord God in the creature: for he is in the mid-point of all things, and all he doeth.

Julian of Norwich (c. 1342–1420),
Revelations of Divine Love, Ch. XI

18. The longing to love the beauty of the world in a human being is essentially the longing for the Incarnation. It is mistaken if it thinks it is anything else. The Incarnation alone can satisfy it. It is therefore wrong to reproach the mystics, as has been done sometimes, because they use love's language. It is theirs by right. Others only borrow it.

> Simone Weil (1909–43),
> *Waiting on God*,
> "Forms of the Implicit Love of God"

19. And thus in this exaltation of the Incarnation of his Son, and the glory of his resurrection according to the flesh, the Father not only made all things beautiful in part, but also, we may well say, clothed them with beauty and dignity.

> John of the Cross (1542–91),
> *A Spiritual Canticle Between the Soul and Christ*, St. V

20. Love is the Christ of God; wherever it comes, it comes as the blessing and happiness of every natural life, as the restorer of every lost perfection, a redeemer from all evil, a fulfiller of all righteousness, and a peace of God which passeth all understanding.

> William Law (1686–1761),
> *The Spirit of Love*, Third Dialogue

21. The prodigious expanses of time which preceded the first Christmas were not empty of Christ: they were imbued with the influx of his power. It was the ferment of his conception that stirred up the cosmic masses and directed the initial developments of the biosphere. It was the travail preceding his birth that accelerated the development of instinct and the birth of thought upon the earth. Let us have done with the stupidity which makes a stumbling-block of the endless eras of expectancy imposed on us by

Messiah; the fearful, anonymous labours of primitive man, the beauty fashioned through its age-long history by ancient Egypt, the anxious expectancies of Israel, the patient distilling of the attar of oriental mysticism, the endless refining of wisdom by the Greeks: all these were needed before the Flower could blossom on the rod of Jesse and of all humanity. All these preparatory processes were cosmically and biologically necessary that Christ might set foot upon our human stage.

Pierre Teilhard de Chardin (1881–1955),
Hymn of the Universe, "Pensées", 2

22. Upon this same manner shall this word "within" be understood. It is commonly said that a soul shall see our Lord within all things and within itself. True it is that our Lord is within all creatures, but not in that manner that a kernel is hid within the shell of a nut, or as a little bodily thing is holden within another such. But he is within all creatures as holding and keeping them in their being, through subtlety and might of his own blessed kind and cleanness unseeable.

Walter Hilton (1300–96),
The Scale of Perfection, Book II, Ch. XXXIII

23. Those who use spiritual discourse without having tasted and experienced the things of which they speak, resemble a man who, in passing through a barren desert in the parching noon of summer, and while tortured with a burning thirst, pictures to his mind some cool fountain of fresh and limpid water, and freely indulges his fancy therewith; or, a man who has never tasted honey, and yet undertakes to describe its sweetness to another.

Macarius (c. 300–390),
Institutes of Christian Perfection, Ch. XVIII

24. Nothing but God himself can explain God to the soul; and this he does in an ineffable manner. He who requires neither words, nor human thought, who, without making himself understood, makes us at least aware that he is incomprehensible, and makes us feel it more vividly and certainly than all the eloquence of human rhetoric.

> François Malaval (1627–1719),
> *A Simple Method of Raising the Soul to Contemplation*, First Treatise

25. As it is now here in this book, when we enter into the darkness that is above mind, we shall not only find the shortening of words, but as it were a madness and a perfect unreasonability of all that we say.

> *Denis Hid Divinity* (late 14th Century), Ch. 3

26. When God speaks to the soul, it is without the aid of the senses. It is in a mighty, strong, and swift communication, in a speech the mind cannot comprehend, unless the mind is so humbled as to take the lowest place amongst created things.

> Mechthild of Magdeburg (1217–82),
> *The Flowing Forth of the Light of the Godhead*

27. If the soul hath freed herself from all intermediate things, if she is stripped of all images, she ought not to tarry with the mediate, but her object must be God in his pure being, and in this essentiality she ought to enter.

> John Tauler (c. 1300–61),
> *The Following of Christ*, 141

28. This alone I know, that I know not what I see, and never can know. And I know not how to name Thee because I know not what Thou art, and did anyone say unto me that Thou wert called by this name or that, by the very fact that he named it, I should know that it was not Thy

name. For the wall beyond which I see Thee is the end of
all manner of signification in names.

Nicholas of Cusa (1401–64),
The Vision of God, Ch. XIII

29. Conscious of this, the sacred writers celebrate It by every
Name while yet they call It Nameless.

Dionysius the Areopagite (c. 500),
The Divine Names, Ch. I, 5

30. For if I were to spend many years in devising how to
picture to myself anything so beautiful, I should never be
able, nor even know how, to do it; for it is beyond the
reach of any possible imagination here below; the
whiteness and brilliancy alone are inconceivable. It is not
a brilliancy which dazzles, but a delicate whiteness and a
brilliancy infused, furnishing the most excessive delight
to the eyes, never wearied thereby, nor by the visible
brightness which enables us to see a beauty so divine. It
is a light so different from any light here below that the
very brightness of the sun we see, in comparison with the
brightness and light before our eyes, seems to be something so obscure, that no one would ever wish to open
his eyes again.

Teresa of Avila (1515–82),
Life, Ch. XXVIII

31. In short, it is such that no man, however gifted he may
be, can ever, in the whole course of his life, arrive at any
imagination of what it is. God puts it before us so
instantaneously, that we could not open our eyes in time
to see it, if it were necessary for us to open them at all.
But whether our eyes be open or shut, it makes no
difference whatever; for when our Lord wills, we must
see it, whether we will or not. No distraction can shut it
out, no power can resist it, nor can we attain to it by any

diligence or efforts of our own. I know this by experience well, as I shall show you.

Teresa of Avila (1515–82),
Life, Ch. XXVIII

32. The steps of a ladder have no proximate relation with the goal and place to which we ascend by it, towards which they are but means; so if he who climbs does not leave behind all the steps so that none remain, or if he rests upon one of them, he will never ascend to the summit, to the peaceful resting of the goal. The soul, therefore, that will ascend in this life to the Supreme Good and Rest must pass beyond these steps of considerations, forms, and notions, because they bear no likeness or proportion to the end, which is God, towards which it tends.

John of the Cross (1542–91),
The Ascent of Mount Carmel, Book II, Ch. XII

33. Moreover, it is in the power of the deiform spouse to strip herself naked of all forms and images, and look into the very Truth and Superessence of all beings throughout the creation. For there is not anything which she looketh at as simply nothing, but in all things doth she see God, as in the greatest so in the least.

Gerlac Petersen (1378–1411),
The Fiery Soliloquy with God, Ch. IX

34. He sat for a long while in thought, and the more he thought the less he could understand what had happened. Then he decided to write about these things as he had been commanded. But all his senses and reason could not express what he had seen; no words could describe it. Then he thought of expressing it in pictures and formulas; but again he could not, for it was beyond all pictures and formulas. Then he thought he would

reason about it and teach by reason and concepts; but it was beyond all reason and all human concepts. The more he thought about it the less he knew, because it was greater than anything he had ever seen or heard of. This amazed him and he said: "O Beloved, tell me what thou meanest. Thou saidst I had to see the origin and then write about it so that men could conceive it. Now thou hast made me see such a great wonder that I cannot express it in words. I have tried with all my reason, but no word will describe it. Nor can I describe where I have been or what I have seen and heard, except for one thing: that I know my heart and my soul are full of an overwhelming joy which frightens me, for I know it will be hard to control."

The *answer* came: "You must do it as far as you can, because men nowadays refuse the divine gifts, not knowing what they are."

Rulman Merswin (c. 1307–82),
The Book of the Nine Rocks, Last Discourse

35. If this is so, we may have to recover for all that creation the Way of the Affirmation of its Images. We shall take no harm from it; we need not be morally nervous; its difficulties are no more, though certainly no less, than the difficulties of the Way of the Rejection of Images which, on the whole, the Christian notabilities have so far preferred.

Charles Williams (1886–1945),
The Image of the City, "Sensuality and Substance"

36. Now, albeit this dialogue pass not betwixt God and the soul in these express and formal terms, yet silently and in spirit they pass in effect and substance within the soul in this her desire of humiliation; the which spiritual effect a man cannot express but by such articulate words.

Benet of Canfield (1562–1610),
The Rule of Perfection, Part II, Ch. IV

37. But the spirit of man, occupying the middle place between the angelic and the brute, has need of a body for
its own advancement in knowledge and for rendering
service to others. Thus, to say nothing of the other bodily
members or their functions, how, I ask, could instruction
be imparted without a corporeal tongue, or attended to
without corporeal ears?

Bernard of Clairvaux (1090–1153),
Sermons, V

38. Suppose that an artist made you a present of a beautiful
picture of the sun, in which he had employed all the
resources of his art so that you could not tear your eyes
away from it, so greatly were you ravished by the beauty
of colour, the boldness of technique, the genius of composition, and all its other beauties; yet I am quite sure
that if you were very cold, your picture of the sun would
not warm you, nor, when you wanted to see or to walk
somewhere, would it furnish you with light. You would
have to go to the sun itself, the subject of your picture,
and not be content with an inanimate and opaque
canvas. This world is a beautiful and impressive picture
of the Divine, but it is from ceaselessly regarding the
original that we draw our heat and light.

François Malaval (1627–1719),
*A Simple Method of Raising the Soul to
Contemplation*, First Treatise

39. My eyes are so clear, My mouth so tender, My cheeks so
radiant and blooming, and all My figure so fair and
ravishing, yea, and so delicately formed, that if a man
were to lie in a glowing furnace till the day of judgement,
only to have one single glance at My beauty, he would
not deserve it. See, I am so deliciously adorned in
garments of light, I am so exquisitely set off with all the
blooming   colours   of   living   flowers,   that   all

May-blossoms, all the beautiful shrubs of all dewy fields, all the tender buds of the sunny meads, are but as rough thistles compared to My adornment.

Henry Suso (c. 1295–1366),
The Little Book of Eternal Wisdom, Ch. VII

40. And yet, when I, the supernatural, immutable good, present Myself to every creature according to its capacity to be susceptible of Me, I bind the sun's splendour, as it were, in a cloth, and give thee spiritual perceptions of Me and of My sweet love in bodily words thus: I set Myself tenderly before the eyes of thy heart; now adorn and clothe thou Me in spiritual perceptions and represent Me as delicate and as comely as thy very heart could wish, and bestow on Me all those things that can move the heart to especial love and entire delight of soul.

Henry Suso (c. 1295–1366),
The Little Book of Eternal Wisdom, Ch. VII

iv *Faith and Heuristic Passion*

Spiritual life, then, requires cultivation, but there can be no investment of labour, no patient progress unless one believes in the first place that the end is attainable; that the fruits will develop; that direct knowledge of God is feasible, as well as desirable.

In this context, I am indebted for the term "heuristic passion" to the philosopher Michael Polanyi, who has done much to explain how fundamentally our passion for knowledge, whether in science or religion, entails necessary, sustaining acts of belief. As human beings we are, says Polanyi, blindly committed to our bodies, which are more complex than we know, but which enable us to learn and understand. We attend, that is, *from* our bodies (in which we believe) *to* the things about which we are learning. Every act of understanding, examined in the light of Polanyi's model, turns out to be based on prior assumptions which are themselves undemonstrable and taken on trust. Learning is therefore an adventure upon which we enter through belief. Although the word "faith" is normally reserved for specifically religious belief, it too is part of the adventure in human learning, for by faith we are called to believe that ultimate reality is knowable.

It is important to understand that faith is not irrational, nor just a matter of emotion. As the scholastic philosophers claim, it is an "intellectual assent": faith completes reason, but does not deny it, just as the scientist's belief in a certain hypothesis gives shape to his enquiry, making it reasonable. Scientists of course do not operate by reason alone, but also by intuition, imagination, trust in their own ability, and a sense of deepening coherency which leads reason towards understanding. Faith operates in a similar manner, and here the mystic resembles the scientist in claiming that faith is justified empirically by results: by a deepening sense of coherency, and the fruits of a human life wherein natural reason finds itself fulfilled.

Thus, our passion for learning entails that we proceed in faith through obscurity, though not irrationally, for the contents of faith are objectively discussible (1–18). At the same time, we must avoid the pitfalls of excessive rationalizing and presumptuous curiosity concerning the hidden things of God (19–21). Desire to know what God is, after all, amounts to a desire to *be* God, for only God can know God fully. We may, however, legitimately desire to know God according to our capacity as creatures.

The narrow way of faith therefore leads us between arrogance and negligence, hope and responsibility, certainty and doubt. It requires us neither to believe doctrines unworthy of God, nor to behave wrongly, making belief our excuse (25–36).

1. For if we rely on other lights, clear and distinct, of the understanding, we have ceased to rely on the obscurity of faith, which has therefore ceased to shine in the dark place of which the Apostle speaks. This place is the intellect, which is the candlestick to hold the light of faith. In this life the intellect must therefore be dark, until the day of our transformation and union with Him, towards whom the soul is travelling; or until the day of the clear vision of God shall have dawned in the next life.

John of the Cross (1542–91),
The Ascent of Mount Carmel, Book II, Ch. XVI

2. That which is wonderful in the saints is the constancy of their faith under every circumstance; without this there would be no sanctity. In the loving faith which makes them rejoice in God for everything, their sanctity has no need of any extraordinary manifestation; this could only prove useful to others who might require the testimony of such signs; but the soul in this state, happy in its obscurity, does in no way rely on these brilliant mani-festations; it allows them to show outwardly for the profit of others, but keeps for itself what all have in common, the will of God, and his good pleasure. Its faith is proved in hiding, and not in manifesting itself, and those who require more proof have less faith.

Jean-Pierre de Caussade (1675–1715),
Abandonment to Divine Providence,
Book II, Ch. I, Sec. V

3. Faith changes the face of the earth; by it the heart is raised, entranced and becomes conversant with heavenly things. Faith is our light in this life. By it we possess the truth without seeing it; we touch what we cannot feel, and see what is not evident to the senses. By it we view the world as though it did not exist. It is the key of the treasure house, the key of the abyss of the science of

God. It is faith that teaches us the hollowness of created things; by it God reveals and manifests himself in all things. By faith the veil is torn aside to reveal the eternal truth.

Jean-Pierre de Caussade (1675–1751),
Abandonment to Divine Providence,
Book I, Ch. II, Sec. I

4. For understanding is the reward of faith. Therefore do not seek to understand in order to believe, but believe that thou mayest understand.

Augustine of Hippo (345–430),
Homilies on the Gospel of John, XXIX, 6

5. Our faith is tried more powerfully in common occurrences, and less exposed to a mixture of pride, than in uncommon and remarkable concerns.

François Fenelon (1651–1715),
Selections, V, "On Faithfulness in Little Things"

6. See now if darkness be not to be esteemed and embraced. What thou oughtest to do amidst them, is to believe, that thou art before the Lord, and in his presence, but thou oughtest to do this with a sweet and quiet attention. Do not desire to know any thing, nor to search after emotions, tenderness or sensible devotions, nor to do anything but what is the good will and pleasure of God. For otherwise thou wilt only make circles all thy life time and not advance one step towards perfection.

Miguel de Molinos (1640–97),
A Spiritual Guide Which Disentangles the Soul,
Book IV, 41

7. A great faith makes a great surrender: we ought to commit ourselves unto God, hoping against all hope.

Madame Guyon (1648–1717),
A Method of Prayer, Ch. V

8. And thus by this means alone, that is faith, God manifests himself to the soul in the divine light, which
surpasses all understanding, and therefore the greater the
faith of the soul the more is that soul united to God. This
is the meaning of St Paul when he said, "He that cometh
to God must believe that he is." Such an one must walk
by faith, with his understanding in darkness, and in the
obscurity of faith only, "for in this darkness God unites
himself to the intellect".

John of the Cross (1542–91),
The Ascent of Mount Carmel, Book II, Ch. IX

9. There is a certain contrivance of perspective which en-
chants the eye by making it see as at a vast distance,
something which is quite close. Faith is that which brings
us nearest to God as well as that which removes us
farthest from him, and therefore the more contemplation
illumines faith, the more it shows us simultaneously a
God present and a God infinite, a God with us, and a
God above us; it puts us in the very heart of God at the
same moment that it plunges us into an abyss of God.
We do not yet distinguish the being of God, faith remaining always obscure, but we see it more clearly than
before.

François Malaval (1627–1719),
A Simple Method of Raising the Soul to Contemplation,
Second Treatise, Discourse XII

10. Thou hast inspired me, Lord, who art the food of the
strong, to do violence to myself, because impossibility
coincideth with necessity, and I have learnt that the place
wherein thou art found unveiled is girt round with the
coincidence of contradictories, and this is the wall of
Paradise wherein thou dost abide. The door whereof is
guarded by the most proud spirit of Reason, and, unless
he be vanquished, the way in will not lie open. Thus 'tis

beyond the coincidence of contradictories that thou
mayest be seen, and nowhere this side thereof. If, then, in
thy sight, Lord, impossibility be necessity, there is
naught that thy sight seeth not.

Nicholas of Cusa (1401–64),
The Vision of God, Ch. IX

11. To begin the way in small things conveniently is better
than to dream of the remote splendours of the vicarious
life; not that they are likely in any case to seem very
splendid when they come. To begin by practising faith
where it is easiest is better than to try and practise it
where it is hardest. There is always somewhere where it
can be done.

Charles Williams (1886–1945),
The Image of the City, "The Way of Exchange"

12. Erasure and reception proceeded together; the past
accumulations of casuistry were erased, and my thought
widened to receive the idea of something beyond all
previous ideas. With disbelief, belief increased. The aspiration and hope, the prayer, was the same as that
which I felt years before on the hills, only it now
broadened.

Richard Jefferies (1848–87),
The Story of My Heart, Ch. VI

13. First of all, faith is not an emotion, not a feeling. It is not
a blind subconscious urge toward something vaguely
supernatural. It is not simply an elemental need in man's
spirit. It is not a feeling that God exists. It is not a
conviction that one is somehow saved or "justified" for
no special reason except that one happens to feel that
way. It is not something entirely interior and subjective,
with no reference to any external motive. It is not just
"soul force". It is not something that bubbles up out of

the recesses of your soul and fills you with an indefinable "sense" that everything is all right. It is not something so purely yours that its content is incommunicable. It is not some personal myth of your own that you cannot share with anyone else, and the objective validity of which does not matter either to you or God or anybody else.

But also it is not an opinion. It is not a conviction based on rational analysis. It is not the fruit of scientific evidence. You can only believe what you do not know. As soon as you know it, you no longer believe it, at least not in the same way as you know it.

Faith is first of all an intellectual assent. It perfects the mind, it does not destroy it. It puts the intellect in possession of Truth which reason cannot grasp by itself. It gives us certitude concerning God as He is in Himself; faith is the way to a vital contact with a God Who is alive, and not to the view of an abstract First Principle worked out by syllogisms from the evidence of created things.

Thomas Merton (1915–68),
New Seeds of Contemplation, Ch. 18, "Faith"

14. I speak boldly yet truly, that an infidel liveth not without faith: for if I demand of him, who is his father or mother, straightways he will tell me, such a man and such a woman: and if I press him further, whether he doth remember the time when he was first conceived, or the hour when he was born into this world, he will answer me, that he never knew or saw any such thing: and yet for all this doth he believe that which he never beheld, seeing he believeth, without all doubt, that such a man was his father, and such a woman his mother.

Gregory the Great (c. 540–604),
The Dialogues, Book IV

15. If, then, faith is nothing else than a preconception of the

mind in regard to what is the subject of discourse, and obedience is so called, and understanding and persuasion; no one shall learn aught without faith, since no one [learns aught] without preconception.

Clement of Alexandria (c. 150–215),
The Miscellanies, Ch. IV

16. Thus I saw and understood that our faith is our light in our night: which light is God, our endless Day.

Julian of Norwich (c. 1342–1420),
Revelations of Divine Light, Ch. LXXXIII

17. And here I understand, that men are incapable of being able to have so much faith in thee, that they should be altogether freed from being solicited to doubt, and therefore God gives them the faith according to their capacity, as we do not put so hot water into a glass vessel, as into one of earth, nor into one of earth, as into one of brass, accommodating it unto the capacity of the vessel, not willing it should be broken.

Juan de Valdes (1490–1541),
The Divine Considerations, CIII

18. Certainly, he who thinks of the Lord in goodness already sees, with the eye of faith, Him who is the beginning of all things.

Richard of St Victor (c. 1123–75),
The Twelve Patriarchs, Ch. III

19. Stand therefore in thy degree, and desire not high things. For if thou desirest to know what God is, thou desirest to be God; the which becomes thee not.

Richard Rolle (1300–49),
The Fire of Love, Ch. VI

20. We may not seek to know the majesty and secrets of

God, being far from our knowledge, and such as God
would not man to meddle withal.

Juan Luis Vives (1492–1540),
Introduction to Wisdom, Diii(v)–Div(r)

21. Son, beware thou dispute not of high matters nor of the
    secret judgements of God, why this man is so left, and that
    man taken into such great favour; why also one is so
    afflicted, and another so eminently exalted. These things are
    beyond all reach of man's faculties: neither can any reason
    or disputation avail to search out the judgement of God.

    Thomas à Kempis (c. 1379–1471),
    Of the Imitation of Christ, Book IV, Ch. LVIII

22. That is, if someone not only in speech or in writing but
    even in thought considers that he should undertake to
    investigate every question about the supreme, un-
    changeable and inscrutable nature, he and every human
    being should be totally restrained and held back from
    such an immense and vain presumption. But to in-
    vestigate these things to the extent that the ability is not
    denied to man or to the degree that it is forbidden a
    faithful man to be ignorant of them, the spirit of the man
    of faith must be helped and exhorted, not discouraged.

    William of St Thierry (c. 1085–1148),
    The Enigma of Faith, 38

23. For God rewards humility by knowledge of the truth;
    but he disdains those who remain incessantly abased
    because of a criminal laziness to raise themselves, who
    bury their talent of faith in an abyss of reasons and
    conceptions, and who, having been created to be the
    image of God, leave God and retain the image.

    François Malaval (1627–1719),
    *A Simple Method of Raising the Soul to
    Contemplation*, Second Treatise, Dialogue IV

24. The main design of Jesus Christ was to promote in us a holy life, as the best and most compendious way to a right belief. He suspends all true acquaintance with God upon doing God's will: "If any man will do his will, he shall know of the doctrine." From what has been said, we may deduce the following inference: "Neither hastily to subscribe to the creed of another; nor hastily to judge another because of his creed."

John Smith (1618–52),
Select Discourses, I

25. He that soars to the heights of faith must soar in love higher than in understanding.

Ramon Lull (c. 1232–1315),
The Tree of Love, Part II, Ch. I, 16

26. No sign can warrant our belief, unless it be in conjunction with a doctrine worthy of God.

Benjamin Whichcote (1609–83),
Select Aphorisms, 240

27. Who will think a man does believe, that does things contrary to what he says he believeth?

Benjamin Whichcote (1609–83),
Select Aphorisms, 105

28. If you would be religious, be rational in your religion.

Benjamin Whichcote (1609–83),
Select Aphorisms, 68

29. If a man be once out of the use of reason, there are no bounds to unreasonableness.

Benjamin Whichcote (1609–83),
Select Aphorisms, 20

30. Precisely, however, for such a faith to be possible, some-

thing further is necessary. The universe must show itself to be capable of kindling and maintaining in us a sufficiently powerful illumination of hope and a sufficient warmth of love. No end awaits man, I said earlier, other than the end of mankind itself; but if this end of mankind is to be worthy of attainment, if it is to be tempting to us, it is essential that it present itself to us (both to our minds and to our hearts) in the form of some issue that opens on to indefinite freedom: an issue that widens out into full consciousness, through all the forces of death and materialization.

> Pierre Teilhard de Chardin (1881–1955),
> *Activation of Energy*,
> "The Sense of the Species of Man"

31. Of the two parts of faith, which are, *to believe*, and *to have confidence*, I understand that of one of them a man's mind is in some manner capable: I would say, that a man is able to bring himself to believe, or at least to persuade himself, that he doth believe. And of the other I understand he is incapable; I would say, he is not able of himself, to reduce himself to have confidence, nor to persuade himself, that he hath confidence. In such sort, he who believes, and hath not confidence, shows that his belief is industry, and human wit, and not divine inspiration. And he who believing hath confidence, shows that his belief is inspiration, and revelation.

> Juan de Valdes (1490–1541),
> *The Divine Considerations*, LXX

32. But what if one has no knowledge of God? Can such ignorance consist with the hope of salvation? Surely not. For we can neither love God without the knowledge of him, nor possess him without the love of him. Therefore, let us know ourselves that we may fear God, and let us know God that we may also love him. The first of these

virtues introduces us to wisdom, the second brings us to its perfection, because "the fear of the Lord is the beginning of wisdom", and "love is the fulfilling of the law". Consequently, it is as necessary to avoid ignorance of God and ignorance of self as it is certain that without the fear and the love of God we cannot save our souls. As regards the knowledge of other objects, that is a matter of indifference; we shall not be condemned for the want of it any more than its possession will save us.

Bernard of Clairvaux (1090–1153),
Sermons, XXXVII

33. Thy unbelief does not take away or make void the truth of God, but faith blows up the spirit of hope, and testifies that we are God's children. The faith is generated in the flesh, and wrestles so long with God, till it overcomes and gets the victory.

Jacob Boehme (1575–1624),
Aurora, Ch. 11

Chapter III

Preliminary Patterns

Mystics tell us that spiritual progress requires moral progress; indeed, certain moral imperatives are laid down as preliminaries to the mystical life. There is no point, for example, in proclaiming a higher love if ordinary love is lacking; there is no point in aspiring to see God if we persecute our neighbour; there is no point in preaching universal peace if we participate in war and cruelty; there is no point in preaching Christ with hatred or wrath in our hearts.

As with so many things human, however, the lines between spiritual and moral cannot be drawn clearly, and it is too much to expect that complete moral perfection precede any degree at all of spiritual aspiration. None the less, as Rudolf Steiner says, one step forward spiritually ought to be prepared by three steps forward in the development of character.

Not surprisingly in this context, mystics stress the fundamental importance of humility. Through it we come to understand, among other things, that however else we excuse violence, war, persecution, tyranny and cupidity, we may not do so by calling them Christian. Our approach to God is rather through charity, the virtue of self-giving love which finds expression also in a moral and patient encounter with ordinary things.

✠

i *Non-Violence*

As we have seen in the previous chapter, we are to avoid rationalizations which would, in the name of faith, excuse acts unworthy of the Christ-impulse. Such a warning is obviously pertinent to those acts of violence and hatred by which Christian persecutors throughout the centuries have sought to enforce their faith. On this subject, the mystics especially assure us that anger is a first fruit of the pride which caused the Fall itself (7), and they proclaim the necessity of non-violence to true religion.

Admittedly, there are exceptions. Bernard of Clairvaux, for instance, wrote a mystical treatise on the love of God, but also preached the second crusade, and there is no dearth of evidence in human history to show how frequently we fail to translate our best knowledge into action. This does not mean that mystics can have no influence at all on history or politics; only that mystics ought not to give allegiance to temporal concerns in which their best insights are betrayed. Clearly, Mother Teresa's rescuing babies from garbage heaps is closer to the mystical way than are the crusades, and history's record of Mother Teresa is commendable: it is the world's acknowledgement, in a sense, of a redemptive energy of selfless love which is the exact opposite of war, persecution and hatred, history's favourite subjects.

Despite aberrations and inconsistencies, then, there remains throughout the literature of mysticism a pre-eminently humanizing, gracious denunciation of war and persecution, proclaiming that where these things are found, God is not (1–14). Excerpts 15–21 develop this theme by reminding us how the Fall is bound up with wrath, and we are asked to remember that anger (like bad faith) readily finds specious justifications disguised as self-righteousness. It follows that the way of the cross is radically pacifist (22–27), and directs us to the conclusion that not only war, but preparation for war, is evil; nuclear weapons, like the racks and gallows of the tormentors, mock at God more offensively even than atheists (25).

Pacifism, of course, implies not only that we desist from violence, but also that we love our neighbour. In so far as we are called upon to forgive our persecutors, we are invited to re-affirm them as God's creatures, bearers also of Christ's image; we do not find him without loving them (28–35). And yet, none of this implies that we should acquiesce in evil. Because war and hatred bring separation and suffering into the world they are hateful, and we must fight against them. We are free to abhor vice in general but not to hate a vicious person; to fight against crime, but not to hate the criminal (36–39). Our conflicts in this arena thus remain spiritual, and we are to find allies among those likewise persuaded that the main struggle is against the impulse to impose one's will on others, the foundation of every tyranny.

1. The Christian who acts in the destroying fury of war, acts in full contrariety to the whole nature and spirit of Christ, and can no more be said to be led by his spirit, or be one with him, than those his enemies who "came forth with swords and staves to take him". Blinded Protestants think they have the glory of slaughtering blind Papists; and the victorious Papist claims the merit of having conquered troops of heretics. But alas! the conquest is equally great on both sides, both are entitled to the same victory; and the glorious victory on both sides, is only that of having gospel goodness equally under their feet.

William Law (1686–1761),
Address to the Clergy, p. 83

2. Look now at warring Christendom, what smallest drop of pity towards sinners is to be found in it? Or how could a spirit all hellish, more fully contrive and hasten their destruction? It stirs up and kindles every passion of fallen nature that is contrary to the all-humble, all-meek, all-loving, all-forgiving, all-saving spirit of Christ. It unites, it drives, and compels nameless numbers of unconverted sinners to fall, murdering and murdered among flashes of fire, with the wrath and swiftness of lightning, into a fire infinitely worse than that in which they died. O sad subject for thanksgiving days, whether in Popish or Protestant churches!

William Law (1686–1761),
Address to the Clergy, p. 89

3. The scandal that is pernicious to him who scandalizeth, is that which the saints of the world do, pretending to do service unto God. And here I learn that I ought to keep my self as from the fire to persecute any man of what manner soever, pretending to do God service therein.

Juan de Valdes (1490–1541),
The Divine Considerations, LXXVI

4. I will not by the noise of bloody wars, and the dethroning of kings, advance you to glory: but by the gentle ways of peace and love. As a deep friendship meditates and intends the deepest designs for the advancement of its objects, so doth it show itself in choosing the sweetest and most delightful methods, whereby not to weary, but please the person it desireth to advance.

Thomas Traherne (c. 1636–74),
Centuries of Meditation, I, 4

5. And the saved man will not suffer any thing to rule that destroys; and so our mind is, and we would that all men

were saved, and come to the knowledge of the truth, which the persecutors are out of.

George Fox (1624–91),
Epistles, CCXLII

6. And if they were in the true faith they would never make racks, and prisons, gaols, and fires to persecute and force others that were not of their faith, for this was not the practice of the true faith of Christ that was witnessed and enjoyed by the apostles and primitive Church; neither had they any such command from Christ and the apostles.

George Fox (1624–91),
Journal, 1668

7. What should God do? Look about and see how most of humanity is eager to slay and murder. You see for yourself that the men in the cities are full of pride and jealousy and hate. They fight and tear among one another. This comes from overweening pride; and because of his pride God hurled Lucifer and his followers into the depths.

Rulman Merswin (c. 1307–82),
The Book of the Nine Rocks,
"Concerning Holy Matrimony"

8. "All by love, nothing by constraint." This was his favourite motto, and the wellspring of his direction to others. He has often said to me that those who try to force human will are exercising a tyranny which is hateful to God and man.

Jean-Pierre Camus (1504–1652),
The Spirit of St Francis de Sales, p. 58

9. Not one syllable of angry resentment nor murmuring complaint; no indignation for such perfect innocence so

causelessly injured and abused; no wishes of revenge, nor no imprecations upon the devoted heads of these brutish men; but even in the extremity of torment, a calm and kind petition to his Father, a word of blessing, and the best excuse alleged in mitigation of their fault, which the guilty themselves could have produced in bar to the condemnation and vengeance due to it. Never was such an instance of meek suffering, never so unwearied a love of enemies, never so kind an intercession for pardon, since the world began. Remember this, my soul, and when thou findest thyself apt to be out of temper for the affronts or wrongs thou sustainest, even when most unkind, even when most undeserved, compare (though in truth there can be no comparison) thy sufferings with thy Lord's.

Anselm (1033–1109),
Meditations, Ch. XII

10. To all other animals, nature, or the God of nature, has given appropriate weapons of offence. . . . But man he brought forth into the world naked from his mother's womb, weak, tender, unarmed, his flesh of the softest texture, his skin smooth and delicate, and susceptible of the slightest injury. There is nothing observable in his limbs adapted to fighting, or to violence.

Desiderius Erasmus (1466?–1536),
Antipolemus

11. Man, whom peace most becomes, and who stands most in need of it, is the only creature that entertains an inveterate hatred against his own kind. Nor is it less remarkable, that nature has furnished all other creatures with arms to fight, as the horse with his feet, bulls with horns, boars with tusks, bees with stings, birds with beaks and talons, and even gnats and flies are not without the power of biting; but thou, O man, whom she has designed for peace and concord, she sent into the world

naked and unarmed, that thou mightest have nothing at all to do harm with. Reflect then how unnatural it is for you to endeavour to be revenged, or to return an injury that has been offered to you, especially with weapons sought without yourself which nature denied you.

Luis de Granada (1504–88),
The Sinners Guide, Book II, Part I, Ch. VII

12. One law Jesus Christ claimed as his own peculiar law, and it was the law of love, or charity. What practice among mankind violates this law so grossly as war?

Desiderius Erasmus (1466?–1536),
Antipolemus

13. He who is convicted judicially, suffers the punishment which the laws impose: but in war, each side treats the other side as guilty, and proceeds to inflict punishment, regardless of law, judge, or jury. In the former case, the evil only falls on him who committed the wrong: the benefit of the example redounds to all; in the latter case the greatest part of the very numerous evils falls on those who deserve no evil at all, on husbandmen, on old people, on mothers of families, on orphans, and on defenceless young females. But if any good at all can be gathered from a thing which is itself the worst of all things, the whole of that good devolves to the share of a few most profligate robbers, to the mercenary pillager, to the piratical privateer. It would be better to let the crime of a few go unpunished than, while we endeavour to chastise one or two by war, in which, perhaps, we may not succeed, to involve our own people, the neighbouring people, and the innocent part of the enemies (for so I may call the multitude) in certain calamity. It is better to let a wound alone, which cannot be healed without injury to the whole body.

Desiderius Erasmus (1466?–1536),
Antipolemus

14. Let it also be remembered, that he who used the sword in defence of his master, very soon after denied and renounced that master. If Peter is to be our model, and if we are so much pleased with the example of Peter *fighting* for Christ, we may probably approve also the example of Peter *denying* Christ.

> Desiderius Erasmus (1466?–1536),
> *Antipolemus*

15. To inquire, or search into the origin of wrath, is the same thing as to search into the origin of evil and sin: for wrath and evil are but two words for one and the same thing. There is no evil in any thing, but the working of the spirit of wrath. And when wrath is entirely suppressed, there can be no more evil, or misery, or sin in all nature and creature. This therefore is a firm truth, that nothing can be capable of wrath, or be the beginning of wrath, but the creature, because nothing but the creature can be the beginner of evil and sin.

> William Law (1686–1761),
> *The Spirit of Love*, First Dialogue

16. And notwithstanding all this, I saw truly that our Lord was never wroth, nor ever shall be. For he is God: good, life, truth, love, peace; his clarity and his unity suffereth him not to be wroth. For I saw truly that it is against the property of his might to be wroth, and against the property of his wisdom, and against the property of his goodness.

> Julian of Norwich (c. 1342–1420),
> *Revelations of Divine Love*, Ch. XLVI

17. And notwithstanding all this, I beheld and marvelled greatly: *What is the mercy and forgiveness of God?* For by the teaching that I had afore, I understood that the mercy of God should be the forgiveness of his wrath

after the time that we have sinned. For methought that to a soul whose meaning and desire is to love, the wrath of God was harder than any other pain, and therefore I took that the forgiveness of his wrath should be one of the principal points of his mercy. But howsoever I might behold and desire, I could in no wise see this point in all the showing.

Julian of Norwich (c. 1342–1420),
Revelations of Divine Love, Ch. XLVII

18. For I saw full surely that where our Lord appeareth, peace is taken and wrath hath no place. For I saw no manner of wrath in God, neither for short time nor for long; for in sooth, as to my sight, if God might be wroth for an instant, we should never have life nor place nor being.

Julian of Norwich (c. 1342–1420),
Revelations of Divine Love, Ch. XLIX

19. As anger produces angry words, so angry words increase anger.

William Law (1686–1761),
A Serious Call, Ch. XV

20. When he says, "Let all anger be taken away from you", he excepts none whatever as necessary or useful for us.

John Cassian (c. 360–434),
The Institutes, Book VIII, Ch. V

21. For if you do not suppress it [anger] in time, it will rise up against you, and make you do that which you will afterwards be sorry for. And what is worst of all, you will scarce be able to know what mischief you do, because an angry man thinks that whatever he does in order to revenge himself, he has always justice on his side; nay, he is often deceived so far as to imagine that

the very heat of his anger is nothing but a zeal for justice, and thus vice hides itself under the colour of virtue.

Luis de Granada (1504–88),
The Sinners Guide, Book II, Part I, Ch. VII

22. I remain pacifist but I quite see that at present the Christian world is not "there" and attempts to preach it at the moment can only rouse resistance and reduce charity. Like you I think the final synthesis must reconcile the lion and the lamb – but meanwhile the crescendo of horror and evil and wholesale destruction of beauty is hard to accept. . . .

Evelyn Underhill (1875–1941),
Letters, Trinity, 1941, To M.C.

23. And he who would be obedient, resigned and submissive to God, must and ought to be also resigned, obedient and submissive to all things, in a spirit of yielding, and not of resistance, and take them in silence, resting on the hidden foundations of his soul, and having a secret inward patience, that enableth him to take all chances or crosses willingly, and whatever befalleth, neither to call for nor desire any redress, or deliverance, or resistance, or revenge, but always in a loving, sincere humility to cry, "Father, forgive them, for they know not what they do!"

Theologia Germanica (c. 1350), Ch. XXIII

24. Therefore all those who unjustly inflict upon us tribulations and anguishes, shames and injuries, sorrows and torments, martyrdom and death, are our friends whom we ought to love much, because we gain eternal life by that which they make us suffer.

Francis of Assisi (1182–1226),
Rules, 22, "Of the Admonition of the Brothers"

25. For only love – which means humility – can exorcize the fear which is at the root of all war.

What is the use of postmarking our mail with exhortations to "pray for peace" and then spending billions of dollars on atomic submarines, thermo-nuclear weapons, and ballistic missiles? This, I would think, would certainly be what the New Testament calls "mocking God" – and mocking Him far more effectively than the atheists do.

Thomas Merton (1915–68),
New Seeds of Contemplation, Ch. 16

26. I told them I was brought off from outward wars. They came down again to give me press-money but I would take none. Then I was brought up to Sergeant Hole's, kept there awhile, and then taken down again. After a while at night the constables fetched me up again and brought me before the Commissioners, and they said I should go for a soldier, but I told them that I was dead to it. They said I was alive. I told them, "Where envy and hatred are there is confusion." They offered me money twice, but I would not take it. Then they were wroth, and I was committed close prisoner without bail or mainprize.

George Fox (1624–91),
Journal, 1651

27. And if it happen (as many times and too often it doth) that thou be troubled or disquieted by any sudden assault, all other things set aside, attend first of all to pacify thy mind, for that being quiet, many things are done, and well done, and without this, thou canst not do any thing of any value; besides that, thou dost thereby lie open to the blows of thine enemies. The devil doth so much fear this peace (as a place where God doth dwell for to work therein wonders) that oftentimes with the banners or ensigns of a friend he attempteth to deceive us with inspirations, which in appearance are good, stirring

up in us sundry good desires. The deceit whereof is known by the effects, because they take from us the peace of our hearts.

Lorenzo Scupoli (1530–1610),
Spiritual Combat, D11–D12

28. He shall say unto thee, "Inasmuch as thou hatest thy brother, it is I whom thou hatest."

Pachomius (–c. 346),
The Instructions, p. 370

29. Praised be my Lord for those who for thy love forgive, and weakness bear and tribulation.

Francis of Assisi (1182–1226),
The Canticle of the Sun

30. And let him not be angry with a brother on account of his offence, but let him advise him kindly and encourage him with all patience and humility.

Francis of Assisi (1182–1226),
Letter to All the Faithful

31. Yet very gently and patiently ought we to bear with one another in all things which are done less perfectly and orderly from without or from within; for to every one is his own calamity which he suffereth sufficiently grievous, whether it be of body or of mind.

Gerlac Petersen (1378–1411),
The Fiery Soliloquy with God, Ch. VI

32. If a man wish to offer Me an acceptable gift, let him strive to exercise himself in these three things. First, let him endeavour to be faithful to his neighbour whenever he is in need or in trouble, and, as much as in him lies, to lessen and excuse all his defects and sins.

Mechthild of Hackborn (1240–98),
Select Revelations, Book IV, Ch. III

33. Apply yourself to love those who appear to hate and calumniate you, and they will thus prepare for you brilliant crowns for eternity.

Bridget of Sweden (1303–73),
Select Revelations, Book II, Ch. III

34. You are all obliged to help one another by word and doctrine, and the example of good works, and in every other respect in which your neighbour may be seen to be in need; counselling him exactly as you would your-selves, without any passion of self-love; and he (a man not loving God) does not do this, because he has no love towards his neighbour; and, by not doing it, he does him, as thou seest, a special injury.

Catherine of Siena (1347–80),
The Dialogue, Ch. VI

35. And every evil also is done by means of his neighbour, for if he do not love Me, he cannot be in charity with his neighbour; and thus, all evils derive from the soul's deprivation of love of Me and her neighbour; whence, inasmuch as such a man does no good, it follows that he must do evil.

Catherine of Siena (1347–80),
The Dialogue, Ch. VI

36. Because I said to thee that it was not lawful for thee to reprove another, except in general (which is the truth), I do not wish thee to think that, when thou actually seest an open sin, thou canst not privately correct the sinner; this thou canst do, if he is so obstinate that he will not correct himself.

Catherine of Siena (1347–80),
The Dialogue, Ch. XV

37. As for these latter sort of enemies [who would entice us

to sin] they are indeed truly such; and their actions we must abhor, and also with discretion avoid their company: but we must not hate their persons, nor be wanting in any office of charity towards them, when occasion is offered.

Augustine Baker (1575–1641),
Sancta Sophia, Treat. 2, Sec. 2, Ch. 5, Part 20

38. Think not that thou canst please God, if thou hatest him whom God loveth.

Juan Luis Vives (1492–1540),
Introduction to Wisdom, H viii

39. This saying is Godly: "I hate, as one ready to love."

Juan Luis Vives (1492–1540),
Introduction to Wisdom, I ii

ii *Spiritual Combat*

Love needs to be protected by the weapons of discretion, as Angela of Foligno says (9), and the difference between spiritual conflict against one's self and physical war against one's neighbour is both sufficiently clear and so clearly necessary, that risks of misinterpreting the metaphors of combat in the literature of mysticism seem minimal. Our hatred, simply, must be confined to all that would put our neighbour further away from redemptive Good, and attacks on our neighbour's wrongdoing should offer the best opportunity for a change of heart. The most radical attack on crime is therefore through love in which the criminal is invited to participate reciprocally, and not through the institutionalized violence by which the authorities contrive to break his neck.

Spiritual combat, however, is far from easy, and calls for unusual patience and forbearance. It requires some understanding that however particular, private and insignificant the battle against one's self (1–13) may seem, it remains part of the cosmic drama of our material world, and of the immense conflicts of force, power and energy in the universe whirling around us. Yet the very smallness of our interior action in such an arena itself may become one of the enemy's weapons, for it can induce a sense of hopelessness. The mystics therefore call us to perseverance (14–18) through the promise that only spiritual victory can bring enduring peace; from war only further war ensues. In the end, the irresistible force is, paradoxically, the most vulnerable (19–30), the one that runs most counter to a literal interpretation of what constitutes victory in battle. Precisely this message, that in literal military victory lies no victory, in persecution lies no religion, in wrath lies no good, constitutes the meaning of spiritual combat.

1. Said Meister Eckhart the preacher, There is no greater valour nor no sterner fight than that for self-effacement, self-oblivion.

Meister Eckhart (1280–1327),
Sayings, 24

2. Remember that there is but one man in the world, with whom you are to have perpetual contention, and be always striving to exceed him, and that is yourself.

William Law (1686–1761),
A Serious Call, Ch. XVIII

3. For it is not an external enemy whom we have to dread. Our fire is shut up within ourselves: an internal warfare is daily waged by us: and if we are victorious in this, all external things will be made weak, and everything will be made peaceful and subdued for the soldier of Christ. We shall have no external enemy to fear, if what is within is overcome and subdued to the spirit.

John Cassian (c. 360–434),
The Institutes, Book V, Ch. XXI

4. We have, it must be admitted, a use for anger excellently implanted in us for which alone it is useful and profitable for us to admit it, viz., when we are indignant and rage against the lustful emotions of our heart, and are vexed at the things which we are ashamed to do or say before men have risen up in the lurking places of our heart, as we tremble at the presence of the angels, and of God himself, who pervades all things everywhere, and fear with the utmost dread the eye of him from whom the secrets of our hearts cannot possibly be hid.

John Cassian (c. 360–434),
The Institutes, Book VIII, Ch. VII

5. The most excellent gift which may be had of God in this world is that the servant of Jesus Christ may know and will to conquer himself, denying his own will.

Catherine of Bologna (1413–63),
The Spiritual Armour, 7

6. The Monastic Church is the one who flees to a special place prepared for her by God in the wilderness, and hides her face in the Mystery of the divine silence, and prays while the great battle is being fought between earth and heaven.

Her flight is not an evasion. If the monk were able to understand what goes on inside him, he would be able to say how well he knows that the battle is being fought in his own heart.

Thomas Merton (1915–68),
The Silent Life, Prologue

7. And he who fighteth against affliction and refuseth to endure it, is truly fighting against God.

Theologia Germanica (c. 1350), Ch. XLVI

8. We cannot be undone but by ourselves.

Benjamin Whichcote (1609–83),
Select Aphorisms, 198

9. If the love of God be not directed with discretion and protected by its weapons, it turneth unto evil. The weapons wherewith the good love of God and one's neighbour may be controlled are given unto man in the transformation of the soul.

Angela of Foligno (c. 1248–1309),
The Divine Consolation, Ch. XXVIII

10. For our fleshly lusts are the weapons with which our enemies make war on us. Idleness and indifference to virtue and the glory of God, these are the causes and the occasions of the struggle. But the weakness of our nature, our carelessness and ignorance of truth, these are the swords with which our enemies often wound, and sometimes conquer us.

John of Ruysbroeck (1293–1381),
Adornment of the Spiritual Marriage, Ch. XXIII

11. And because thou aspiring to the top of so great perfection, must use force with thy self, and courageously overcome thy own will, both in great and little things: it behoveth thee of necessity with all readiness of mind to prepare thy self to this combat, since the crown of so great a victory is not given, but to them that fight valiantly. This battle, as of all others it is the hardest, so the victory gotten by the same, is of all others most glorious and most dear unto God.

Lorenzo Scupoli (1530–1610),
The Spiritual Combat, Ch. 1

12. The distrust of ourselves, although in this battle it be so needful as we have said before, yet not withstanding, if

we have but it only, either we shall run away from the battle, or abiding still, be vanquished and overcome of our enemies. And therefore, besides this, it is also necessary to have our whole trust and confidence in God, hoping and expecting from him alone all good and help whatsoever.

Lorenzo Scupoli (1530–1610),
The Spiritual Combat, Ch. 3

13. Hence it cometh to pass that very few attain to the state of perfection, because like cowardly soldiers they will not stand fast, and constantly fight, and suffer the dints, which the resistance of an infinite number of their self wills bringeth with it, which doth always fight against them: but retiring back, leave their weapons and themselves in the power of their enemies who tyrannize over them.

Lorenzo Scupoli (1530–1610),
The Spiritual Conflict, Ch. 6

14. Never was a skilful knight in a tournament so gazed at as a man who suffers well is gazed at by all the heavenly court. All the saints are on the side of the suffering man; for, indeed, they have all partaken of it before him, and they call out to him with one voice that it contains no poison, but is a wholesome beverage.

Henry Suso (c. 1295–1366),
The Little Book of Eternal Wisdom, Ch. XIII

15. Our enemy is a great clatterer, do not trouble yourself at all about him; he cannot hurt you, I well know. Mock at him and let him go on. Do not strive with him, ridicule him, for it is all nothing. He has howled round about the Saints, and made plenty of hubbub; but to what purpose? In spite of it all, there they are, seated in the place which he has lost, the wretch!

François de Sales (1567–1622),
The Spiritual Conferences, Book III,
Letters to Widows, VII, To Madame de Chantal

16. Courage, then, it will come to an end at last; provided he
    enter not, it matters not. And meanwhile it is an excel-
    lent sign when the enemy beats and blusters at the door;
    for it is a sign that he has not got what he wants. If he
    had it, he would not cry out any more, he would enter
    and stay. Take note of this, so as not to fall into scruple.

    François de Sales (1567–1622),
    The Spiritual Conferences, Book III,
    Letters to Widows, XI, To Madame de Chantal

17. The second power is the power of anger, which man
    should be able to control in all things. He should always
    think that another is more likely to be right than he, and
    thus avoid strife. He must learn forbearance, and how to
    be quiet and kindly wherever he may be. One man may
    be sitting alone, or in an assembly, while others are
    sitting there, who are noisy and seldom silent. Ye must
    learn to be forbearing and to endure, and to commune
    with your own hearts. A man cannot work at a trade
    without having learnt it. If any one wanted to be an
    umbrella-maker, and would not learn his trade, he might
    do great harm to the work if he tried to carry it on before
    he had learned it; thus it is in all adversities, we must
    learn how to struggle.

    John Tauler (c. 1300–61),
    The Inner Way, Sermon XX

18. All that takes place in our days is the consequence of this
    war. Monster follows monster out of the pit, which
    swallows, and vomits them forth again amidst incessant
    clouds of smoke. The combat between St Michael and
    Lucifer, that began in Heaven, still continues. The heart
    of this once magnificent angel has become, through
    envy, an inexhaustible abyss of every kind of evil. He
    made angel revolt against angel in Heaven, and from the
    creation of the world his whole energy is exerted to make

more criminals among men to fill the ranks of those who
have been swallowed up in the pit.

> Jean-Pierre de Caussade (1675–1751),
> *Abandonment to Divine Providence*,
> Book II, Ch. IV, 12

19. It is thus that by bending gently, cedars are broken, and
    rocks overthrown. Who amongst creatures can resist a
    faithful, gentle, and humble soul? These are the only
    arms to be taken if we wish to conquer all our enemies.
    Jesus Christ has placed them in our hands that we may
    defend ourselves; there is nothing to fear if we know
    how to use them.

> Jean-Pierre de Caussade (1675–1751),
> *Abandonment to Divine Providence*,
> Book II, Ch. IV, 10

20. It is impossible but to love him that loveth. Love is so
    amiable that it is irresistible. There is no defence against
    that arrow, nor any deliverance in that war, nor any
    safeguard from that charm. Wilt thou not live unto him?
    Thou must of necessity live unto some thing. And what
    so glorious as his infinite love? Since therefore laws are
    requisite to lead thee, what laws can thy soul desire, than
    those that guide thee in the most amiable paths to the
    highest end?

> Thomas Traherne (c. 1636–74),
> *Centuries of Meditation*, I, 71

21. The perfect victory is to triumph over ourselves. For he
    that keeps himself in such subjection that his senses be
    obedient to reason, and his reason in all things to Me, is
    truly conqueror of himself and lord of the world.

> Thomas à Kempis (c. 1379–1471),
> *Of the Imitation of Christ*, Book IV, Ch. LIII

22. For if thou desire true delight and to be more plentifully comforted by Me, behold in the contempt of all worldly things and in the cutting off all base delights shall be thy blessing, and abundant consolation shall be rendered to thee. And the more thou withdrawest thyself from all solace of creatures, the sweeter and more powerful consolations shalt thou find in Me. But at first thou shalt not without some sadness nor without toil of conflict attain unto them.

Thomas à Kempis (c. 1379–1471),
Of the Imitation of Christ, Book IV, Ch. XII

23. Love, who is good and great, bade the Lover weep for the great and evil love that still endures in this world, though it pertains to the Beloved and was created by him for his own honour. The Lover wept, and in his tears he strove against that great and evil love, and he said to Love, that is good and great, and with his tears he could neither destroy that false love nor enslave it. Then answered Love: "If thy weeping avail not against that great and evil love as touching other men, it may avail at the least as touching thyself, since thy Beloved and I find therein honour and glory."

Ramon Lull (c. 1232–1315),
The Tree of Love, Part I, Ch. II, 3

24. Desire nothing but God: seek for nothing but God: and you shall taste of peace: you shall taste it in defiance of the world.

François Fenelon (1651–1715),
Pious Reflections, The Seventeenth Day

25. Jesus Christ alone is able to give peace to man. He makes him consistent with himself.

François Fenelon (1651–1715),
Pious Reflections, The Seventeenth Day

26. Love worketh wisely and softly in a soul where he will, for he slayeth mightily ire and envy and all passions of angriness and melancholy in it, and bringeth into the soul virtues of patience and mildness, peaceability, and love.

Walter Hilton (1300–1396),
The Scale of Perfection, Book II, Ch. XXXVIII

27. No carnal weapon or outward battelier can compare with these that are to be exercised as divine archers in the faith. In the Lamb's battles no noise is to be heard, but all softness and meekness is, by which the arrows do hit, and whereby the great Goliath doth fall, so that his conquest shall appear not to be of man, but God shall here act from the stillness of his own deep, wherein he will manifest himself to be all in all.

Jane Lead (1623–1704),
The Ascent to the Mount of Vision, XLVII

28. The way to procure and strengthen love is by fixing their minds upon the mercies, goodness and perfections of God, and to contradict or forget all arguments or motives of servile fear, the greatest enemy of love.

Augustine Baker (1575–1641),
Sancta Sophia, Treat. 3, Sec. 3, Ch. 5, Part 1

29. If then the bias of a love of the world inclines ever so little the balance of the scales which are in the heart, the evil word goes forth from the lips, and the mind, like one who shoots from a bow, strikes its neighbour with its tongue; nay, the evil sometimes reaches to the hands, and extends to wounds, and even to murder.

Macarius (c. 300–90),
Institutes of Christian Perfection, Ch. XXIII

30. When, therefore, any one yields an obedient ear to God, and loosens himself from the engagements of worldly life, and renounces all carnal pleasures, cleaving to God and adhering to him with entire application of mind; he then is enabled to discover that there is still another conflict, a secret war of thoughts, which is carried on in the recesses of the heart: and, by seeking the mercy of Christ with persevering prayer and with much faith and patience, he is enabled, by the powerful succour of God, to effect his deliverance from his inward chains and prison-house, and from the darkness of the spirits of wickedness, which are the influences of his own secret passions.

Macarius (c. 300–90),
Institutes of Christian Perfection, Ch. XXVII

iii *Humility*

The self-effacement required for spiritual combat leads us directly to humility, sometimes referred to as queen of the virtues. Humility can be described as knowledge of ourselves as we really are, and confronts us both with our moral weakness as fallen beings, and with our radical dependency as creatures. Humility is also essential to charity (which is self-giving love), for without humility the good that we do threatens merely to swell into self-regard. And when mystics claim that God makes available to some people an extraordinary, experiential sense of his presence, they claim also that humility is the ballast preventing the personality from capsizing into a chaos of ego-inflation. Without humility the entire mystical enterprise is not only insecure, but positively dangerous (1–15).

Humility can also be understood as a certain kind of unself-conscious action, such as highly trained performers bring to their special skill or art. The great painter, or musician or surgeon is taken out of himself while performing at his highest and best. There is nothing of mere individualism in what he does, for individualism and originality are opposites. Seen in this light, humility entails disciplined self-effacement and submission to rigorous training, but it is not just a sentimental or gratuitous self-abasement; rather it is the loss of that kind of self-regard which would prohibit our potential for creative expression.

Humility is thus as elusive as it is fundamental, for although it involves the casting out of self-will, we must be careful not to pursue it too directly or too wilfully. Our desire to be humble, like our requirement of humility in others, comes close to implying either that we deserve to be humble, or that we are important enough for others to heed our advice on this matter. We cannot presume to be pleased with ourselves on account of humility, though neither should we relinquish the vigilance required in disposing ourselves towards it, poised delicately as it is between hypocritical individualism and weak-sided inertia. It seems that although we are free to admire it in others, we cannot really know this virtue directly in ourselves (16–28).

Excerpts 29–34 deal with some varieties of false humility, and how closely it can ape the true virtue while encouraging covert self-esteem, hypocrisy or pride. Self-love remains the destroyer of paradise, wreathing its colours among even our fairest flowers. Humility is this serpent's bane; without it, virtue's flowers, and even the special graces of illumination, carry poison about them, all the more dangerous for being unseen.

1. Humility in itself is naught else but a true knowing and feeling of a man's self as he is.
   The Cloud of Unknowing (late 14th Century), Ch. 13

2. This virtue is so essential to the right state of our souls,

that there is no pretending to a reasonable or pious life without it. We may as well think to see without eyes, or live without breath, as to live in the spirit of religion without the spirit of humility. And although it is thus the soul and essence of all religious duties, yet is it, generally speaking, the least understood, the least regarded, the least intended, the least desired and sought after, of all other virtues, amongst all sorts of Christians.

William Law (1686–1761),
A Serious Call, Ch. XVI

3. For the fuller of pride any one is himself, the more impatient will he be at the smallest instances of it in other people. And the less humility any one has in his own mind, the more will he demand and be delighted with it in other people. You must therefore act by a quite contrary measure, and reckon yourself only so far humble, as you impose every instance of humility upon yourself, and never call for it in other people – so far an enemy to pride, as you never spare it in yourself, nor ever censure it in other persons. Now, in order to do this, you need only consider that pride and humility signify nothing to you, but so far as they are your own; that they do you neither good nor harm, but as they are the tempers of your own heart.

William Law (1686–1761),
A Serious Call, Ch. XVI

4. True patience and tranquillity is neither gained nor retained without profound humility of heart: and if it has sprung from this source, there will be no need either of the good offices of the cell or of the refuge of the desert. For it will seek no external support from anything, if it has the internal support of the virtue of humility, its mother and guardian. But if we are disturbed when attacked by anyone it is clear that the foundations of

humility have not been securely laid in us, and therefore at the outbreak of even a small storm, our whole edifice is shaken and ruinously disturbed.

John Cassian (c. 360–434),
Conference of Abbot Piamun, Ch. XIII

5. All visions, revelations and impressions of heaven, however much the spiritual man may esteem them, are not equal in worth to the least act of humility: for this brings forth the fruits of charity, which never esteems nor thinks well of self, but only of others.

John of the Cross (1542–91),
Spiritual Maxims, 316

6. Unless you make up your minds to this, never expect to make much progress, for as I said humility is the foundation of the whole building and unless you are truly humble, our Lord, for your own sake, will never permit you to rear it very high lest it should fall to the ground.

Teresa of Avila (1515–82),
The Interior Castle, Seventh Mansions, Ch. IV, 12

7. I know this, for I have passed through this state myself. However deep humility may be, it neither disquiets, wearies, nor disturbs the soul, but brings peace, sweetness and serenity. Although the sight of our wickedness grieves us and proves to us that we deserve to be in hell and that in justice all mankind should hate us, so that we hardly dare to beg for mercy, yet if it is a right humility this pain is accompanied by suavity, content and joy, and we do not wish to be without it; indeed, it ought to be prized since it brings self-knowledge.

Teresa of Avila (1515–82),
The Way of Perfection, Ch. XXXIX

8. We would fain be humble; but not despised. To be

despised and rejected is the heritage of virtue. We would be poor too, but without privation. And doubtless we are patient, except with hardships and with disagreeables. And so with all the virtues. The willing poor, unsolaced by corruptibles, descend into the valley of humility. They are pursued by insult and adversity, the best school of self-knowledge. And self-knowledge gets God-knowledge.

Meister Eckhart (1260–1327),
Sermons and Collations, XII

9. Vain is all prayer without humility; for, after prayer, humility is the thing most needful unto man.

Angela of Foligno (c. 1248–1309),
The Divine Consolation, Ch. XXIV

10. This lowliness of heart is mother of all the virtues, whence springeth even the exercising of these virtues, as the trunk and branches spring from the root. So precious is this virtue of humility and so firm its foundation (upon which is built up the whole perfection of the spiritual life), that the Lord did especially desire that we should learn it direct of him.

Angela of Foligno (c. 1248–1309),
The Divine Consolation, Ch. XXIV

11. For though there be some wise among you, yet through the simple hath He added to Him the wise, who once by men that were fishers subdued unto Himself the kings and philosophers of the world.

William of St Thierry (c. 1085–1148),
The Golden Epistle, Ch. 1, 2

12. So, then, henceforward, since we have not courage, let us at least have humility.

François de Sales (1567–1622),
The Spiritual Conferences, Book VI,
Various Letters, XLV, To a Lady

13. On wings of humility the love of Lover and Beloved rises and likewise sinks.

Ramon Lull (c. 1232–1315),
The Tree of Love, Part II, Ch. IXX

14. It is chiefly by this that all the saints have been and are men after God's heart. In short, the whole discipline of Christian wisdom is contained in this virtue. If thou dost not desire nor strive to be humble, in vain thou persuadest thyself that thou hast charity.

Louis de Blois (1506–65),
The Spiritual Mirror, Ch. VIII

15. For it is very much better for thee to be one among a crowd of a thousand people and to possess a very little humility, than to be a man living in the cave of a hyena in pride.

Pachomius (–c. 346),
The Instructions, p. 379

16. But the will of the soul must without ceasing, in this fiery driving, sink into nothing, viz., into the deepest humility in the sight of God. For no sooner doth the will of the soul in the least measure go on in its own speculation or searching, but Lucifer layeth hold of it in the centre of the forms of life, and sifteth it, so that it entereth into self. It must therefore continue close to resigned humility, as a well doth to its spring, and must suck and drink of God's fountain, and not depart from the ways of God at all.

Jacob Boehme (1575–1624),
The Way to Christ,
"Of True Resignation", Ch. II, 11

17. Firstly, as it is a want of humility to desire what you have never deserved, I do not think any one who longs for

these graces can be really humble: a common labourer never dreams of wishing to be made a king – the thing seems impossible and he is unfit for it; a lowly mind has the same feeling about these divine favours. I do not believe God will ever bestow these gifts on such a person, as before doing so He always gives thorough self-knowledge.

Teresa of Avila (1515–82),
The Interior Castle, Sixth Mansions, Ch. IX, 13

18. In this life, however, to promise or to hope for the perfection of the vision or knowledge of God is the height of vain presumption.

William of St Thierry (c. 1085–1148),
Exposition on the Song of Songs, Preface, 23

19. Nevertheless, brethren, let all highness be far from the judgement of your conscience, from your littleness and humility, and from your lips; because to be high-minded is death; and easy it is for him that in high places doth contemplate himself to become dazzled and so to suffer jeopardy of his life. Set another name to your profession, write another title upon your order.

William of St Thierry (c. 1085–1148),
The Golden Epistle, Ch. 2, 6

20. Hoar-frost is the desire to be somewhat or the belief that one is somewhat; or to be attached to one's self, or to suppose that we have earned these consolations and are worthy of them. This is hoar-frost, which may destroy the flowers and fruits of all the virtues.

John of Ruysbroeck (1293–1381),
Adornment of the Spiritual Marriage, Ch. XX

21. The distrust of thy self is obtained three manner of ways. First, that thou acknowledge and consider deeply thine

own vileness and nothing, and that indeed thou canst not obtain any thing that is good of thy self: a man being no more able to do any good meritorious work, than a stone that (I may so say) is able of itself to go upwards, and we having no less inclination to evil, than the said stone to the centre of the earth.

Lorenzo Scupoli (1530–1610),
The Spiritual Conflict, Ch. 2

22. The very meek behold not other men's sins, but their own; and not their good deeds, but other men's they praise. The rejected truly do the reverse; for they see rather other men's sins than their own, and in comparisons they count their own sins as little or none; but their good deeds – if any happen – they praise before all others, whose goodness they desire to lessen if they cannot fully destroy it.

Richard Rolle (1300–49),
The Fire of Love, Ch. XXVII

23. So that in all things nothing is left for man to boast concerning himself, either concerning his own virtue, or his own operation, but all his glorying is in the wholeness of God, and that the only thing which belongs to himself is nothing. By this means he becometh wholly lost in himself, and cannot in any way find himself, but in God he findeth himself whole, in whom he dwelleth with enough of quietness and security.

Gerlac Petersen (1378–1411),
The Fiery Soliloquy with God, Ch. X

24. Out of this grows the love of our neighbours, for we now esteem them, and no longer judge them as we used to do, when we looked upon ourselves as exceedingly fervent, and upon others as not. Now we see nothing but our

own misery, which we keep so constantly before our eyes
that we can look upon nothing else.

John of the Cross (1542–91),
The Dark Night of the Soul, Book I, Ch. XII

25. Only madmen and fools are pleased with themselves: no
wise man is good enough for his own satisfaction.

Benjamin Whichcote (1609–83),
Select Aphorisms, 13

26. None so empty as those who are full of themselves.

Benjamin Whichcote (1609–83),
Select Aphorisms, 215

27. He, who is truly sensible that nothing is due to him,
never thinks himself ill used.

François Fenelon (1651–1715),
Pious Reflections, The Eleventh Day

28. If thou wouldst bear thy neighbour's faults, cast thine
eyes upon thine own. And if thou thinkest to thyself, that
thou hast made any progress in perfection by thyself,
know that thou art not humble at all, nor hast yet made
one step in the way of the spirit.

Miguel de Molinos (1640–97),
A Spiritual Guide Which Disentangles the Soul,
Ch. X, 103

29. This consideration of the not-being of creatures out of
God, and the all-being of God, be indeed the true and
most proper ground of perfect humility.

Augustine Baker (1575–1641),
Sancta Sophia, Treat. 2, Sec. 2, Ch. 13, Part 14

30. For it is not to the humbled but to the humble that God
gives his grace. The humble man is he who converts

humiliation into humility, and it is only such can say to God, "It is good for me that Thou hast humbled me."

Bernard of Clairvaux (1090–1153),
Sermons, XXXIV

31. Lay aside a certain reticence which some people maintain towards Him under the impression that it is humility. Humility would not lead you to refuse a favour from the king, but would make you accept and take pleasure in it although you recognized how little it was your due. What humility! I receive in my house the Emperor of heaven and earth who comes to show me kindness and to rejoice with me, and because of my *humility*, I neither answer nor remain with him, nor accept his gifts, but go away and leave him alone! And though he begs and even bids me to petition him, yet through humility I remain in my poverty, and even permit him to depart.

Teresa of Avila (1515–82),
The Way of Perfection, Ch. XXVIII

32. False humility as much displeases God as does true pride, nay more, because the former is also hypocrisy.

Miguel de Molinos (1640–97),
A Spiritual Guide Which Disentangles the Soul,
Ch. XI, 116

33. To praise humility is to cause it to be desired from a secret self-love and to invite people to enter its domain through the wrong door.

Jean-Pierre Camus (1584–1652),
The Spirit of St Francis de Sales, p. 143

iv *The Transformation of Eros*

Humility, as we see, is the mother of charity, or selfless love. The traditional opposite to charity is cupidity, or love of things for some end other than God. In this sense we should interpret Jesus's proclamation that we cannot love both God and the world, for love is either God-directed (charity), or world-directed (cupidity). As St Augustine puts it, our love is our weight, and we are carried by it according to the impulse which impels it, either towards God, or towards something else (1–10).

The opposition between charity and cupidity does not mean that we may not love the world at all or, for instance, that erotic love is wrong. As Charles Williams says, Eros need not be on his knees to Agape, for he has a right to his own delights, and marriage can be part of the mystical way to God (12). All things can be loved in charity, which means in humility rather than possessively, and for the glory they give to their creator rather than for the pleasure they give us.

Far from being austere or chilly, this attitude to love is energetic and demanding, partly because it discourages us from treating others as instruments for our own gratification. We are required, rather, to acknowledge another person as a God-created free agent like ourselves. Only a spiritual love will sufficiently acknowledge another's spiritual need and dignity. Far from curtailing the scope of love, the mystics demand here an extension of its privileges and pleasures towards infinite richness and variety (11–20).

Physical love and the love of nature are therefore not to be valued in themselves but in God, which is to say, in the fullest possible manner. Clearly, that is a tall order, and although the distinction between charity and cupidity remains plain, most people's love makes numerous dizzying turns between the two. We all have some selfless and some possessive moments, so that normal human love is intermittent. The transformation of cupidity into charity is therefore a continuing test, to which the mystics call us because the best love does most good in the world, and it does so when most consistent, both in variety and intensity.

The well-known bridal imagery throughout the literature of Western mysticism indicates also that the transformation of Eros is not just a repression of Eros (21–30). Comparison between the soul's consummation in selfless, mystical love of God and the physical consummation of marriage is to be taken seriously though not literally. Spiritual union is emphatically spiritual, and is not fully amenable to description through images. But in so far as union is describable, marriage is a just comparison. Indeed, images are insufficient only because they fall short of the reality they indicate, and the mystics claim that spiritual marriage is more pleasurable, more fulfilling, more complete, than its analogue. We are not asked to deny love, but to increase it.

Just as marriage is preceded by courtship and trial, so is spiritual marriage. Such preliminaries partly constitute our education in charity, a process which, as we have seen, is normally full of intermittent worldliness. Nor do we enter into these trials alone, any more than the soul can be a bride without a bridegroom. The relationship is, somehow, mutual, even though the descriptions of bridal mysticism do not suggest that spiritual marriage is between equals. The bridegroom, after all, is Love itself (22), God condescending to grant us the favour of his presence. However much the images of mystical union suggest that the soul becomes as God, the mystics also like to point out that the soul retains its created essence, and is not absorbed into God, losing itself completely.

1. The highest degree, which the mystics call transformation or essential and immediate union with God, is

the reality of pure love in which there is no self-interest.

François Fenelon (1651–1715),
Maxims of the Mystics, Article XLV

2. By love, I do not mean any natural tenderness, which is more or less in people, according to their constitutions; but I mean a larger principle of the soul, founded in reason and piety, which makes us tender, kind and benevolent to all our fellow-creatures, as creatures of God, and for his sake.

William Law (1686–1761),
A Serious Call, Ch. XX

3. I mean by charity that affection of the mind which aims at the enjoyment of God for His own sake, and the enjoyment of one's self and one's neighbour in subordination to God; by cupidity I mean that affection of the mind which aims at enjoying one's self and one's neighbour, and other corporeal things, without reference to God.

Augustine of Hippo (345–430),
Of Christian Doctrine, Book III, Ch. X, 16

4. All our carnal affections are but self-love. That which cometh not of charity cometh, as St Augustine often saith, of carnal desire. Thus, it is against this self-love, the root of all our evil-doing, that the jealousy of God warreth.

François Fenelon (1651–1715),
Maxims of the Mystics,
"Of the Different Kinds of Love"

5. Wherefore, my dear children, there is nothing in this world, neither man nor devil nor any other thing, which I do fear as greatly as I fear love. For love penetrateth the soul more than any other thing, neither is there anything

which doth so fill the mind and the whole heart as doth love.

Angela of Foligno (c. 1248–1309),
The Divine Consolation, Ch. XXVII

6. Lord, thy glance is love. And just as thy gaze beholdeth me so attentively that it never turneth aside from me, even so is it with thy love. And since 'tis deathless, it abideth ever with me, and thy love, Lord, is naught else but thy very Self, who lovest me.

Nicholas of Cusa (1401–64),
The Vision of God, Ch. IV

7. Thou shalt call none other thy mother, and thy love shall be thy mother. And as children suck their mothers' breasts, even so shalt thou suck from My love inward consolation and unutterable health, and My love shall also feed thee, and clothe thee, and provide for thee in all thy wants, like a mother who provideth for her only daughter.

Mechthild of Hackborn (1240–98),
Select Revelations, Book II, Ch. IV

8. The Lover went to seek his Beloved, and he found a man who was dying without love. And he said: "How great a sadness is it that any man should die without love!" So the Lover said to him that was dying: "Say, why dost thou die without love?" And he replied: "Because I lived without love."

Ramon Lull (c. 1232–1315),
The Book of the Lover and the Beloved, 84

9. There dare no flesh-fly rest upon the pot's brink boiling on the fire; right so there may no fleshly delight rest upon a clean soul, that is wrapped and warmed all in the fire of love.

Walter Hilton (1300–96),
The Scale of Perfection, Book II, Ch. XLII

10. Little matter and much love, Philothea, and the fire will light itself so often that at last it will remain always lighted.

> François Malaval (1627–1719),
> *A Simple Method of Raising the Soul to Contemplation*, Second Treatise, Dialogue XII

11. Suppose a curious and fair woman. Some have seen the beauties of heaven in such a person. It is a vain thing to say they loved too much. I dare say there are ten thousand beauties in that creature which they have not seen. They loved it not too much but upon false causes. Nor so much upon false ones, as only upon some little ones. They love a creature for sparkling eyes and curled hair, lily breasts and ruddy cheeks; which they should love moreover for being God's image, queen of the universe, beloved by angels, redeemed by Jesus Christ, an heiress of heaven, and temple of the Holy Ghost: a mine and fountain of all virtues, a treasury of graces, and a child of God. But these excellencies are unknown. They love her perhaps, but do not love God more: nor men as much: nor heaven and earth at all.

> Thomas Traherne (c. 1636–74),
> *Centuries of Meditation*, II, 68

12. It is not to make us heavy and solemn; Eros need not for ever be on his knees to Agape; he has a right to his delights; they are a part of the Way. The division is not between Eros of the flesh and the Agape of the soul; it is between the moment of love which sinks into hell and the moment which rises to the in-Godding.

> Charles Williams (1886–1945),
> *Religion and Love in Dante*, p. 40

13. Marriage might be the most common exposition of the Way; as, no doubt, in many unknown homes it is. And if

so high a potentiality lies in so many lovers' meetings, then those lovers might well be encouraged to believe in the Way and to become aware of what potentialities they hold.

Charles Williams (1886–1945),
Religion and Love in Dante, p. 40

14. But I wretched, most wretched, in the very commencement of my early youth, had begged chastity of Thee, and said, "Give me chastity and continency, only not yet." For I feared lest Thou shouldest hear me soon, and soon cure me of the disease of concupiscence, which I wished to have satisfied, rather than extinguished.

Augustine of Hippo (345–430),
Confessions, Book VIII, 18

15. For we lose not our delights, but change them from body to soul, from the senses to the conscience.

William of St Thierry (c. 1085–1148),
The Golden Epistle, Ch. 8, 23

16. And our spirit, by God's working and by the power of love, presses and inclines itself into God: and, thereby, God is touched. From these two contacts there arises the strife of love, at the very deeps of this meeting; and in that most inward and ardent encounter, each spirit is deeply wounded by love. These two spirits, that is, our own spirit and the Spirit of God, sparkle and shine one into the other, and each shows to the other its face. This makes each of the spirits yearn for the other in love. Each demands of the other all that it is; and each offers to the other all that it is and invites it to all that it is.

John of Ruysbroeck (1293–1381),
Adornment of the Spiritual Marriage, Ch. LIV

17. For charity is a bond of love, in which we are drawn up

to God, and through which we renounce ourselves, and whereby we are united with God and God is united with us. But natural love turns back towards itself, and towards its own profit, and ever abides alone. Nevertheless, in its outward works, natural love is as like unto charity as two hairs from the same head; but the intentions are different. For the good man always seeks and means and desires, with an aspiring heart, to glorify God; but in natural love a man has always himself and his own profit in mind.

John of Ruysbroeck (1293–1381),
Adornment of the Spiritual Marriage, Ch. LXVI

18. So the love which grows out of sensuality ends in sensuality; that which is of the spirit ends in the Spirit of God, and makes it grow. This is the difference between these two loves, that men may distinguish between them.

John of the Cross (1542–91),
Spiritual Maxims, 131

19. You would not have your love to be a hermit; yet see you have her not a harlot. You seek a unique love; see that it be uniquely chosen. You know that love is fire, and fire must have fuel if it is to burn; but have a care that you throw not on it what gives but smoke and stench. It is a property of love that it must resemble that which it loves; and by the very fellowship of loving you will be in some measure transformed into the likeness of that to which you are united by its power. And so, my soul, give heed to your beauty and understand what sort of beauty you should love. Your face is not invisible to you; your eye sees nothing well, if it sees not itself; for when it is made very clear for contemplating itself, no foreign image from without or shadowy fantasy of truth has power to deceive it. And if perchance your inner vision is dimmed by neglect, and you have no power to con-

template yourself as is fit and profitable, why do you not at least use another's judgement to consider what you should think about yourself?

Hugh of St Victor (c. 1096–1141),
The Soul's Betrothal Gift, p. 10

20. For, if a carnal conjugal love can so detach men from their fathers, and mothers, and brethren, that if they continue to love them it is only with a superficial love, but their whole inclination and affection is devoted to the wife with whom they live; if, I say, a carnal love can thus loosen a man from every other worldly affection, how much rather shall those who have been touched with *that love*, cease to be held by the love of any object of this world?

Macarius (c. 300–90),
Institutes of Christian Perfection, Book V, Ch. IX

21. This is in truth the alliance of a holy and spiritual marriage. But it is saying too little to call it an alliance: it is rather an embrace. Surely we have then a spiritual embrace when the same likes and the same dislikes make one spirit out of two? Nor is there any occasion to fear lest the inequality of the persons should cause some defect in the harmony of wills, since love knows nothing of reverence. Love means an exercise of affection, not an exhibition of honour. Honour is given by him who is awe-stricken, who is astounded, who is terrified, who is filled with admiration.

Bernard of Clairvaux (1090–1153),
Sermons, LXXXIII

22. It must also be remembered that this Bridegroom is not only loving, but is Love itself.

Bernard of Clairvaux (1090–1153),
Sermons, LXXXIII

23. You have often heard that God spiritually espouses souls: may he be praised for his mercy in thus humbling himself so utterly. Though but a homely comparison, yet I can find nothing better to express my meaning than the sacrament of matrimony although the two things are very different. In divine union everything is spiritual and far removed from anything corporal, all the joys our Lord gives and the mutual delight felt in it being celestial and very unlike human marriage, which it excels a thousand times. Here all is love united to love; its operations are more pure, refined, and sweet than can be described, though our Lord knows how to make the soul sensible of them.

Teresa of Avila (c. 1515–82),
The Interior Castle, Fifth Mansions, Ch. IV, 1

24. It was our Lord's will that in this vision I should see the angel in this wise. He was not large, but small of stature, and most beautiful – his face burning, as if he were one of the highest angels, who seem to be all of fire: they must be those whom we call cherubim. Their names they never tell me; but I see very well that there is in heaven so great a difference between one angel and another, and between these and the others, that I cannot explain it.

I saw in his hand a long spear of gold, and at the iron's point there seemed to be a little fire. He appeared to me to be thrusting it at times into my heart, and to pierce my very entrails; when he drew it out, he seemed to draw them out also, and to leave me all on fire with a great love of God. The pain was so great that it made me moan; and yet so surpassing was the sweetness of this excessive pain that I could not wish to be rid of it. The soul is satisfied now with nothing less than God. The pain is not bodily, but spiritual; though the body has its share in it, even a large one. It is a caressing of love so sweet which now takes place between the soul and God,

that I pray God of His goodness to make him experience
it who may think that I am lying.

Teresa of Avila (1515–82),
Life, Ch. XXIX, 16–17

25. Then, by the virtue of love, is the lover transformed in the
beloved and the beloved is transformed in the lover, and
like unto hard iron which so assumeth the colour, heat,
virtue, and form of the fire that it almost turneth into fire,
so doth the soul, united with God through the perfect
grace of divine love, itself almost become divine and
transformed in God. Nevertheless, it changeth not its own
substance, but its whole life is transformed in the love of
God, and thus doth it almost become divine in itself.

Angela of Foligno (c. 1248–1309),
The Divine Consolation, Ch. VI

26. There is, then, a corporeal kiss, a spiritual kiss, and an
intellectual kiss. The corporeal kiss is made by the
impression of the lips; the spiritual kiss by the union of
spirits; the intellectual kiss through the Spirit of God, by
the infusion of grace.

Aelred of Rievaulx (c. 1110–67),
Spiritual Friendship, II, 24

27. When, therefore, the Eternal Wisdom or Uncommutable
Truth showeth us his face, his incomparable riches, all
beauty, and all that is desirable, and how he who beholdeth his face desireth nothing further; then our interior face striveth with such vehement love to be pressed
against his face in an interior kiss and embrace, chaste
and powerful, as if wholly it ought to pass into it and be
transformed, and in a certain manner itself become what
that face of his is in itself.

Gerlac Petersen (1378–1411),
The Fiery Soliloquy with God, Ch. XXXI

28. And the holy cross itself, like a true bed, hath four corners, towards which the sacred members of the Son of God were stretched, that thereby it might be given us clearly to understand, that he embraceth the whole race of man; that is, all men, in one common love, and that he, as a true lover, desireth to draw them all to himself upon his bed, from the four corners of the world.

John Tauler (c. 1300–61),
Meditations on the Life and Passion, Ch. 34

29. But the soul does not enter the garden of perfect transformation, the glory and the joy of the spiritual nuptials, without passing first through the spiritual espousals, the mutual faithful love of the betrothed. When the soul has lived for some time as the affianced bride of the Son, in perfect and sweet love, God calls it and leads it into his flourishing garden for the celebration of the spiritual marriage. Then the two natures are so united, what is divine is so communicated to what is human, that, without undergoing any essential change, each seems to be God – yet not perfectly so in this life, though still in a manner which can neither be described nor conceived.

John of the Cross (1542–91),
*A Spiritual Canticle Between the
Soul and Christ*, St. XXII

30. The present Church is, as it were, the house in which the betrothed of God are made ready for their future marriage; the heavenly Jerusalem is the king's chamber in which those marriages are celebrated.

Hugh of St Victor (c. 1096–1141),
The Soul's Betrothal Gift, p. 31

31. When we have the most complete possession of bodily pleasure, the bond is weak and loose compared with this union. For the senses, and what is connected with them,

only touch the accidents that are outside – we only see the colour, hear the sound, taste the sweet or bitter, touch the soft or hard. But when God embraces the soul, he wholly penetrates it throughout, passes through its secret divisions and unites himself with its most intimate being; there becoming, as it were, its soul, he embraces it most intimately.

Luis de Leon (1528–91),
The Names of Christ, 110

v *Intense Ordinariness*

Real love is particular. The romantic lover is more a lover in relationship to *this* person of the opposite sex, than in claiming to love the *whole* opposite sex. And although we may claim, say, to love spaniels, our relationship to Sparky is more complete because he is our dog. Indeed, hatred characteristically generalizes in order to distance its object. It is more difficult to put a child in a gas chamber than to think of one's self as expediting the Final Solution to a political problem.

In some such sense, the growth in charity to which the mystics call us is accompanied by a developing appreciation of particulars. This is a different quality of experience from the "seed" or spark of insight by which we are suddenly surprised in our solitude (II, ii). The experience of "intense ordinariness" is less a flash than a steady attitude of attentive wonder in which even the most banal occurrences are experienced as eternally precious. The mystics insist that small things, far from being inconsequential, are of special significance. It is as if love's energy is released most powerfully by attention to the atomic; that is, to the tiniest particles which unleash the most dynamic force. Only by such care for the small does charity itself become mature, for one sign of maturity is knowing how the health of the whole depends on the detailed adjustment of many parts. Thus, a mature thinker grasps instantaneously the implications for a whole system of ideas of a modification of one small idea. So it is with love: whoever despises the littlest things begins to unravel the whole web (1–18).

An enhanced appreciation of detail can, however, easily become an appalling burden if seen as mere duty rather than an occasion of delight. Puritan diaries of seventeenth-century England, like over-scrupulous examinations of conscience preceding confession, can show an obsessive concern with the possibly damning or redeeming consequences of ordinary domestic events. The way to obsessional neurosis lies through such self-conscious pursuit of the absolute significance of details; we must, rather, allow to providence its mystery, and not presume to grasp beyond our reach. Consequently, the word "Intense" in the heading to this section indicates a certain pleasure – let us say, joy – quite the opposite of neurotic, cerebral introspection. We may discover such joy in a sense of the infinite richness of particular things – in the detection of a timeless energy in the play of boys and girls in the street, as Thomas Traherne says; in the beauty of a hazel nut or a leaf; or in knowing ourselves immersed with all things in a sea of created glory (19–27).

1. And if this is so, nay, because it is so in great and deep matters, how much more will it be so in matters of least moment, and in the circumstances and events of every day.

> Gerlac Petersen (1378–1411),
> *The Fiery Soliloquy with God*, Ch. XVI

2. It is the nature of abandonment always to lead a mysterious life, and to receive great and miraculous gifts from

God by means of the most ordinary things, things that may be natural, accidental, or that seem to happen by chance, and in which there seems no other agency than the ordinary course of the ways of the world, or of the elements. In this way the simplest sermons, the most commonplace conversations, and the least high-toned books, become to these souls, by the virtue of God's will, sources of knowledge and of wisdom. This is why they carefully gather up the crumbs that sceptics trample underfoot. Everything is precious in their eyes, everything enriches them. They are inexpressibly indifferent towards all things, and yet neglect nothing, having a respect for, and making use of all things.

> Jean-Pierre de Caussade (1675–1751),
> *Abandonment to Divine Providence*,
> Book II, Ch. IV, Sec. IV

3. That which is sent us at the present moment is the most useful because it is intended especially for us.

> Jean-Pierre de Caussade (1675–1751),
> *Abandonment to Divine Providence*,
> Book I, Ch. II, Sec. VIII

4. He who knows that a certain person in disguise is the king, behaves towards him very differently to another who, only perceiving an ordinary man, treats him accordingly. In the same way the soul that recognizes the will of God in every smallest event, and also in those that are most distressing and direful, receives all with an equal joy, pleasure and respect. It throws open all its doors to receive with honour what others fear and fly from with horror. The outward appearance may be mean and contemptible, but beneath this abject garb the heart discovers and honours the majesty of the king. The deeper the abasement of his entry in such a guise and in secret the more does the heart become filled with love. I

cannot describe what the heart feels when it accepts the divine will in such humble, poor, and mean disguises.

> Jean-Pierre de Caussade (1675–1751),
> *Abandonment to Divine Providence*,
> Book I, Ch. II, Sec. II

5. Indeed, Smallness is the elementary Cause of all things; for you will never find any part of the world but participates in that quality of Smallness. This, then, is the sense in which we must apply this quality to God. It is that which penetrates unhindered unto all things and through all things, energizing in them and reaching to the dividing of soul and spirit, and of joints and marrow; and being a Discerner of the desires and the thoughts of the heart, or rather of all things, for there is no creature hid before God. This Smallness is without Quantity or Quality; it is Irrepressible, Infinite, Unlimited, and, while comprehending all things, is Itself Incomprehensible.

> Dionysius the Areopagite (c. 500),
> *The Divine Names*, Ch. IX, 3

6. Try and see your ordinary daily life as the medium through which He is teaching your soul, and respond as well as you can. Then you won't need, in order to receive His lessons, to go outside your normal experience. So too the type of prayer best for you is that to which you feel drawn in your best and quietest times and in which it is easiest to you to remain with God. Whether you do or don't use words or books is not very important. But there should be confidence and self-surrender in it, and of course prayer and self-offering for those you love and who need you.

> Evelyn Underhill (1875–1941),
> *Letters*, January 1928, To A.B.

7. Though this means seems inefficient, yet it gives great strength to the soul. We must keep watch over ourselves carefully in the most insignificant matters.

Teresa of Avila (1515–82),
The Way of Perfection, Ch. X

8. After this I think the greatest safeguard is to be very careful and to watch how we advance in virtue; we must notice whether we are making progress or falling back in it, especially as regards the love of our neighbour, the desire to be thought the least of all and how we perform our ordinary, everyday duties.

Teresa of Avila (1515–82),
The Interior Castle, Fifth Mansions, Ch. IV, 8

9. And then they will find that, whether married or unmarried, they have but one business upon their hands; to be wise, and pious, and holy, not in little modes and forms of worship, but in the whole turn of their minds, in the whole form of all their behaviour, and in the daily course of common life.

William Law (1686–1761),
A Serious Call, Ch. X

10. The one who is ending his week of service shall do the cleaning on Saturday. He shall wash the towels with which the brethren wipe their hands and feet; and this server who is ending his week, aided by the one who is about to begin, shall wash the feet of all the brethren. He shall return the utensils of his office to the cellarer clean and in good condition, and the cellarer in turn shall consign them to the incoming server, in order that he may know what he gives out and what he receives back.

Benedict of Nursia (c. 480–c. 547),
Rule for Monasteries, Ch. 35

11. The second coming of Christ our Bridegroom takes place every day within good men; often and many times, with new graces and gifts, in all those who make themselves ready for it, each according to his power.

John of Ruysbroeck (1293–1381),
Adornment of the Spiritual Marriage, Ch. VI

12. Let us advance, meanwhile, let us advance; let us make our way through these low valleys of the humble and little virtues; we shall see in them the roses amid the thorns, charity which shows its beauty among interior and exterior afflictions; the lilies of purity, the violets of mortification: what shall we see not? Above all, I love these three little virtues, sweetness of heart, poverty of spirit, and simplicity of life; and these substantial exercises, visiting the sick, serving the poor, comforting the afflicted, and the like: but the whole without eagerness, with a true liberty. No, our arms are not yet long enough to reach the cedars of Lebanon; let us content ourselves with the hyssop of the valleys.

François de Sales (1567–1622),
The Spiritual Conferences, Book VI,
Various Letters, VII, To Madame de Chantal

13. Some are kept from great temptations, and in small daily ones are often overcome, that they may be humbled, and never trust themselves in great matters, who break down in such trifles.

Thomas à Kempis (c. 1379–1471),
Of the Imitation of Christ, Book I, Ch. XIII

14. If thou mount a horse, think thou upon his oats.

Ramon Lull (c. 1232–1315),
The Tree of Love, Part II, Ch. I, 39

15. Despising small things does not, as some assert, arise

from greatness of mind; but, far otherwise, from a short-sightedness, esteeming things small which in their tendency and consequences have a very extensive reach and effect.

François Fenelon (1651–1715),
Selections, V, "On Faithfulness in Little Things"

16. Man is very liable to become beguiled by little things, because he looks on them as matters of indifference, and imagines himself free from any powerful attachment to them; but when God commands him to forsake them, he finds, by painful experience, how inordinate and unwarrantable were his attachment and practice respecting them.

François Fenelon (1651–1715),
Selections, V, "On Faithfulness in Little Things"

17. That our sanctification did not depend upon changing our works, but in doing that for God's sake, which we commonly do for our own. That the most excellent method he had found of going to God, was that of doing our common business without any view of pleasing men (as far as we are capable) purely for the love of God.

Brother Lawrence (c. 1605–91),
Conversations, IV, 25 November 1667

18. That we ought not to be weary of doing little things for the love of God, who regards not the greatness of the work, but the love with which it is performed.

Brother Lawrence (c. 1605–91),
Conversations, IV, 25 November 1667

19. Your enjoyment of the world is never right, till you so esteem it, that every thing in it is more your treasure than a king's exchequer full of gold and silver. And that exchequer yours also in its place and service. Can you

take too much joy in your father's works? He is himself in every thing. Some things are little on the outside, and rough and common, but I remember the time, when the dust of the streets were as precious as gold to my infant eyes, and now they are more precious to the eye of reason.

Thomas Traherne (c. 1636–74),
Centuries of Meditation, I, 25

20. The men! O what venerable and reverend creatures did the aged seem! Immortal cherubims! And young men glittering and sparkling angels and maids strange seraphic pieces of life and beauty! Boys and girls tumbling in the street, and playing, were moving jewels. I knew not that they were born or should die. But all things abided eternally as they were in their proper places. Eternity was manifest in the light of the day, and some thing infinite behind every thing appeared, which talked with my expectation and moved my desire.

Thomas Traherne (c. 1636–74),
Centuries of Meditation, III, 3

21. Also in this He showed me a little thing, the quantity of an hazel-nut, in the palm of my hand; and it was as round as a ball. I looked thereupon with eye of my understanding, and thought: *What may this be?* And it was answered generally thus: *It is all that is made.* I marvelled how it might last, for methought it might suddenly have fallen to naught for littleness. And I was answered in my understanding: *It lasteth, and ever shall last for that God loveth it.* And so All-thing hath the Being by the love of God.

Julian of Norwich (c. 1342–1420),
Revelations of Divine Love, Ch. V

22. Praised be my Lord for our sister, mother earth, the

which sustains and keeps us, and brings forth diverse
fruits with grass and flowers bright.

Francis of Assisi (1182–1226),
The Canticle of the Sun

23. There is not a single atom on the earth, not a single drop
in all the depths of the seas, not a particle in the air, or a
point in the globes of the heavens, where God, Father,
Son, and Holy Spirit, is not, whole and complete. He is
also complete and entire in animals, plants, minerals,
and in all their smallest parts, of which there is an
infinity in each one of his creatures. It is, therefore, an
article of faith that God is in all things, or to speak more
exactly and according to the rigour of theology, that all
things are in God; for we do not say that the sea is in the
sponge, but we say, on the contrary, that the sponge is in
the sea, of which it is full within, without, on every side,
and in all its substance.

François Malaval (1627–1719),
*A Simple Method of Raising the Soul to
Contemplation*, First Treatise

24. As the hot sands take up the heat, so would I take up that
soul-energy. Dreamy in appearance, I was breathing full
of existence; I was aware of the grass blades, the flowers,
the leaves on hawthorn and tree. I seemed to live more
largely through them, as if each were a pore through
which I drank. The grasshoppers called and leaped, the
greenfinches sang, the blackbirds happily fluted, all the
air hummed with life. I was plunged deep in existence,
and with all that existence I prayed.

Richard Jefferies (1848–87),
The Story of My Heart, Ch. I

25. And let us go on and on endlessly increasing our
perception of the hidden powers that slumber, and the

infinitesimally tiny ones that swarm about us, and the immensities that escape us because they appear to us simply as a point.

From all these discoveries, each of which plunges him a little deeper into the ocean of energy, the mystic derives an unalloyed delight, and his thirst for them is unquenchable; for he will never feel himself sufficiently dominated by the powers of the earth and the skies to be brought under God's yoke as completely as he would wish.

Pierre Teilhard de Chardin (1881–1955),
Hymn of the Universe, "Pensées", 4

26. For, if thou wilt contemplate even the leaf of a tree, thou wilt discover in it a work of stupendous skill. Thou wilt see how fitly it is strongest where it is nearest to the branch of the tree; thou wilt see how beautifully it spreads out, and forms itself, how skilfully it is guarded all round by serrated teeth, and interwoven here and there with ribs; compare any one with another of the same kind; thou wilt find as many teeth in one as in the other, as many ribs in one as in the other; and the same shape in both. What, again, is fairer than light? What pleasanter than the serene sky? What more glorious than the brilliant sunshine? What more perfect than the order of the moon and the stars?

Louis de Blois (1506–65),
The Rule of the Spiritual Life, Ch. XXVIII

27. The wonder, the thrill, of a shoulder or a hand awaits its proper exploration. At present we have simply nothing to say to anyone in a state of exaltation, watching for "meaning", except something which sounds very much like: "Well, don't look too intently." The hungry sheep look up for metaphysics, the profound metaphysics of the awful and redeeming body, and are given morals.

Charles Williams (1886–1945),
The Image of the City, "Sensuality and Substance"

Chapter IV

The Redemption of Psyche

This chapter deals with the advice mystics give on some issues where a balanced relationship needs to be preserved between opposing goods. The first such issue is the perennial opposition between individualism and authority on the question of finding a way to God; second is the relationship between transforming insight and secure identity; third is the cultivation of detachment which is neither callous unconcern nor zealous advocacy of a special interest; fourth is the manner in which Christ is in us, and we in him.

The chapter clarifies how a mystical pursuit of holiness does not seek to avoid tension, but to discover the kind of tension best enabling psychic health, from which is released, consequently, the most untrammelled and world-transforming energy.

✠

i *Threading the Labyrinth*

Experience of spiritual progress gives rise to the idea of a mystical way. I use the word "labyrinth" here, because it captures the idea that a variety of paths leads to the centre, and that every path is potentially puzzling. Some may even be dead ends.

None the less, there is a centre, and those who have found it leave us assorted rules for the road. A body of traditional wisdom has thus developed, providing, among other things, safeguards against wrong turnings and treacherous bypaths (1–5).

Still, instruction in how to avoid failure is not the same as instruction in how to succeed, and although mystics offer certain traditional warnings, they also insist that mystical experience cannot be reduced to a system of rules. The requirements of no two persons need be quite the same; we find what is right for us as we proceed, and threading the labyrinth remains a personal adventure (6–15).

Inevitably, there is tension between ecclesiastical authority (the corporate way) and a mystic who claims to have been led on his own (individual) way. On the one hand, the Church provides an opportunity for critical judgement by which mystics can come to understand and assess their experience. For this reason, it is impossible to discuss mysticism intelligently outside some framework of belief – an intellectual and critical tradition, that is, providing language to establish the very identity of the experience. On the other hand, the mystic will often feel that ecclesiastical authorities are bent on reducing his experience in order to classify it, and are unfairly sceptical. A balance therefore must be found between variety threatening to collapse into disorientation, and judgement threatening to harden into tyranny (16–24). Nor, it seems, should we hope for relaxation of this tension while we are engaged on our earthly journey, for one enduring fact about the mystical way is its insecurity. The very desire to find security *en route* bodes ill, we are assured, for our successful arrival at the end (25–30).

1. For even so a man that taketh a journey any whither, if he holdeth to one sure road, shall quickly come thither

whither he goeth and make an end of his journey and of his toil. But if he essay many roads, he wandereth and maketh never an end of his toil, because of such wandering there is no end.

William of St Thierry (c. 1085–1148),
The Golden Epistle, Ch. 9, 26

2. And they should not follow strange paths or singular ways; but they should follow the track of love through all storms to that place whither love shall lead them. And if they abide the time, and persevere in all virtues, they shall behold the Mystery of God and take flight towards It.

John of Ruysbroeck (1293–1381),
Adornment of the Spiritual Marriage, Ch. XXVII

3. Let us seek no fresh path; we should lose ourselves in ways of ease. It would be a strange thing to fancy we should gain these graces by any other road than that by which Jesus and all his saints have gone before.

Teresa of Avila (1515–82),
The Interior Castle, Seventh Mansions,
Ch. IV, 17

4. I have walked in this world by three ways, and if any one desire to imitate Me, he must follow Me perfectly in these three ways. The first is dry and narrow; the second is full of flowers, and planted with fruit trees; the third is full of thorns and thistles. Now the first way is that of voluntary poverty, which I followed and loved in the highest degree all the days of My life. The second is that of My zealous and praiseworthy conversation; the third that of My hard and cruel passion. Therefore must every one who desireth to follow Me embrace poverty, and desire to possess nothing in this world. Secondly, he

must be praiseworthy in his behaviour. Thirdly, he must gladly suffer for My love both pains and tribulations.

Mechthild of Hackborn (1240–98),
Select Revelations, Book IV, Ch. X

5. That which is greatest and most eminent in religion is indeed easiest of all. The most necessary sacraments are the easiest. This is also true in natural things. Would you go to sea? Then take a boat upon a river, and you shall get at it insensibly and without trouble. Would you go to God? Take this so very sweet and easy way, and you shall shortly come at him in a manner that will surprise you.

Madame Guyon (1648–1717),
A Method of Prayer, Ch. XII

6. I say this because there are some who make a kind of art of all these rules and counsels, seeming to think that, as one learning the duties of an office, by keeping strictly its rules, will quickly become a good office-bearer, so, by virtue of these religious counsels strictly kept, that one may attain to all one can desire, without observing that this is to make grace into an art, and to attribute to human rules and plans that which is only of the free gift and mercy of God. On this account, therefore, we should be careful to treat these practices not as a matter of art, but as a matter of grace; because, by taking it in this way, a man will learn that the principal means required for this is a profound humility and consciousness of one's own pitiful condition together with the fullest trust in the divine mercy.

Peter of Alcantara (1499–1562),
A Golden Treatise of Mental Prayer, Part II, Ch. V

7. Generally, mystic authors write according to their own experience in their own souls when they treat of the

several degrees of prayer, and the several manners of
divine operations in souls in such degrees; as if the same
instructions **would** serve indefinitely for all others.
Whereas such is the inexplicable variety of internal dis-
positions, that the same course and order in all things
will scarce serve any two souls.

Augustine Baker (1575–1641),
Sancta Sophia, Treat. 1, Sec. 2, Ch. 3, Part 8

8. Those therefore that have not, and indeed are not
capable of much light in their interior, and so are not fit
to be guided by divine inspirations, are the more in need
to have certain rules from without, at least for the exterior. And for such it is God's will and direction that
they should more depend on external guides.

Augustine Baker (1575–1641),
Sancta Sophia, Treat. 1, Sec. 2, Ch. 2, Part 17

9. That is why God so wisely directs the work of our
salvation that he takes us by the hand without letting us
see the way he is leading us, save what is necessary to the
capacity of each one.

François Malaval (1627–1719),
A Simple Method of Raising the Soul to Contemplation,
Second Treatise, Dialogue III

10. God leads every soul by a separate path, and you will
scarcely meet with one spirit which agrees with another
in one half of the way by which it advances.

John of the Cross (1542–91),
The Living Flame of Love, St. III

11. And in that Love which is wayless, we shall wander and
stray, and it shall lead us and lose us in the immeasurable
breadth of the love of God. And herein we shall flee forth

and flee out of ourselves, into the unknown raptures of
the goodness and riches of God. And therein we shall
melt and be melted away, and shall eternally wander and
sojourn within the glory of God. Behold! by each of
these images, I show forth to God-seeing men their being
and their exercise, but none else can understand them.
For the contemplative life cannot be taught. But where
the eternal Truth reveals itself within the spirit all that is
needful is taught and learnt.

> John of Ruysbroeck (1293–1381),
> *The Sparkling Stone*, Ch. III

12. Now understand this well: that measureless splendour of
God, which together with the incomprehensible
brightness, is the cause of all gifts and of all virtues – that
same uncomprehended light transfigures the fruitive
tendency of our spirit and penetrates it in a way that is
wayless; that is, through the uncomprehended light. And
in this light the spirit immerses itself in fruitive rest; for
this rest is wayless and fathomless, and one can know of
it in no other way than through itself – that is, through
rest.

> John of Ruysbroeck (1293–1381),
> *Adornment of the Spiritual Marriage*, Ch. LXIV

13. A monk is a man who has been called by the Holy Spirit to
relinquish the cares, desires and ambitions of other men,
and devote his entire life to seeking God. The concept is
familiar. The reality which the concept signifies is a
mystery. For in actual fact, no one on earth knows
precisely what it means to "seek God" until he himself has
set out to find Him. No man can tell another what this
search means unless that other is enlightened, at the same
time, by the Spirit speaking within his own heart.

> Thomas Merton (1915–68),
> *The Silent Life*, Prologue

14. God leads people by different ways and the same con-
fessor may not understand them all. I assure you there
will always be holy persons ready to guide and to comfort your souls if you live as you ought, however poor
you may be. God, Who sustains your bodies and supplies
them with food, will incite some one with the good will
to enlighten your souls.

Teresa of Avila (1515–82),
The Way of Perfection, Ch. V

15. Philothea, I have attempted to take you into the garden of
the Bridegroom, but not to describe to you the fruits and
flowers. This garden of contemplation is vast and great; it is
for him to lead you along its paths as it pleases him. Be
faithful to God, and God will be liberal to you. Never try to
go before God; follow him always, and do not trouble about
anything but loving him, never mind if you cannot see him.

François Malaval (1627–1719),
*A Simple Method of Raising the Soul to
Contemplation*, Second Treatise, Dialogue XII

16. Christ, the true and universal Way, contains, as far as
lies with him, all these varieties. Some are flat and open,
with no fear of stumbling, in which the weak walk easily.
He has narrower paths which go uphill for stronger
souls; circuitous routes for those they suit; and as many
straight, short cuts for those who wish to hasten on.

Luis de Leon (1528–91),
The Names of Christ, 20

17. So that the "Way" is used in four senses besides that of a
path: as a tendency, a business or office, an action, and
the law or precepts, for each of these leads man to some
end and he aims at some object by their means.

Luis de Leon (1528–91),
The Names of Christ, 19

18. In short, thou wilt be drawn to different practices at different times, and it will be good for thee to follow now one and now another form of exercises. For the Holy Spirit influences the interior of man in various ways, and leads him by divers paths to the embraces of divine love; and we must ever be most watchful for his calls and impulses, that we may always bend to his will, utterly abandoning our own choice.

Louis de Blois (1506–65),
The Rule of the Spiritual Life, Ch. XXV

19. Union with the will of God is the universal means. It does not act by one method only, but all methods and all ways are, by its virtue, sanctified. The divine will unites God to our souls in many different ways, and that which suits us is always best for us.

Jean-Pierre de Caussade (1675–1751),
Abandonment to Divine Providence,
Book II, Ch. II, Sec. I

20. Our blessed Father never told me the name of this director, nor even gave me the slightest hint as to who he was, and I therefore sought no further explanation, contenting myself with admiring the ways of God and his various desires for the good of the souls whom he calls to his service. I became penetrated, too, with the conviction that by many different routes we can reach one and the same goal.

Jean-Pierre Camus (1584–1652),
The Spirit of St Francis de Sales, p. 401

21. I can assure you, Philothea, that one encounters many more lazy souls who never go so far as God would like to draw them, than weaklings who go beyond their strength. For one imaginative soul who deceives herself, there are a hundred proud souls who draw back from the

ways of God, and pride is much more general than illusion. But there is this difference between the two, that God often leaves the proud in their pride while he withdraws the simple from their illusion. Seek to please God in everything you undertake, and you will never deceive yourself in anything.

François Malaval (1627–1719),
A Simple Method of Raising the Soul to Contemplation, Second Treatise, Dialogue XII

22. You will observe that some rivers move gravely and slowly, and others with greater velocity; but there are rivers and torrents which rush with frightful impetuosity, and which nothing can arrest. All the burdens which might be laid upon them, and the obstructions which might be placed to impede their course, would only serve to redouble their violence. It is thus with souls. Some go on quietly towards perfection, and never reach the sea, or only very late, contented to lose themselves in some stronger and more rapid river, which carries them with itself into the sea. Others, which form the second class, flow on more vigorously and promptly than the first. They even carry with them a number of rivulets; but they are slow and idle in comparison with the last class, which rush onward with so much impetuosity, that they are utterly useless: they are not available for navigation, nor can any merchandise be trusted upon them, except at certain parts and at certain times. These are bold and mad rivers, which dash against the rocks, which terrify by their noise, and which stop at nothing. The second class are more agreeable and more useful; their gravity is pleasing, they are all laden with merchandise, and we sail upon them without fear or peril.

Madame Guyon (1648–1717),
Spiritual Torrents, Part I, Ch. I

23. I do not mean that divine communication and inspirations received in this mansion are the same as those I shall describe later on; God here speaks to souls through words uttered by pious people, by sermons or good books, and in many other such ways. Sometimes he calls souls by means of sickness or troubles, or by some truth he teaches them during prayer, for tepid as they may be in seeking him, yet God holds them very dear.

Teresa of Avila (1515–82),
The Interior Castle, Second Mansions, Ch. I, 5

24. A man's life without his learning, is able to work a far more excellent effect than his learning without his life. For, the one profits, even though he be silent; whereas, the other occasions disorder, notwithstanding his intelligence. But, if his learning and his life keep pace together and unite, they then complete the whole structure of philosophy.

Macarius (c. 300–90),
Sayings, 8

25. Human life which is to be acceptable to God cannot exist without tribulation; just as the body cannot exist without the soul, the soul without grace, the earth without the sun.

Miguel de Molinos (1640–97),
A Spiritual Guide Which Disentangles the Soul,
Book III, Ch. III, 67

26. Many souls have undertaken, and daily do undertake, this way, and they persevere while they keep the sweet relish of their primitive fervour; yet this sweetness and sensible delight is scarce done, but presently, when they are overtaken by the storms of trouble, temptation and aridity (which are necessary things to help a man up the high mountain of perfection) they falter and turn back: a

clear sign that they sought themselves, and not God or perfection.

Miguel de Molinos (1640–97),
A Spiritual Guide Which Disentangles the Soul,
Book III, Ch. III, 18

27. The love of one that makes distinction between the trials and the joys that he has of love cannot soar to the heavens.

Ramon Lull (c. 1232–1315),
The Tree of Love, Part II, Ch. I, 8

28. Thou hast not here an abiding city, and wheresoever thou mayest be thou art a stranger and pilgrim; neither shalt thou ever have rest: unless thou be inwardly united unto Christ.

Thomas à Kempis (c. 1379–1471),
Of the Imitation of Christ, Book II, Ch. I

29. For whatever plans I devise for my peace, my life cannot be without war and sorrow.

Thomas à Kempis (c. 1379–1471),
Of the Imitation of Christ, Book IV, Ch. XII

30. Never promise thyself security in this life, although thou seem to be a good monk or a devout hermit. Oftentimes those who are better in the judgement of men, have fallen into greater danger by overmuch self-confidence.

Thomas à Kempis (c. 1379–1471),
Of the Imitation of Christ, Book I, Ch. XX

ii *Novelty and Stability*

Tradition is concerned to classify and judge, but individuals must engage the adventure in whatever terms it presents itself. The Church needs its mystics if it is to remain vital, just as mystics need the Church if they are to understand and test their experiences. Neither, it seems, is complete without the other, and so it is with knowledge of spiritual things in general. Novelty, surprise, illumination and variety are all expressions of energy, but mere variety without form, like surprise without context, is quickly disorienting. If every experience struck us as novel, we could not so much as make our way to the front door, for we would lose our sense of direction in the sheer, unclassifiable immediacy of whatever our gaze or our touch happened to encounter. Too much novelty is nightmarish, as the states of mind sometimes produced by hallucinogenic drugs suggest, and novelty is most pleasurable when it is, somehow, kept safe. Thus, we are free to enjoy the excitement of, say, a roller-coaster because we are safely held, believing that the machinery is reliable and in two minutes we will get off. But the smallest mechanical failure – the merest suggestion that the machinery is out of control – converts excitement instantly to terror.

This example can apply to a wide range of phenomena in the spiritual life, taking us back even to God's nature. The creator is at once unified and stable, yet infinitely various and new (1–5). So it seems that in our encounters with godlike things, we inevitably experience some such combination of exact care and thrilling energy. If one of these poles is surrendered, the wholeness – or holiness – of the experience itself is threatened.

The extensive use of metaphors in this section – the flight of birds and butterflies, the activity of bees, colour and light, circles, fountains, cups, and so on – addresses the tension between novelty and stability partly by exemplifying it. As Romantic poets and philosophers especially tell us, imagination's function is to express with fresh insight the necessary relationship between whole and part. Metaphor therefore not only describes, but also enacts new, individual perception bringing to life some general, stable truth (6–23).

1. Yea, 'tis a common and undifferenced activity of the whole Godhead that it is wholly and entirely communicated unto each of them that share it and unto none merely in part; even as the centre of a circle is shared by all the radii which surround it in a circle; and as there are many impressions of a seal all sharing in the seal which is their archetype while yet this is entire, nor is it only a part thereof that belongeth unto any of them.

Dionysius the Areopagite (c. 500),
The Divine Names, Ch. II, 5

2. For the Divine Peace remains indivisible and shows forth all its power in a single act, and permeates the whole world without departing from its own Identity. For it goes forth to all things and gives to all things of itself (according to their kinds), and overflows with the abundance of its peaceful fecundity, and yet through the transcendence of its unification it remains wholly and entirely in a state of Absolute Self-Unity.

Dionysius the Areopagite (c. 500),
The Divine Names, Ch. XI, 2

3. And so all theology is said to be stablished in a circle, because any one of his attributes is affirmed of another, and to have is with God to be, and to move is to stand, and to run is to rest, and so with the other attributes. Thus, although in one sense we attribute unto him

movement and in another rest, yet because he is himself the
Absolute Ground, in which all otherness is unity, and all diversity is identity, that diversity which is not identity proper,
to wit, diversity as we understand it, cannot exist in God.

Nicholas of Cusa (1401–64),
The Vision of God, Ch. III

4. An essential work is when the essence of the soul is one
   and simple, and is placed in complete silence. And
   through simplicity it hath communion with all things; for
   what is most simple is most universal, and imparts itself to
   all things, and yet remains undivided and unmoved in
   itself. And to communicate and divide with all things is
   called an essential working; and in this working one work
   is all works, and all works are one work. For just as God
   seeth all things with one glance, and it worketh without
   any movement of himself, so doeth also an essential will.

John Tauler (c. 1300–61),
The Following of Christ, Part I, 157

5. Great and overflowing is the love of God, that never
   standeth still, but floweth on for ever and without ceasing,
   with no labour or effort, but freely and fully, so that our
   little vessel is full and over-full. If we do not stop the channel
   by our self-will it will never slacken in its flowing, but the
   gift of God will ever make our cup to run over.

Mechthild of Magdeburg (1217–82),
The Flowing Forth of the Light of the Godhead, p. 125

6. But the fire which is God, although it consumes, yet does
   not afflict, burning sweetly, blissfully devastating. For it is
   truly a "desolating fire", which, however, so exercises its
   destructive energy against sin, that it acts on the soul as a
   healing unction.

Bernard of Clairvaux (1090–1153),
Sermons, LVII

7. For that vitality of understanding in the soul of a contemplative at one time goes out and comes back with marvellous quickness, at another time bends itself, as it were, into a circle, and yet at another time gathers itself together, as it were, in one place and fixes itself, as it were, motionless. Certainly if we consider this rightly, we see the form of this thing daily in the birds of the sky. Now you may see some raising themselves up on high; now others plunging themselves into lower regions and often repeating the same manner of their ascent and descent.

Richard of St Victor (c. 1123–75),
The Mystical Ark, Book I, Ch. V

8. Oh, to see the restlessness of this charming little butterfly, although never in its life has it been more tranquil and at peace! May God be praised! It knows not where to stay nor take its rest.

Teresa of Avila (1515–82),
The Interior Castle, Fifth Mansions, Ch. II, 6

9. Love is infinitely delightful to its object, and the more violent the more glorious. It is infinitely high, nothing can hurt it. And infinitely great in all extremes of beauty and excellency. Excess is its true moderation: activity its rest: and burning fervency its only refreshment. Nothing is more glorious yet nothing more humble; nothing more precious, yet nothing more cheap; nothing more familiar, yet nothing so inaccessible; nothing more nice, yet nothing more laborious; nothing more liberal, yet nothing more covetous; it doth all things for its object's sake, yet it is the most self-ended thing in the whole world.

Thomas Traherne (c. 1636–74),
Centuries of Meditation, II, 54

10. In the highest light of mental gnosis, therein the ground
    of beatitude lies. Accordingly there springs up and grows
    within the will a prelude of delights which the vision
    adorns as bloom does youth, and therein is revealed to
    all creatures the splendour and majesty of his estate, and
    concerning it he says, "Behold I make all things new."

    Meister Eckhart (1260–1327),
    Sermons and Collations, XVII

11. So the wise man will do like the bee, and he will fly forth
    with attention and with reason and with discretion,
    towards all those gifts and towards all that sweetness
    which he has ever experienced, and towards all the good
    which God has ever done to him. And in the light of love
    and with inward observation, he will taste of the
    multitude of consolations and good things; and will not
    rest upon any flower of the gifts of God, but, laden with
    gratitude and praise, will fly back into the unity, wherein
    he wishes to rest and to dwell eternally with God.

    John of Ruysbroeck (1293–1381),
    Adornment of the Spiritual Marriage, Ch. XXI

12. Now understand this: God comes to us without ceasing,
    both with means and without means, and demands of us
    both action and fruition, in such a way that the one
    never impedes, but always strengthens, the other. And
    therefore the most inward man lives his life in these two
    ways: namely, in work and in rest. And in each he is
    whole and undivided; for he is wholly in God because he
    rests in fruition, and he is wholly in himself because he
    lives in activity: and he is perpetually called and urged
    by God to renew both the rest and the work.

    John of Ruysbroeck (1293–1381),
    Adornment of the Spiritual Marriage, Ch. LXV

13. Love forsooth has a diffusive, unitive and transformative

strength. In *Diffusion* truly: for it spreads the beams of its goodness not only to friends and neighbours, but also to enemies and strangers. In *Union* truly: for it makes lovers one in deed and will; and Christ and every holy soul it makes one. He truly that draws to God is one spirit, not in nature but in grace, and in onehood of will. Love has also a *Transforming* strength, for it turns the loving into the loved, and ingrafts him.

Richard Rolle (1300–49),
The Fire of Love, Ch. XVII

14. Without method, yet most exact; without rule, yet most orderly; without reflexion, yet most profound; without skill, yet thoroughly well constructed; without effort, yet everything accomplished; and without foresight, yet nothing better suited to unexpected events. Spiritual reading with the divine action, often contains a meaning that the author never thought of. God makes use of the words and actions of others to infuse truths which might otherwise have remained hidden. If he wishes to impart light in this way, it is for the submissive soul to avail itself of this light. Every expedient of the divine action has an efficacy which always surpasses its apparent and natural virtue.

Jean-Pierre de Caussade (1675–1751),
Abandonment to Divine Providence,
Book II, Ch. IV, Sec. IV

15. She said nothing, know that I do not lie, for much she feared that evil people, if she had spoken it, would at once have said that it was an invention, a mad thing newly invented.

Elizabeth of Schonau (1138–65),
"Poem on the Assumption"

16. Love, without losing its simplicity, becometh in turn all

the different virtues. Yet love desireth not to become any
virtue of them all, simply for the sake of being virtuous.

François Fenelon (1651–1715),
Maxims of the Mystics, Article XXXIII

17. Know that the diversity of conditions amongst those that be
spiritual consists only in a different manner of dying.

Miguel de Molinos (1640–97),
A Spiritual Guide Which Disentangles the Soul,
Ch. VIII, 74

18. As a bottom of silk is unwound, and wrought out into
diverse beautiful figures in a garment of needlework: such is
thy life, thy whole story, O saint. Divine love spun forth
from the glorious heart of God, as silk from the curious
worm, is wound up into a bottom in the promise. This rich
bottom worketh out itself into all thy motions and rests, into
all thy changes and chances through thy whole course, as
into so many exact and shining figures of eternal glories.
Thus love maketh itself the entire history of thy life; of that
history and life it maketh for thee a garment to wear in
heaven, becoming the bride of the great king.

Peter Sterry (c. 1614–72),
*The Rise, Race, and Royalty of the Kingdom of God
in the Soul of Man*, p. 353

19. It is true that it is a suspension, but it is a suspension of
distinct and particular acts, in order to give place to a general
and universal act of the presence of God; thus the soul is
always occupied and always filled. It is to suspend a lesser
good for a more perfect good; or to express it better, it is to
free the soul from the weight of its many thoughts and
reasonings, to enlighten and purify it rather than to suspend
it.

François Malaval (1627–1719),
*A Simple Method of Raising the Soul to
Contemplation*, Second Treatise, Dialogue III

20. One distinguishes colours according to their kinds, but light remains in its nature always the same, though it can be greater or less according as it is more or less diffuse and as the subject in which it is found has more or less capacity for reflecting it. The presence of God produces light in the soul, or to speak more correctly it is this light itself which keeps alive in us a perpetual belief that God is, without particularizing as to what he is.

François Malaval (1627–1719),
A Simple Method of Raising the Soul to Contemplation, Second Treatise, Dialogue III

21. There is neither height nor depth nor summit nor surface in the soul of man because, being spiritual, it has neither parts nor divisions. So that what I now tell you is very true, that the whole of your soul is just as much at the point of one of your fingers as in the whole of your body.

François Malaval (1627–1719),
A Simple Method of Raising the Soul to Contemplation, Second Treatise, Dialogue III

22. As when several lamps are lighted with the same oil and the same fire, all do not always give forth their light in the same measure; so, the graces of the different virtues derive different degrees of splendour from one and the same good Spirit. And, as of many who inhabit one and the same city, and partake of the same bread and the same water, some are men and some infants, some are youths and some aged; or, as corn sown in one and the same field brings forth various and diverse ears, yet all are brought to the same threshing-floor, and are laid up in the same granary.

Macarius (c. 300–90),
Institutes of Christian Perfection, Book IV, Ch. X

23. My love is of that sort which is not diminished in unity, nor confounded in multiplicity. I am entirely concerned and

occupied with thee alone, with the thought how I may at all times love thee alone, and fulfil everything that appertains to thee, as though I were wholly disengaged from all other things.

Henry Suso (c. 1295–1366),
The Little Book of Eternal Wisdom, Ch. VII

iii *Holy Indifference*

Holy indifference is basically an attitude to love: the practice of charity, that is, makes us indifferent to everything that happens to us. Yet love alone makes the indifference holy, which otherwise would collapse into cynical apathy. Only if you love courageously, for instance, are you indifferent to the consequences for yourself of contracting leprosy by handling a leper's wounds.

Without love, indifference falls away on the one hand into neglect. But over-zealous concern for some special interest can be equally distortive in the opposite direction, for it can cause us cruelly to ignore those who do not share that special interest. Thus the mystics insist that although love is particular we should love the particulars in God, each according to its capacity and without preference (1–7).

Holy indifference is well described also as disinterested love (8), and is often associated with the idea of abandonment to God's providence, wherein we have no concern for the fruits of our actions, but only for the fact that in our actions we attempt to love God fully. One result is a certain detachment, though as with holy indifference we ought not to mistake detachment for mere withdrawal. It is, rather, freedom from self-concern: we do not rescue a child from a burning building if we are so apprehensive about falling off the ladder that we dare not climb it (8–13).

As excerpts 14–25 suggest, holy indifference – with the

allied notions of disinterested love, abandonment and detachment – is commendable not because making us less human,
but more so. The results show up as courage, peacefulness,
freedom from agitation and readiness to serve one's neighbour.
In calling attention to such qualities of character, the mystics
once again declare that progress in charity is accompanied not so
much by high feelings or dramatic illuminations, as by a transformed moral disposition. In this sense alone, they suggest, love
is blind; true lovers are always indifferent to consequences.

1. The proof and sign of the death of all that is external is a sort
   of indifference, or rather of insensibility with regard to
   exterior goods, pleasures, reputation, relations, friends, etc.
   This insensibility becomes, by the help of grace, so complete,
   and so profound that one is tempted to imagine it purely
   natural; and God permits this to prevent the artifices of self-
   complacency, and to make us in all things, walk in the
   obscurity of faith, and in a great abandonment.

   Jean-Pierre de Caussade (1675–1751),
   Spiritual Counsels, Seventh Book,
   "The Last Trials", Letter XV

2. That we may always stand in the state of indifference, willing
   only what God from eternity hath willed, and be indifferent
   as to all things that regard either the body or the soul,
   temporal or eternal riches; forgetting what is past, giving up
   the time present to God, and leaving to his providence that
   which is to come; making ourselves content in the actual
   moment, seeing it brings along with it the eternal order of
   God concerning us, and makes for us a declaration of his will
   as infallible as it is common and inevitable for all: not
   attributing anything that befalls us to the creature, but
   beholding all things in God, and considering them as coming
   infallibly from his hand, our own sin only excepted.

   Madame Guyon (1648–1717),
   A Method of Prayer, Ch. VII

3. Indifference is to be practised in things belonging to the natural life, as in health, sickness, beauty, deformity, weakness, strength: in the affairs of the spiritual life, as in dryness, consolations, relish, aridity; in actions, in sufferings – briefly, in all sorts of events.

François de Sales (1567–1622),
Treatise on the Love of God, Book IX, Ch. V

4. Resignation prefers God's will before all things, yet it loves many other things besides the will of God. Indifference goes beyond resignation: for it loves nothing except for the love of God's will: insomuch that nothing can stir the indifferent heart, in the presence of the will of God.

François de Sales (1567–1622),
Treatise on the Love of God, Book IX, Ch. IV

5. The profession of aspiring to perfection in a contemplative life requires not only patience and indifference in such crosses as we cannot avoid, but also that we be not solicitous in seeking to avoid them.

Augustine Baker (1575–1641),
Sancta Sophia, Treat. 2, Sec. 2, Ch. 7, Part 8

6. The forsaking of one's own will causes a man to live without preference for either this or that, in doing or leaving undone, in those things which are strange and special in the saints, in their precepts and in their practice; but it makes him to live always according to the glory and the commandments of God, and the will of his prelates, and in peace with all men in his neighbourhood, so far as true prudence permits.

John of Ruysbroeck (1293–1381),
Adornment of the Spiritual Marriage, Ch. XIV

7. And so when death has been brought upon a saint, we

ought not to think that an evil has happened to him but a thing indifferent, which is an evil to a wicked man, while to the good it is rest and freedom from evils.

John Cassian (c. 360–434),
Conference of Abbot Theodore, Ch. VI

8. Holy indifference, which is naught else than the disinterestedness of love, becometh under the severest trials that which the holy mystics have called *abandon*, meaning that the disinterested soul doth wholly and without reserve abandon itself to God for all that concerneth its own interest; yet never doth it renounce either love or any other thing which toucheth the glory and good pleasure of its Beloved.

François Fenelon (1651–1715),
Maxims of the Mystics, Article VIII

9. "The disinterested soul", as St Francis de Sales said of the Mère de Chantal, "doth not cleanse itself of its faults for the sake of being pure; doth not deck itself with virtues for the sake of being fair; but in order to please the Bridegroom; the soul would have preferred ugliness had it pleased Him better." In this sense we may say that the passive and disinterested soul no longer desireth even love itself as being its perfection and its happiness, but only as being that which God willeth for us. Hence it cometh that St Francis de Sales saith that "we make self our object, when it is love that we love instead of the Beloved".

François Fenelon (1651–1715),
Maxims of the Mystics, Article XXXIII

10. Oh! my God, give me grace to be faithful in the action, and indifferent as to the success.

François Fenelon (1651–1715),
Pious Reflections, The Thirteenth Day

11. Holy indifference, which is but the disinterestedness of love, so far from excluding disinterested desires, is the real and positive principle of all the disinterested desires which the written law enjoineth, as well as those which are prompted by grace.

> François Fenelon (1651–1715),
> *Maxims of the Mystics*, Article VI

12. And therefore if I might get a watchful and a busy beholding to this spiritual work within in my soul, I would then have an indifference in eating and in drinking, in sleeping and in speaking, and in all mine outward doings. For surely I believe that I should rather come to discretion in them by such an indifference than by any busy beholding to the same things.

> *The Cloud of Unknowing* (late 14th Century), Ch. 42

13. And in all other sweetness and comforts, bodily or spiritual, be they never so pleasing nor so holy (if it be courteous and seemly to say), we should have a manner of indifference. If they come, welcome them; but lean not too much on them for fear of feebleness; for it will take much of thy powers to bide any long time in such sweet feelings and weepings. And peradventure thou mayest be stirred to love God for the sake of them.

> *The Cloud of Unknowing* (late 14th Century), Ch. 50

14. Such men become so godlike and so well-regulated, so truly resigned, virtuous, peaceful and calm, that no one is ever conscious of any infirmity in them, either in words or deeds; and yet they look upon themselves as nothing, and heed all as little as if it had taken place in some one a thousand miles away.

> John Tauler (c. 1300–61),
> *The Inner Way*, Sermon XXIV

15. Nor have I any great care in this respect, how it may happen unto me in outward matters, whether, namely, I am clothed in sackcloth or in good clothes, whether I dwell in a corner at home or otherwise, whether I be despised or had in reverence, whether others be preferred before me or not; for all these things in whatsoever way they may happen, cannot touch me. For small and slight indeed is still the spiritual conversation of a man, and weak and nigh unto destruction the state of his mind, if he be yet agitated by such outward things, or vacillate to and fro between what is to be followed and what is to be avoided.

> Gerlac Petersen (1378–1411),
> *The Fiery Soliloquy with God*, Ch. XXV

16. The worth of love does not consist in high feelings; but in detachment: in patience under trials for the sake of God whom we love.

> John of the Cross (1542–91),
> *Spiritual Maxims*, 56

17. The weak in spirit and he that is yet in a manner carnal and inclined to sensible things can hardly withdraw himself altogether from earthly desires. And therefore he is often afflicted when he would withdraw himself, and is easily made angry if anyone thwart his wish.

> Thomas à Kempis (c. 1379–1471),
> *Of the Imitation of Christ*, Book I, Ch. VI

18. He that seeks no witness for himself without, has clearly committed himself wholly unto God.

> Thomas à Kempis (c. 1379–1471),
> *Of the Imitation of Christ*, Book II, Ch. VI

19. A soul which has true liberty will leave its exercise with an equal countenance, and a heart gracious towards the importunate person who has inconvenienced her. For it is

all one to her whether she serve God by meditating, or serve him by bearing with her neighbour: both are the will of God, but the bearing with her neighbour is necessary at that time.

François de Sales (1567–1622),
The Spiritual Conferences, Book III,
Letters to Widows XI, To Madame de Chantal

20. If you do great works, you are raised high by mercy. If you do no great work, perhaps you are wholesomely humbled. He knows better than you what will help you: and on that account, if you wish to feel rightly about him, understand that every thing which is done for you by him is well done.

Hugh of St Victor (c. 1096–1141),
The Soul's Betrothal Gift, p. 33

21. Oh, by all that love that constrained thee, who art the life of all that live, thyself to submit to die, be pleased to put to death in me all that is unpleasing to thee.

Gertrude the Great (1256–1301),
Prayers on the Passion, IX

22. It is therefore of the first importance to love God and his will, and to love this will in whatever way it is made manifest to us, without desiring anything else. The soul has no concern in the choice of different objects, that is God's affair, and whatever he gives is best for the soul. The whole of spirituality is an abridgement of this maxim, "Abandon yourself entirely to the over-ruling of God, and by self-oblivion be eternally occupied in loving and serving him without any of those fears, reflexions, examens, and anxieties which the affair of our salvation, and perfection sometimes occasion."

Jean-Pierre de Caussade (1675–1751),
Abandonment to Divine Providence,
Book II, Ch. II, Sec. I

23. Our surrender then ought to be an entire leaving of ourselves in the hands of God, both in respect to the outward and inward state, forgetting ourselves in a great measure, and thinking on God only: by this means the heart remains always free, contented, and disengaged.

Madame Guyon (1648–1717),
A Method of Prayer, Ch. V

24. 'Tis likewise of great importance for the soul to go to prayer with courage, and that it bring along with it a pure and disinterested love: let it not go so much to receive anything from God, as to please him and do his will.

Madame Guyon (1648–1717),
A Method of Prayer, Ch. IV

25. Whether he gives sweetness or bitterness, darkness or light, whatever he lays upon the scale, the man balances it evenly; all things are equal to him, save sin alone, which is for ever cast out. When such utterly resigned men have thus been deprived of all consolation, and believe that they have lost all virtues, and are forsaken of God and of all creatures: then if they are able to reap them, all kinds of fruit, the corn and vine, are ready and ripe.

John of Ruysbroeck (1293–1381),
Adornment of the Spiritual Marriage, Ch. XXVIII

iv *The Mystical Body*

Each of us shares a common humanity: we are, so to speak, parts of one another. In realizing this, the mystics place themselves with us in a physical and spiritual web, where we live and move and have our being. Charles Williams uses the

the word "coinherence" (11) to describe this idea, and he has done much to explore the possibility of our love and suffering so affecting the web that we may be said, even literally, to bear one another's burdens in suffering, and to promote one another's good in love.

The familiar theological reassurances that Christ is in us and we in him are relevant here, for Christ, as we have seen, can be conceived as the entire course of good in human history which would redeem our separation from God, and which found unique incarnation in Jesus of Nazareth. In so far as we contribute to dividing ourselves or others from God, we may be said therefore to crucify the Good itself. And in so far as that Good made man in Jesus brings self-giving love to its ultimate test in the unspeakable suffering of crucifixion, it remains also in us when we suffer in its name. The crucifixion, mystically understood, thus goes on through the history of suffering itself, just as redemptive love remains alive to the degree that Christ is imitated. He is in us, and we in him through every act of love and suffering endured to bring men closer to God. Such acts of course are innumerable and mostly nameless in the world's complexity, but they join us in one mystical body of such intricacy that its convergent design towards a single redeemed humanity can be grasped only obscurely and in faith (1–8).

Evidences, however, of our mystical coinherence are not entirely withheld, even in ordinary experience. They are discovered in the simple fact that mutual joy is more fulfilling than isolated pleasure, that we can comfort one another, inspire one another, be pleased for one another, and so on. At such moments, the bonds of love and suffering which bring us into relationship may also touch upon a further, deeper interconnectedness passing into mystery, and the promise of meaning (9–16).

In the context of such interpenetration, the eucharist also finds its place, for food shared commemoratively and in charity is our incorporation in Christ, who takes on our burdens as we take on his love, which is his being. We are thus, in a mystical sense, one in Christ's body in so far as we are one in the love that would overcome our separation from God. And yet, while we live in this world, love must be expressed as plainly as bread and wine. As the old catechetical anecdote puts it, in hell they must eat with eight-foot-long spoons and so can never eat at all; in heaven they also use eight-foot-long spoons, but to feed one another (17–26).

1. Here saw I a great oneing betwixt Christ and us, to mine understanding: for when he was in pain, we were in pain. And all creatures that might suffer pain, suffered with him: that is to say, all creatures that God hath made to our service. The firmament, the earth, failed for sorrow in their nature in the time of Christ's dying. For it belongeth naturally to their property to know him for their God, in whom all their virtue standeth.

Julian of Norwich (c. 1342–1420),
Revelations of Divine Love, Ch. XVIII

2. And thus all saints are in me, and I in them. And thus all angels and the eternity and infinity of God are in me for evermore, I being the living temple and comprehensor of them. Since therefore all other ways of in-being would be utterly vain, were it not for this. And the Kingdom of God (as our Saviour saith, this way) is within you; let us ever think and meditate on him, that his conception, nativity, life and death may be always within us.

Thomas Traherne (c. 1636–74),
Centuries of Meditation, I, 100

3. O Marguerite, my sister, while I, given body and soul to

the positive forces of the universe, was wandering over continents and oceans, my whole being passionately taken up in watching the rise of all the earth's tints and shades, you lay motionless, stretched out on your bed of sickness; silently, deep within yourself, you were transforming into light the world's most grievous shadows.

Pierre Teilhard de Chardin (1881–1955),
Activation of Energy,
"The Spiritual Energy of Suffering"

4. A little carrying of the burden, a little allowing our burden to be carried; a work as slow, as quiet, even as dull as by agreement to take up or give up a worry or a pain – a compact of substitution between friends – this is the beginning of the practice. The doctrine will grow in us of itself.

Charles Williams (1886–1945),
The Image of the City, "Exchange"

5. For all the saints that have ever been, have suffered no more than flowed in upon them through Christ united to them his members; who communicated to them his own afflictions. Truly it was he who suffered in them, rather than they themselves. For he drew upon himself the affliction of all the saints, out of his great love for his members, and marvellous compassion, and he felt them with far more interior agony than any of the saints.

John Tauler (c. 1300–61),
Meditations on the Life and Passion, Ch. 46

6. O wonderful and incomprehensible exchange! The Lord of glory, for our poor human weakness, gave his own most high Godhead! The maker of all creatures did not abhor to take upon him the form of a servant.

John Tauler (c. 1300–61),
Meditations on the Life and Passion, Ch. 2

7. So also, if a man return thanks for the thirst wherewith upon the cross He thirsted for man's salvation, He will receive it as if He had refreshed His thirst. Moreover, whosoever shall return thanks to Him for having hung nailed upon the cross, it will be as grateful to Him as if he had loosened Him from the cross and freed Him from all pains.

> Mechthild of Hackborn (1240–98),
> *Select Revelations*, Book II, Ch. V

8. It is to me a species of scourging, when their impatience prevents their bearing the least thing for My love. The thorns of their pride lacerate My head, for they wish to be greater than I. Their voluntary habit of offending is to Me as the weight of the cross.

> Bridget of Sweden (1303–73),
> *Select Revelations*, Book I, Ch. XIV

9. For when the light is spread abroad the heat is divided over the earth; because when righteousness is openly preached, the anxious desire of the heart to seek God is spread forth in the practice of virtues; so that one person shines forth in the word of wisdom, another in the word of knowledge; one is mighty in the grace of healing, another in the working of mighty deeds; and that thus, while they severally receive unequally the gifts of the Spirit, they are all necessarily united to each other, and unanimously inflamed.

> Gregory the Great (c. 540–604),
> *Morals on the Book of Job*, Book XXIX, 41

10. In planetary terms, the human forms but one. It is therefore as one body (that is, in a unanimous movement) that it must abandon the mirage of a mysticism of relaxation and conform to the particular type of spirit determined for it by the immutable axes of a *convergent universe*.

> Pierre Teilhard de Chardin (1881–1955),
> *Activation of Energy*, "A Clarification:
> Reflections on Two Converse Forms of Spirit", VI

11. In the second place there arises within one a first faint
    sense of what might be called "loving from within". One
    no longer merely loves an object; one has a sense of
    loving precisely from the great web in which the object
    and we are both combined. There is, if only transitorily,
    a flicker of living within the beloved. Such sensations
    are, or are not; they are, in themselves, of no importance.
    But they do for a moment encourage us, and they may
    assist us to consider still more intensely the great co-
    inherence of all life.

    Charles Williams (1886–1945),
    The Image of the City, "The Way of Exchange"

12. So, in this perfect love possessed by the countless angels
    and blessed souls, where none shall love another less
    than he loves himself, every one shall rejoice in every
    other as much as he rejoices in himself. And if the heart
    of man shall hardly contain his own joy over such great
    good, how shall it hold delights so many and so great.

    Bonaventure (1221–74),
    The Breviloquium, VII, 7, 8

13. For to be loved and to love is a sweet change; the delight
    of all man's life, and of angel's, and of God's; and also
    the reward of all blessedness. If therefore thou desirest to
    be loved, love; for love gainyields itself. No man has ever
    lost by good love who keeps in view the end of love.
    Truly he that knows not to burn in love knows not to be
    glad. Therefore never is a man more blessed than he that
    is borne without himself by the might of love, and by the
    greatness of God's love receives within himself a songful
    sweetness of everlasting praising.

    Richard Rolle (1300–49),
    The Fire of Love, Ch. XXV

14. Souls, which are attracted to pure love, may be as dis-

interested for themselves as for their neighbours, because
they seek in themselves, as much as in their least-known
neighbour, the glory and good pleasure of God and the
fulfilment of his promises. In this sense such souls are, as it
were, strangers to themselves; they only love themselves, as
they love other creatures, in the due order of pure charity.

> François Fenelon (1651–1715),
> *Maxims of the Mystics*, Article XII,
> "Of loving self for love of God"

15. True love weighs all alike: where true love reigns, no man
seeks preferment, no man steals from his well-beloved,
accounting all such things to be with himself which are with
his friend.

> Juan Luis Vives (1492–1540),
> *Introduction to Wisdom*, H ii

16. Ye must be faithful unto Him who was faithful unto you,
and in faithful love must ye be united with your neighbour,
for he who is faithful unto God will also be faithful unto his
neighbour. How greatly, purely and faithfully this holy Man
of Sorrows hath loved us hath been made clearly evident by
His life, teaching, and death.

> Angela of Foligno (c. 1248–1309),
> *The Divine Consolation*, Ch. XVII

17. Let us, then, consider that one and simple nature of the
peaceful Unity which unites all things to itself, to themselves
and to each other, and preserves all things, distinct and yet
interpenetrating in an universal cohesion without confusion. Thus it is that the Divine Intelligences derive that
Unity whereby they are united to the activities and the
objects of their intuition; and rise up still further to a
contact, beyond knowledge, with truths which transcend
the mind.

> Dionysius the Areopagite (c. 500),
> *The Divine Names*, Ch. XI, 2

18. For if religion requires me to love all persons, as God's
    creatures, that belong to him, that bear his image, enjoy
    his protection, and make parts of his family and house-
    hold; if these are the great and necessary reasons why I
    should live in love and friendship with any one man in
    the world; and, consequently, I offend against all these
    reasons, and break through all these ties and obligations,
    whenever I want love towards any one man. The sin,
    therefore, of hating, or despising any one man, is like the
    sin of hating all God's creation; and the necessity of
    loving any one man, is the same necessity of loving every
    man.

    William Law (1686–1761),
    A Serious Call, Ch. XX

19. That indeed seems to be one of the magical Laws of this
    very creation in which we live; that the thing we know
    already, the thing we have said to ourselves a hundred
    times, when said by *someone else* becomes suddenly
    operative. It is part of C. Williams' doctrine, isn't it? –
    that no one can paddle his own canoe but everyone can
    paddle someone else's. . . .

    C. S. Lewis (1898–1963),
    Letters, 26 December 1951, To a Lady

20. I would say that those men are beasts rather than human
    beings who declare that a man ought to live in such a
    way as to be to no one a source of consolation, to no one
    a source even of grief or burden; to take no delight in the
    good fortune of another, or impart to others no
    bitterness because of their own misfortune, caring to
    cherish no one and to be cherished by no one.

    Aelred of Rievaulx (c. 1110–67),
    Spiritual Friendship, II, 52

21. The man said: "Tell me, Beloved, what is the reason that

the men on this ninth rock shine inwardly like bright angels?" The *answer* came: "God has filled these men with luminous grace so that it must shine forth from them; but they neither know it nor wish to know." The man said: "Beloved, are there many of these men, for I think them to be the righteous men?" The *answer* came: "I will tell you. As few as they are, for their sake God permits Christendom to continue. You see, if these men were gone, God would immediately let Christendom perish."

Rulman Merswin (c. 1307–82),
The Book of the Nine Rocks, "On the Ninth Rock"

22. He will draw up the lowest powers to the highest, and lead the lowest with the highest unto Himself. If we do this, He will draw us after Himself into His highest and most secret place. For thus it must needs be; if I am to come to Him, I must receive Him into myself. So much of mine, so much of His; it is an equal bargain.

John Tauler (c. 1300–61),
The Inner Way, Sermon XX

23. And thus hath it come to pass when they look into the essence of the soul, where God is, that God lifteth and embraceth them, and they embrace God. And each sitteth down to table, and wisheth to partake, and each one inviteth the other to eat and to drink. They all eat and drink, and are all filled in common. One letteth himself be moved by another, what one willeth the other willeth, and all agree. Therefore Christ said, "When I am lifted up I draw all things to Me."

John Tauler (c. 1300–61),
The Following of Christ, Part II, 52

24. In the holy Eucharist the Son of God, in his overflowing mercy, not content with having made himself the Son of

Man, a sharer in our humanity and our brother, has invented a wondrous way of communicating himself to each one of us in particular. By this he incorporates himself in us, and us in him. He dwells in us, and makes us dwell in him, becoming our food and support, flesh of our flesh, and bone of our bone, by a grace which surpasses every other grace, since it contains in itself the author of all grace! Truly, we possess in this divine mystery, though veiled and hidden under the sacramental species, him whom the angels desire to see, even while they see him continually.

Jean-Pierre Camus (1584–1652),
The Spirit of St Francis de Sales, pp. 390–1

25. Love fell sick, and the Lover tended him with patience, perseverance, obedience and hope. Love grew well, and the Lover fell sick; and he was cured by his Beloved, who made him to remember his virtue and honour.

Ramon Lull (c. 1232–1315),
The Book of the Lover and the Beloved, 239

26. Therefore let us all love the One singly, that all may be singly loved by the One, for no other beside that One is fit to be singly loved by all. And let all men love themselves as one in the One, and they may be made one in the loving of One. That love is single, but not private; alone, yet not solitary; shared, but not divided; common and singular; a single love of all and the whole love of each; growing no less by sharing, failing not through use nor growing old by time, ancient and new, desirable in affection, sweet in experience, eternal in fruit, full of mirth, refreshing and satisfying, and never cloying.

Hugh of St Victor (c. 1096–1141),
The Soul's Betrothal Gift, pp. 18–19

Chapter V

Prayer

Prayer lies at the heart of mystical life, and this chapter deals with some of its varieties and stages. Especially among theologians, discussions on this subject can become technical, but the mystics insist also on certain enabling kinds of simplicity. Prayer, for instance, should not be a harsh or merely external observance, but the expression and refinement of our general human impulses of gratitude, trust, delight, longing, anguish and understanding. This is not to say that prayer is without difficulty, but its first aim, and its last, is the expression of, and participation in, God's glory.

✠

i *Elevation to God*

Prayer is defined as an elevation of the heart and mind to God. It follows that those familiar forms of prayer wherein we make requests are the most rudimentary, and indeed sometimes may not be prayers at all. Even the beautiful set prayers of the liturgy are inadequate if they do not promote an intention to submit our wills to God out of a desire to be united to him. This does not mean that prayers of petition are always spurious, or that the liturgy is an empty formality, but the mystics would have us reflect on our basic intention in prayer, and the desire from which it springs. Seen in such a light, the very effort to dispose ourselves to pray can itself be a prayer, and the person who admits an inability to pray may be closer to true prayer than one who prays unreflectingly and by habit. It follows also that prayer is not confined to words. Our desires and affections can be offered to God, and so can our actions. Indeed, a person desiring God's will in all things, and referring every daily activity to that end, is perpetually in prayer (1–11).

We are asked, therefore, to appreciate a variety of possibilities, rather than approach prayer as a confining, systematic discipline. Prayer has the complexity of a living relationship (12), and is based on an affirmation of life, variety and energy. To force it in directions which deny these foundations, is to pervert it (12–23).

Despite such emphases, however, the mystics have done much to classify different kinds and degrees of prayer. While they assure us that the actual terrain we will cross in the way of prayer is unique to ourselves, they assume that maps are helpful. As we might expect, the maps they provide vary in scale and detail, but they also offer some consistent guidelines.

One major, generally accepted landmark is the distinction between meditation and contemplation. Meditation is comparable to speech, for it proceeds discursively, uses imagination, and is directed by our will and intelligence. Contemplation is comparable to sight, for it grasps its object intuitively, does not resort to imagination, and is given to us rather than generated by us.

The mystics also distinguish between higher and lower forms of contemplation. The lower develops from meditation and is guided by our own effort and will, which enable prayer to pass beyond images and discourse. In the higher form, God comes to us and we are elevated in a manner beyond our capacity to achieve. The exact point at which our own seeking thus passes over into God's finding is difficult to define, and has occasioned much discussion. It is not un-reasonable to suggest that the complexity of the debate itself indicates how the point of transformation varies among different temperaments.

A small number of terms has developed from this debate, and they are part of a common vocabulary. The prayer of meditation is described as *active*, *acquired*, *imperfect* and *natural*. Contemplation, by contrast, is *passive, infused, perfect* and *supernatural*. In the elusive intermediate stage, these terms are frequently supplemented by others, and used in a sense best derived from context. The first set of words, however, clearly suggests that we are the initiators of prayer which is within our capacity as free creatures desiring God; the second set makes clear that our own efforts are inade-quate to effect the final union we seek. Rather, we must wait upon a power which pours itself into us (*infusion*), and through which alone our prayer is perfected. This power is usually described as *grace*, and because it is experienced as coming to us from a source higher than our created nature, it is also called *supernatural* (24–39).

1. When I pray for aught my prayer goes for naught; when I pray for naught I pray as I ought. When I am one with that wherein are all things, past, present and to come, all the same distance and all just the same, then they are all in God and all in me. There is no thought of Henry or of Conrad. Praying for aught save God alone is idolatry and unrighteousness. They pray aright who pray in spirit and in truth. When praying for someone, for Henry or Conrad, I pray at my weakest. When praying for no one I pray at my strongest, and when I want nothing and make no request I am praying my best, for in God is no Henry nor no Conrad.

Meister Eckhart (1260–1327),
Sermons and Collations, V

2. The most powerful prayer, one wellnigh omnipotent, and the worthiest work of all is the outcome of a quiet mind. The quieter it is the more powerful, the worthier, the deeper, the more telling and more perfect the prayer is. To the quiet mind all things are possible. What is a quiet mind? A quiet mind is one which nothing weighs on, nothing worries, which, free from ties and from all self-seeking, is wholly merged into the will of God and dead as to its own. Such an one can do no deed however small but it is clothed with something of God's power and authority.

Meister Eckhart (1260–1327),
In Collationibus, 2

3. The first and principal thing which a man ought in prayer to do, is to rectify his intention, that is, to take it in hand only because God would have it so, without any other end or motive whatsoever; and to continue the same only end and motive.

Benet of Canfield (1562–1610),
The Rule of Perfection, Part II,
"Advice Touching Prayer"

4. For prayer is a right understanding of that fulness of joy that is to come, with well-longing and sure trust.

Julian of Norwich (c. 1342–1420),
Revelations of Divine Love, Ch. XLII

5. Prayer oneth the soul to God.

Julian of Norwich (c. 1342–1420),
Revelations of Divine Love, Ch. XLIII

6. Our part in prayer is to try to raise our minds and hearts to God, to spend time making the effort. "Trying to pray" is prayer, and it is very good prayer. The will to try is also His gift.

Basil Hume (1923–),
To Be a Pilgrim, "Prayer"

7. For prayer is naught else but a rising desire of the heart into God, by withdrawing of the heart from all earthly thoughts. And so is prayer likened to a fire which of its own kind leaveth the lowness of the earth and always rises up into the air. Right so desire in prayer, when it is touched and lightened of the spiritual fire which is God, it is ever rising to Him that it came from.

Walter Hilton (1300–96),
The Scale of Perfection, Book I, Ch. XXV

8. Hence, before every endeavour, more especially if the subject be Divinity, must we begin with prayer: not as though we would pull down to ourselves that Power which is nigh both everywhere and nowhere, but that, by these remembrances and invocations of God, we may commend and unite ourselves thereunto.

Dionysius the Areopagite (c. 500),
The Divine Names, Ch. III, 1

9. For just as the crown of the building of all virtues is the perfection of prayer, so unless everything has been united and compacted by this as its crown, it cannot possibly continue strong and stable. For lasting and continual calmness in prayer, of which we are speaking, cannot be secured or consummated without them, so neither can those virtues which lay its foundations be fully gained without persistence in it.

John Cassian (c. 360–434),
First Conference of Abbot Isaac, Ch. II

10. Prayer, which consisteth in the reference of all our deliberate acts to God, can be perpetual in the sense that it can last so long as such acts can last.

François Fenelon (1651–1715),
Maxims of the Mystics, Article XXV

11. Prayer is no other thing but the application of the heart to God, and the inward exercise of love.

Madame Guyon (1648–1717),
A Method of Prayer, Ch. I

12. Prayer should never be regarded as a science or reduced to a system – that ruins it, because it is essentially a living and personal relationship, which tends to become more personal and also more simple, as one goes on.

Evelyn Underhill (1875–1941),
Letters, 12 April 1939, To S.P.

13. Thus it does not follow, because all the nuns in this convent practise prayer, that they must all be contemplatives. It is impossible and it would greatly discourage those who are not so if they did not understand the truth that contemplation is a gift of God which is not necessary for salvation nor for earning our eternal reward, nor will any one here require them to possess it.

Teresa of Avila (1515–82),
The Way of Perfection, Ch. XVII, 2

14. I am certainly unfit to advise anyone else on the devotional life. My own rules are (1) To make sure that, wherever else they may be placed, the main prayers should *not* be put "last thing at night". (2) To avoid introspection in prayers – I mean not to watch one's own mind to see if it is in the right frame, but always to turn the attention outwards to God. (3) Never, never to try to generate an emotion by will power. (4) To pray without words when I am able, but to fall back on words when tired or otherwise below par. With renewed thanks. Perhaps *you* will sometimes pray for *me*?

C. S. Lewis (1898–1963), *Letters*,
31 July 1954, To Mrs Ursula Roberts

15. You say you do not know how to pray. Experience has taught me that persons of good will who speak in this way know better than others how to pray, because their prayer is more simple and humble, but, on account of its simplicity it escapes their observation. To pray like this is to remain by faith in the presence of God, with a hidden, but constant desire to receive his grace according to our needs. As God sees all our desires, and as, according to St Augustine, to desire always is to pray always, so in this consists our great prayer. Follow the leading of simplicity in prayer, there can never be excess of it, for God loves to see us like little children in his presence.

Jean-Pierre de Caussade (1675–1751),
Spiritual Counsels, Fourth Book, Letter VII

16. Therefore you must learn a kind of prayer which can be made at all times, which does not divert from outward business, and which princes, kings, prelates, priests, magistrates, soldiers, children, artisans, labourers, women and sick persons, may all perform. This is not the prayer of the head, but the prayer of the heart. It is not a prayer of thought only, because the spirit of man is so bounded that while he thinks on one thing he cannot think on another; but it is the prayer of the heart, which is not at all interrupted by all the occupations of the mind: nothing but irregular affections can interrupt the prayer of the heart: and 'tis almost impossible for the soul which has once tasted God and the sweetness of his love, to relish anything else but him.

Madame Guyon (1648–1717),
A Method of Prayer, Ch. I

17. Be not cast down if God does not in this life raise thee to high degrees of contemplation; but beseech him earnestly to give thee a good, humble, and resigned will, and to keep it in thee to the end; ask of him that thou mayest

ever live according to his gracious good pleasure. And since thou hast not strength wherewith to take a lofty flight, do thou remain under the wings of the most loving eternal Wisdom incarnate for thee, as a little chicken remains under the wings of the hen.

> Louis de Blois (1506–65),
> *The Spiritual Mirror*, Ch. X

18. For according to the degree of the purity to which each soul attains, and the character of the state in which it is sunk owing to what happens to it, or by its own efforts renewing itself, its very prayers will each moment be altered: and therefore it is quite clear that no one can always offer up uniform prayers.

> John Cassian (c. 360–434),
> *First Conference of Abbot Isaac*, Ch. VIII

19. And assuredly, a man of good will who always acts rightly, and refers all his works to the honour of God, is ever praying.

> Louis de Blois (1506–65),
> *The Spiritual Mirror*, Ch. X

20. And even of ourselves and of what we do we have to be forgetful for, as said one of the fathers of old, "That is the perfect prayer, when the one who is praying does not remember that he is praying."

> Peter of Alcantara (1499–1562),
> *A Golden Treatise of Mental Prayer*, Part I, Ch. V

21. But unless humility, simplicity and goodness adorn our lives, and are associated with prayer, the mere formality of prayer will avail us nothing. And this I say, not of prayer only, but of every other outward exercise or labour undertaken with a notion of virtue.

> Macarius (c. 300–90),
> *The Institutes of Christian Perfection*,
> Book I, Ch. IX

22. To force the mind to pray, and to persevere in the practice of prayer, will cause it to pray with joy and with repose; but the force must proceed from our own will, the joy and repose will follow of grace.

Macarius (c. 300–90),
Sayings, 10

23. A fervent contemplating sounds better in My ears than merely a praising with words, and a heartfelt sighing sounds better than a lofty appeal. A total subjection of one's self under God and all mankind, in the wish to be as nothing in their sight, is a sound for Me above all sweet sounds.

Henry Suso (c. 1295–1366),
The Little Book of Eternal Wisdom, Ch. XXV

24. Contemplation may also be defined as a loving wisdom which tastes God perfect.

François Malaval (1627–1719),
*A Simple Method of Raising the Soul to
Contemplation*, Second Treatise, Dialogue XII

25. The reasoning of meditation resembles speech; it is formed of one thought after another and is thus always in some kind of motion. Contemplation, on the contrary, is more like sight; it attains its object in one instant, and it reposes in that object without speech and without thought.

François Malaval (1627–1719),
*A Simple Method of Raising the Soul to
Contemplation*, Second Treatise, Dialogue XII

26. This doctrine being thus established, I say that if contemplation is supernatural, the soul is passive in the exercise of contemplation because of the principle of the gift or of the help which is infused in it, whether actually

or habitually. But if the contemplation is only acquired, that is to say if it is a habit of holding oneself in the presence of God, with more or less facility according to the progress of each soul, then the soul is not passive, because its principle is produced and acquired in its own depths and is nothing but a habit of regarding God always present.

François Malaval (1627–1719),
*A Simple Method of Raising the Soul to
Contemplation*, Second Treatise, Dialogue III

27. This [third degree of attention] comes not till a soul be arrived to perfect contemplation, by means of which the spirit is so habitually united to God, and besides, the imagination so subdued to the spirit, that it cannot rest upon any thing that will distract it.

Augustine Baker (1575–1641),
Sancta Sophia, Treat. 3, Sec. 1, Ch. 3, Part 4

28. Wherefore, saith the holy teacher, meditation goes its way and brings forth fruit with labour, but contemplation bears fruit without labour. The one seeketh, the other findeth, the one consumeth the food, the other enjoys it; the one discourseth, and maketh reflections, the other is contented with a simple gaze upon the things, for it hath in possession their love and joy. Lastly, the one is as the means, the other as the end: the one as the road and journeying along it, the other as the end of the road and of the journeying. From this to be inferred a very common thing, which all masters of the spiritual life teach, although it is little understood of those who learn it; which is this, that as the means cease when the end has been attained, as the voyaging is over when the port has been touched, so when, through the working out of our meditation, we have come to the repose and sweet savour of contemplation, we ought then to cease from

that pious and laborious searching; and being satisfied with the simple gaze upon, and thought of, God – as though we had him there present before us – we should rest in the enjoyment of that affection then given, whether it be of love, or of admiration, or joy, or other like sentiment.

Peter of Alcantara (1499–1562),
A Golden Treatise of Mental Prayer, Part I, Ch. V

29. When some persons hear the prayer of silence, they groundlessly imagine that therein the soul is placed in a state of dullness, and is lifeless and inactive. But certain it is that therein the soul acteth more nobly and with more enlargement than ever it did hitherto.

Madame Guyon (1648–1717),
A Method of Prayer, Ch. XXI

30. Simple, pure, infused and perfect contemplation, therefore, is a known and inner manifestation which God gives of himself, of his goodness, of his peace, and of his sweetness, whose object is God, pure, ineffable, abstracted from all particular thoughts, within an inward silence.

Miguel de Molinos (1640–97),
A Spiritual Guide Which Disentangles the Soul,
Ch. XIII

31. There are, moreover, two ways of contemplation: the one imperfect, active and acquired; the other infused and passive. The active (whereof we have treated hitherto) is that which may be achieved by our own diligence, the divine grace also assisting, and we gathering together the faculties and senses and preparing ourselves for everything God wills.

Miguel de Molinos (1640–97),
A Spiritual Guide Which Disentangles the Soul,
Third Admonition

32. Good reason have the saints to say that meditation operates with toil, and with fruit; contemplation without toil, but with quiet, rest, peace, delight, and far greater fruit. Meditation sows, and contemplation reaps; meditation seeks, and contemplation finds; meditation prepares the food, contemplation savours it and feeds on it.

Miguel de Molinos (1640–97),
A Spiritual Guide Which Disentangles the Soul,
Second Admonition

33. Active is the lower, and contemplative is the higher. Active life hath two degrees, a higher and a lower; and also contemplative life hath two degrees, a lower and a higher. These two lives be so coupled together, that although they differ in part, yet neither of them may be had fully without some part of the other.

The Cloud of Unknowing (late 14th Century), Ch. 8

34. Whatever man or woman thinks to come to contemplation without many such sweet meditations beforehand of their own wretchedness, the passion, the kindness, the great goodness and the worthiness of God, surely he shall err and fail of his purpose. And yet, a man or woman that hath long time been practised in these meditations, must nevertheless leave them, and put them and hold them far down under the cloud of forgetting, if ever he shall pierce the cloud of unknowing betwixt him and his God.

The Cloud of Unknowing (late 14th Century), Ch. 7

35. Meditation tends to contemplation, as means to an end. So when the end is attained, the means are laid aside; men rest at the end of their journey; thus, when the state of contemplation has been attained, meditation must cease.

John of the Cross (1542–91),
Spiritual Maxims, 242

36. Contemplatives call it infused contemplation, or mystical theology, whereby God secretly teaches the soul and instructs it in the perfection of love, without efforts on its own part beyond loving attention to God, listening to his voice and admitting the light he sends, without understanding how this is infused contemplation.

John of the Cross (1542–91),
The Dark Night of the Soul, Book II, Ch. V

37. Just as when the surface of the sea has been struck by a stone, one circle produces another circle, and others follow from the impulse of the first; even so, the soul is not purely suspended by the act of contemplation, but gently and imperceptibly plunged in its object.

François Malaval (1627–1719),
A Simple Method of Raising the Soul to
Contemplation, Second Treatise, Dialogue III

38. So prayer is named Meditation until it has produced the honey of devotion, and then it is converted into Contemplation. For as the bees fly through their meadows, settling here and there and gathering honey, which having heaped together, they work in it for the pleasure they take in its sweetness, so we meditate to gather the love of God, but having gathered it we contemplate God, and are attentive to his goodness, by reason of the sweetness which love makes us find in it. The desire we have to obtain divine love makes us meditate, but love obtained makes us contemplate; for by love we find so agreeable a sweetness in the thing beloved, that we can never satiate our spirits in seeing and considering it.

Francois de Sales (1567–1622),
Treatise on the Love of God, Book VI, Ch. III

39. This prayer is no work of ours; it is supernatural and

utterly beyond our power of attainment. The surest way to prolong it is to recognize that we can neither dismiss nor obtain it, and, unworthy as we are, we can but receive this grace with thanksgiving – and this, not by much speaking, but by raising our eyes like the publican.

Teresa of Avila (1515–82),
The Way of Perfection, Ch. XXXI, 5

ii *The Cross and its Passing*

The cross is Christianity's central sign. It reminds us that suffering is unavoidable, and the tension suggested by its intersecting arms is often taken to represent the paradoxes of faith, the incomplete knowledge which we must endure while separated from God in this life. The theologian Paul Tillich also suggests that the sign of the cross shows an insufficiency in signs themselves, which are always to some degree dependent on space and time, and therefore impede the direct, mystical vision beyond images.

The cross, however, is also a historical fact, and the founder of Christianity was executed by this cruel device reserved by the Romans for enemies of the state. Consequently, Christian devotion may run special risks by seeming to glorify a torture, and even in certain circumstances by seeming to approve of suffering: crusaders, after all, march beneath the banner of a red cross. But to the mystics especially belongs the privilege of interpreting the cross in a spiritual sense as part of the life of prayer, in a manner designed to prevent the imposition of suffering on others, while doing justice to the fact that the cross is a true sign of our material condition where suffering and paradox are unavoidable (1–16).

The cross is thus associated among the mystics with a surrender of ego-assertion, and only spiritual combat should be undertaken in its name, for the contemplative is at war with the limitations of signs and images, the impediments to vision inherent in space and time. Consequently, the cross is associated with meditation, that form of discursive prayer wherein we deploy imagination as a means of elevating the heart and mind to God. Mystics insist that although we must attend to images, these are means to a higher end, and will pass away before contemplative vision, just as faith passes away in the full experience of love (17–26).

The cross reminds us, therefore, that we are required to inhabit a material world, to suffer, and to die. It is the central motif for meditation among the Western mystics because these facts of our human condition are fundamental, and must be faced honestly. Indeed, attempts to avoid the inevitable crosses of death and suffering are a major source of the kind of fear which would cause us to seek for scapegoats. If we shrink from bearing the cross faithfully, we will impose it on others, and precisely in such imposition lies the self-willed urge for power to which the mystics stand so radically opposed.

1. Now as it was the spirit of the world that nailed our Blessed Lord to the Cross; so every man that has the Spirit of Christ, that opposes the world as he did, will certainly be crucified by the world, some way or other.

William Law (1686–1761),
A Serious Call, Ch. XVII

2. You are quite willing to have a cross, but you want to have the choice.

François de Sales (1567–1622),
The Spiritual Conferences, Book VI,
Various Letters, II, To Madame de Chantal

3. As the soul is strong with the strength of God himself, God lays upon it more crosses and heavier ones than

before; but they are borne divinely. Formerly the cross charmed it; it was loved and cherished; now it is not thought of, but is suffered to go and come; and the cross itself becomes God, like all other things. This does not involve the cessation of suffering, but of the sorrow, the anxiety, the bitterness of suffering. It is true that the crosses are no longer crosses, but God.

Madame Guyon (1648–1717),
Spiritual Torrents, Part I, Ch. IX

4. Theotimus, Mount Calvary is the mount of lovers. All love that takes not its beginning from Our Saviour's Passion is frivolous and dangerous. Unhappy is death without the love of the Saviour, unhappy is love without the death of the Saviour! Love and death are so mingled in the Passion of Our Saviour that we cannot have the one in our heart without the other. Upon Calvary one cannot have life without love, nor love without the death of Our Redeemer. But, except there, all is either eternal death or eternal love: and all Christian wisdom consists in choosing rightly; and to assist you in that, I have made this treatise, by Theotimus.

François de Sales (1567–1622),
Treatise on the Love of God, Book XII, Ch. XIII

5. His lordly couch was the hard cross, on which he leapt with such joy and burning love, and with such delight, as never bridegroom took on couch of ivory and silk. On this couch of love he is still waiting for thee with desire unutterable. But if now thou desirest to be his bride, thou must utterly renounce all delight, and approach to him on his little bed of sorrow, on which love hath placed him, and join thyself to his side, which love hath wounded.

Mechthild of Hackborn (1240–98),
Select Revelations, Book IV, Ch. XII

6. This casting off is a weary Cross, and the heavier and stronger the clinging is, the heavier the Cross will also be. For all the pleasure and delight that ye have in the creature, however holy and divine it may appear to be, or is called, or as it may seem to thee – all must be cast off, if thou desirest to be truly lifted up and drawn to God.

John Tauler (c. 1300–61),
The Inner Way, Sermon XXI

7. Whoso obtaineth the grace that is in Christ and in His Passion, to him all mediation disappeareth, so that all things are known to him immediately. That we do not know all in truth comes from this, that we still have mediation; if we were free from this we should certainly know the pure truth. But its purity we obtain in Christ and in His Passion.

John Tauler (c. 1300–61),
The Following of Christ, Part II, 57

8. Although he may with but moderate affection read or meditate on any point of the Life and Passion of Christ, he cannot but derive great benefit from it; as he who handles flour must of necessity have his fingers sprinkled with it. But he who contemplates the same Passion of our Lord with many tears, but yet neglects true humility, patience, resignation, and charity, will certainly reap little or no fruit from his meditation.

Louis de Blois (1506–65),
The Spiritual Mirror, Ch. X

9. He who seeks not the cross of Christ, seeks not the glory of Christ.

John of the Cross (1542–91),
Spiritual Maxims, 10

10. And the higher a man hath mounted in the Spirit the heavier crosses he will often find, because the punishment of his exile increases with love.

Thomas à Kempis (c. 1379–1471),
Of the Imitation of Christ, Book II, Ch. XII

11. Walk where thou wilt, seek what thou wilt, thou wilt find no higher way above, nor safer way below, than the way of the holy cross. Dispose and order all things as thou wilt and seest, yet shalt thou only learn that thou must always suffer, willingly or unwillingly, so shalt thou always find the cross.

Thomas à Kempis (c. 1379–1471),
Of the Imitation of Christ, Book II, Ch. XII

12. If thou carry the cross cheerfully it will carry thee, and lead thee to the desired end, namely where there shall be an end of suffering, though here there shall be none.

Thomas à Kempis (c. 1379–1471),
Of the Imitation of Christ, Book II, Ch. XII

13. And all the creatures that are under heaven serve and know and obey their creator in their own way better than you. And even the demons did not crucify him, but you together with them crucified him and still crucify him by taking delight in vices and sins.

Francis of Assisi (1182–1226),
Admonitions

14. Souls that really love truth and God cannot endure the smallest intermission of that love, but are wholly and always (as it were) fixed to his cross, watching the sense of spiritual improvement taking place in themselves.

Macarius (c. 300–90),
Institutes of Christian Perfection, Book VI, Ch. XXV

15. Notwithstanding, the bleeding continued till many things were seen and understood. The fairness and the lifelikeness is like nothing but the same; the plenteousness is like to the drops of water that fall off the eaves after a great shower of rain, that fall so thick that no man may number them with bodily wit; and for the roundness, they were like to the scale of herring, in the spreading on the forehead. These three came to my mind in the time: pellets, for roundness, in the coming out of the blood; the scale of herring, in the spreading in the forehead, for roundness; the drops off eaves, for the plenteousness innumerable.

This Showing was quick and life-like, and horrifying and dreadful, sweet and lovely. And of all the sight it was most comfort to me that our God and Lord that is so reverend and dreadful, is so homely and courteous: and this most fulfilled me with comfort and assuredness of soul.

Julian of Norwich (c. 1342–1420),
Revelations of Divine Love, Ch. VII

16. They live in unknowing and desire not to know. They have not looked into the origin, nor do they desire to do so, because they think themselves too unworthy. The devil has beset them with all kinds of temptations that men can conceive and beyond human conception; yet they have no desire except what God gives them, and that they receive joyfully. To them all creaturely things have become crosses and they have endured them. If God gave them the cross again, they would receive it with joy, because they know that their Lord and their God has gone before them with the cross. Other than that, they desire nothing till they die. These men are unknown to the world, but the world is well known to them.

Rulman Merswin (c. 1307–82),
The Book of the Nine Rocks, "On the Ninth Rock"

17. That the innocent Christ did not suffer, to quiet an angry Deity, but merely as co-operating, assisting and uniting with that love of God, which desired our salvation. That he did not suffer in our place or stead, but only on our account, which is a quite different matter. And to say, that he suffered in our place or stead, is as absurd, as contrary to Scripture, as to say, that he rose from the dead, and ascended into heaven in our place and stead, that we might be excused from it. For his sufferings, death, resurrection and ascension, are all of them equally on our account, for our sake, for our good and benefit, but none of them possible to be in our stead.

William Law (1686–1761),
The Spirit of Love, Second Dialogue

18. Die! die as the silkworm does when it has fulfilled the office of its creation, and you will see God and be immersed in his greatness, as the little silkworm is enveloped in its cocoon. Understand that when I say "you will see God", I mean in the manner described, in which he manifests himself in this kind of union.

Teresa of Avila (1515–82),
The Interior Castle, Fifth Mansions, Ch. II, 5

19. That cross is a tree set on fire with invisible flame, that illuminateth all the world. The flame is love. The love in his bosom who dies on it. In the light of which we see how to possess all the things in heaven and earth after his similitude.

Thomas Traherne (c. 1636–74),
Centuries of Meditation, I, 60

20. I understood that we be now, in our Lord's meaning, in his cross with him, in his pains and his passion, dying; and we, willingly abiding in the same cross with his help and his grace unto the last point, suddenly he shall

change his cheer to us, and we shall be with him in heaven. Betwixt that one and that other shall be no time, and then shall all be brought to joy. And thus said he in this showing: *Where is now any point of thy pain, or thy grief?* and we shall be full blessed.

Julian of Norwich (c. 1342–1420),
Revelations of Divine Love, Ch. XXI

21. Certainly in this exercise a man should lay hold of good images to help him; such as the Passion of our Lord and all those things that may stir him to greater devotion. But in the possession of God, the man must sink down to that imageless Nudity which is God; and this is the first condition, and the foundation, of a ghostly life.

John of Ruysbroeck (1293–1381),
The Sparkling Stone, Ch. II

22. My unfathomable love shows itself in the great bitterness of My Passion, like the sun in its brightness, like the fair rose in its perfume, like the strong fire in its glowing heat. Therefore, hear with devotion how cruelly I suffered for thee.

Henry Suso (c. 1295–1366),
The Little Book of Eternal Wisdom, Ch. I

23. If thou hast no liking to meditate on My Passion with weeping eyes, because of the bitter agony I suffered, then oughtest thou to meditate on it with a laughing heart, because of the joyous benefit thou wilt find in it. But if thou hast no mind either to laugh or to cry, thou oughtest to meditate on it in the dryness of thy heart, to My honour and praise, by doing which thou wilt have done no less than if thou hadst been dissolved in tears or steeped in sweetness; for then thou actest from love of virtue, without regard to thyself.

Henry Suso (c. 1295–1366),
The Little Book of Eternal Wisdom, Ch. XIV

24. Lo! here mayest thou see that thou must sorrowfully desire for to forego the feeling of thyself, and painfully bear the burden of thyself as a cross, ere thou mayest be oned to God in ghostly feeling of himself, the which is perfect charity.

Epistle of Privy Counsel (late 14th Century), Ch. 8

25. God gives us the cross and the cross gives us to God.

Madame Guyon (1648–1717),
A Method of Prayer, Ch. VII

26. For this end, that is useful which I spoke of before: we must not show ourselves as labouring after spiritual consolations; come what may, to embrace the cross is the great thing. The lord of all consolation was himself forsaken: they left him alone in his sorrows. Do not let us forsake him; for his hand will help us to rise more than any efforts we can make; and he will withdraw himself when he sees it to be expedient for us, and when he pleaseth will also draw the soul forth out of itself, as I said before.

Teresa of Avila (1515–82),
Life, Ch. XXII, 15

iii *Divine Dark*

Not surprisingly, the stages of prayer wherein we encounter most fully the loneliness and abandonment of the cross are compared by the mystics to a dark night. St John of the Cross distinguishes between two phases: a dark night of sense, and a dark night of spirit. The first is fairly common, consisting of a relinquishment of the senses in so far as they impede the soul's harmony with its own spiritual nature. The second is rare, and is a purification of spirit so that the soul is in harmony with God. The main experience in both cases is one of appalling aridity, anguish, and deprivation. It is as if the enterprise of prayer itself were futile, unsupported by nature or God. Such afflictions, the mystics tell us, are symptoms of the fact that we must, at some point, cast off altogether our reliance on created things (1–15).

Darkness, however, has another signification. If it is true, as the mystics claim, that there is knowledge beyond discourse and vision beyond images, then such knowledge is impossible to describe, and it is often compared to a kind of darkness. Thus we are to discover at the heart of our abandonment in the spiritual night a wholly other kind of apprehension, which so enables us to find our way around in the dark that the heart of darkness itself becomes bright. The mystics are fond of images suggesting how visionary knowledge is a brilliantly intense night, a darkness so bright that it dazzles. Such knowledge, however, remains a privilege, and because it is God's gift we ought not to desire it impatiently, for experiencing it in this life is not necessary for salvation. Indeed, recognition that we must relinquish the desire itself for contemplative vision is part of the denudation of self-will of which the dark night consists (16–25).

The mystics thus remain our guides, and obscurity remains our home ground. Perhaps we do not need to be reminded too strenuously of the darkness around us, the suffering and need. But we might conceivably live with these things more easily if they were all we knew, for hope is our great disturber of acquiescence and instigator of protest. The mystics would at least stimulate hope by asking us to take seriously the promise that, in the last resort, we need not be lost in the dark.

1. If, then, one cannot achieve God and yet cannot and will not do without Him, from these two things there arise in such men tumult and restlessness, both without and within. And so long as a man is thus agitated, no

creature, neither in heaven nor on earth, can give him rest or help him.

John of Ruysbroeck (1293–1381),
Adornment of the Spiritual Marriage, Ch. XXIII

2. How the poor heart is afflicted when being as it were abandoned by love, she seeks everywhere, and yet seems not to find it. She finds it not in the exterior senses, they not being capable of it; nor in the imagination, which is cruelly tortured by conflicting impressions; nor in the understanding, distracted with a thousand obscurities of strange reasonings and fears; and though at length she finds it in the top and supreme region of the spirit where it resides, yet the soul does not recognize it, and thinks it is not love, because the greatness of the distress and darkness hinders her from perceiving its sweetness. She sees it without seeing it, meets it but does not know it, as though all passed in a dream only, or in a type. In this way Magdalen, having met with her dear Master, received no comfort from him, because she thought that it was not he indeed, but the gardener only.

François de Sales (1567–1622),
Treatise on the Love of God, Book IX, Ch. XII

3. God willeth that we know that he keepeth us even alike secure in woe and in weal. And for profit of man's soul, a man is sometime left to himself; although sin is not always the cause: for in this time I sinned not wherefore I should be left to myself – for it was so sudden. Also I deserved not to have this blessed feeling. But freely our Lord giveth when he will; and suffereth us to be in woe sometime. And both is one love.

Julian of Norwich (c. 1342–1420),
Revelations of Divine Love, Ch. XV

4. You must not suppose, sisters, that the effects I

mentioned always exist in the same degree in these souls, for as far as I remember, I told you that in most cases our Lord occasionally leaves such persons to the weakness of their nature. The venomous creatures from the moat round the castle and the other mansions at once unite to revenge themselves for the time when they were deprived of their power.

Teresa of Avila (1515–82),
The Interior Castle, Seventh Mansions, Ch. IV, 1

5. There is no consolation. There is no relief. There is no hope certain; the whole system is a mere illusion. I, who hope so much, and am so rapt up in the soul, know full well that there is no certainty. The tomb cries aloud to us – its dead silence presses on the drum of the ear like thunder, saying, Look at this, and erase your illusions.

Richard Jefferies (1848–87),
The Story of My Heart, Ch. XI

6. This law holds in foul and accursed joy; this in permitted and lawful joy; this in the very purest perfection of friendship; this, in him who was dead, and lived again; had been lost, and was found. Everywhere the greater joy is ushered in by the greater pain. What means this, O Lord my God, whereas thou art everlastingly joy to thyself, and some things around thee evermore rejoice in thee? What means this, that this portion of things thus ebbs and flows alternately displeased and reconciled?

Augustine of Hippo (345–430),
Confessions, Book VIII, 8

7. Prayer in this degree is extremely painful, because the soul being no longer able to make use of its own powers, of which it seems to be entirely deprived, and God having taken from it a certain sweet and profound calm which supported it, is left like those poor children

whom we see running here and there in search of bread, yet finding no one to supply their need, so that the power of prayer seems to be as entirely lost as if we had never possessed it; but with this difference, that we feel the pain occasioned by the loss, because we have proved its value by its possession, while others are not sensible of the loss, because they have never known its enjoyment. The soul, then, can find no support in the creature; and if it feels itself carried away by the things of earth, it is only by impetuosity, and it can find nothing to satisfy it.

Madame Guyon (1648–1717),
Spiritual Torrents, Part I, Ch. VII

8. But because thou art not reformed, therefore when thy soul cometh in from all bodily things, and findeth naught but darkness and heaviness, thou thinkest it an hundred winters till thou be out again by some bodily delight or vain thought, and that is no wonder. For whoso cometh home unto his house, and findeth nothing therein but stink and smoke and a chiding wife, he would soon run out of it. Right so thy soul, when it findeth no comfort in itself but black smoke of spiritual blindness and great chiding of fleshly thoughts crying upon thee that thou mayest not be in peace, truly it is soon weary till it be out again. This is the darkness of conscience.

Walter Hilton (1300–96),
The Scale of Perfection, Book I, Ch. LIII

9. Outward showing profiteth but little, unless by an inwardly keen glance we learn by experience which way to go. And this is why we remain dry and in darkness, without the illumination of truth, because we have not arrived at that which is essential in all things, because of which all external things are made and are, even those that are mystical and spiritual.

Gerlac Petersen (1378–1411),
The Fiery Soliloquy with God, Ch. XXVI

10. But it may be said: Why do we call the divine light, which enlightens the soul and purges it of its ignorances, the Dark Night? I reply, that the Divine Wisdom is, for two reasons, not night and darkness only, but pain and torment also to the soul. The first is, the Divine Wisdom is so high that it transcends the capacity of the soul, and therefore is, in that respect, darkness. The second reason is based on the meanness and impurity of the soul, and in that respect the Divine Wisdom is painful to it, afflictive and obscure also.

John of the Cross (1542–91),
The Dark Night of the Soul, Book II, Ch. V

11. This night – I have already said that it is contemplation – produces in spiritual men two sorts of darkness or purgations conformable to the two divisions of man's nature into sensitive and spiritual. Thus one night or sensitive purgation, wherein the soul is purified or detached, will be of the senses, harmonizing them with the spirit. The other is that night or spiritual purgation wherein the soul is purified or detached in the spirit, and which harmonizes and disposes the soul for union with God in love. The sensitive night is common, and the lot of many: these are the beginners, of whom I shall first speak. The spiritual night is the portion of very few; and they are those who have made some progress, exercised therein, of whom I shall speak hereafter.

John of the Cross (1542–91),
The Dark Night of the Soul, Book I, Ch. VIII

12. It is evident that the faith is a dark night of the soul, and it is thus that it gives it light; the more it darkens the soul the more does it enlighten it. It is by darkening that it gives light, according to the words of the prophet, "If you will not believe", that is, "if you do not make yourselves blind you shall not understand" – that is, you

shall have no light, the high and supernatural knowledge.

> John of the Cross (1542–91),
> *The Ascent of Mount Carmel*, Book II, Ch. III

13. In these and many such like ways the faithful servant of the Lord is tried: how far he can deny and break himself in all things.

> Thomas à Kempis (c. 1379–1471),
> *Of the Imitation of Christ*, Book IV, Ch. XLIX

14. And think not, because I call it a darkness or a cloud, that it is any cloud congealed of the vapours that fly in the air, or any darkness such as is in thine house on nights when the candle is out. For such a darkness and such a cloud mayest thou imagine with curiosity of wit.

> *The Cloud of Unknowing* (late 14th Century), Ch. 4

15. The pain and anguish that good souls suffer from these aridities is very grievous, being a kind of continual martyrdom.

> Augustine Baker (1575–1641),
> *Sancta Sophia*, Treat. 3, Sec. 3, Ch. 5, Part 23

16. Yea some souls there are conducted by almighty God by no other way, but only by such prayer of aridity, finding no sensible contentment in any recollections, but on the contrary continual pain and contradiction. And yet by a privy grace and courage imprinted deeply in the spirit, cease not for all that, but resolutely break through all difficulties and continue, the best they can, their internal exercises to the great advancement of their spirit.

> Augustine Baker (1575–1641),
> *Sancta Sophia*, Treat. 3, Sec. 3, Ch. 5, Part 18

17. A man, provided only he does his part, should not withdraw himself because of spiritual dryness. For the salvation of that soul which by God's will suffers from spiritual dryness is often accomplished as nobly in the light of pure faith alone, as in great sweetness.

Henry Suso (c. 1295–1366),
The Little Book of Eternal Wisdom, Ch. XXIII

18. Guide us to that topmost height of mystic lore which exceedeth light and more than exceedeth knowledge, where the simple, absolute and unchangeable mysteries of heavenly Truth lie hidden in the dazzling obscurity of the secret Silence, outshining all brilliance with the intensity of their darkness, and surcharging our blinded intellects with the utterly impalpable and invisible fairness of glories which exceed all beauty!

Dionysius the Areopagite (c. 500),
The Mystical Theology, Ch. I

19. Unto this darkness which is beyond light we pray that we may come, and may attain unto vision through the loss of sight and knowledge, and that in ceasing thus to see or to know we may learn to know that which is beyond all perception and understanding (for this emptying of our faculties is true sight and knowledge), and that we may offer Him that transcends all things the praises of a transcendent hymnody, which we shall do by denying or removing all things that are.

Dionysius the Areopagite (c. 500),
The Mystical Theology, Ch. II

20. The soul delighteth unspeakably therein, yet it beholdeth naught which can be related by the tongue or imagined in the heart. It seeth nothing, yet seeth all things, because it beholdeth this Good darkly – and the more darkly and secretly the Good is seen, the more certain is it, and

excellent above all things. Wherefore is all other good which can be seen or imagined doubtless less than this, because all the rest is darkness.

Angela of Foligno (c. 1248–1309),
The Divine Consolation, Treatise III, Seventh Vision

21. Hence I observe how needful it is for me to enter into the darkness, and to admit the coincidence of opposites, beyond all the grasp of reason, and there to seek the truth where impossibility meeteth me. And beyond that, beyond even the highest ascent of intellect, when I shall have attained unto that which is unknown to every intellect, and which every intellect judgeth to be most far removed from truth, there, my God, art Thou, who art Absolute Necessity. And the more that dark impossibility is recognized as dark and impossible, the more truly doth his Necessity shine forth, and is more unveiledly present, and draweth nigh.

Nicholas of Cusa (1401–64),
The Vision of God, Ch. IX

22. But you are going to ask me what you should do. Nothing, nothing, my daughter, but to let God act, and to be careful not to obstruct by an inopportune activity the operation of God; to abstain even from sensible acts of resignation, except when you feel that God requires them of you. Remain then like a block of wood, and you will see later the marvels that God will have worked during that silent night of inaction. Self-love, however, cannot endure to behold itself thus completely despoiled, and reduced to nothing.

Jean-Pierre de Caussade (1675–1751),
Spiritual Counsels, Seventh Book, Letter X, 1733,
To Sister Charlotte Elizabeth Bourcier
de Monthureux Luneville

23. And therefore shape thee to bide in this darkness as long as thou mayest, evermore crying after him whom thou lovest. For if ever thou shalt see him or feel him, as it may be here, it must always be in this cloud and in this darkness.

The Cloud of Unknowing (late 14th Century), Ch. 3

24. There are two sorts of darknesses; some unhappy, and others happy: the first are such as arise from sin, and these are unhappy, because they lead the Christian to eternal death. The second are those which the Lord suffers to be in the soul, to establish and settle her in virtue; and these are happy, because they illumine the soul, fortify her, and give her greater light.

Miguel de Molinos (1640–97),
A Spiritual Guide Which Disentangles the Soul,
Book I, Ch. VI

25. This state of trouble and darkness, which is but for a while, hath ever its peaceful respites, flashes of grace illuminating the black night of storm and leaving no trace behind them.

François Fenelon (1651–1715),
Maxims of the Mystics, Article IX

iv *Grace*

In a broad sense, grace means any action coming from outside our conscious selves and promoting our spiritual good. Our existence itself is thus a grace, for God does not owe us anything, not even life. Grace is always a gift, for if it is not free, we either deserve it or earn it and it ceases to be grace, or gratuitous. Conversely, what is true of gifts is true also of grace. Gifts, that is, are gratifying because they are free. The old adage that nothing worth having in this life is easy of acquisition remains generally true, but not of gifts, which are very much worth having, and easy to receive. Although we are not free to demand a gift, however, we are free to refuse one.

Clearly, spiritual gifts, like other kinds, vary in their power to affect us. If grace is, as Jean-Pierre de Caussade says, God's work in the soul making it like himself (8), there are degrees of intensity in such work. Not surprisingly, a complex theological literature has developed, attempting to classify some of these degrees, and the debate is analogous to that among mystics on the stages of prayer between meditation and contemplation. Indeed, it is at times the same debate, for the transition between meditation and contemplation is another way of describing the relationship between nature and grace.

In general, then, any experience promoting our spiritual good by assistance freely offered and accepted by our conscious selves, is an experience of grace. At the heights of contemplative prayer, such experience is not different in kind but in intensity from many more ordinary experiences of illumination and insight. In contemplation, however, the mystics tell us that the act of self-disclosure, the gratuitous, divine condescension, enables us to participate in God's nature itself. The word "supernatural" is frequently used in this context to indicate the limitations of our human capacity: we need assistance to experience the divine secrets (1–20).

At this point, we encounter the perennial issue of whether or not we can do anything to deserve grace if grace is free, and therefore undeserved. In logical terms, the answer must be "No", and our personal encounter with that "No" will, perhaps, be our introduction to the dark night of which the mystics speak. But the question itself is less usefully considered in strictly logical terms than as a clash of competing goods. On the one hand, we are naturally free creatures; on the other, God is supernaturally free to sanctify us. The mystics do not advise a relinquishment of this tension, but a heightening of it, a discovery of the point of maximum energy between our autonomous desire for God, and his self- disclosure.

The term "co-operation" is relevant here, though it should be used cautiously, for it does not imply that God and man are equal partners in a joint venture (21–32). But it does indicate that we are free to refuse grace just as we are free to refuse a gift. Also, it implies that we can prepare ourselves for the reception of a gift by removing obstacles which would impede its coming to us. When we go sailing, as someone has said, we cannot command the wind, but we must raise our sails if we are to enable the wind to carry us along.

The means by which our freedom encounters God's self-disclosure are thus perpetually intricate and personal, but the Western mystics emphatically require that we deny neither side of the operation. On the one hand, for our spiritual health we must realize our insufficiency to effect union with the Divine, and such a realization encourages humility and fraternalism, for it shows us that we are not above our fellow men merely because we pray. On the other hand, spiritual health is thwarted if we relinquish responsibility, for then the moral life would not be relevant to mysticism at all.

1. But the spirit of prayer, the spirit of love, and the spirit of humility, or of any other virtue, are only to be attained by the operation of the light and spirit of God, not outwardly teaching, but inwardly bringing forth a new-born spirit within us.

    William Law (1686–1761),
    The Spirit of Love, Third Dialogue

2. If this work is to be done, God alone must do it, and thou must undergo it. Where from thy willing and knowing thou truly goest out, God with his knowing

surely and willingly goes in and shines there clearly. Where God thus knows himself thy knowledge is of no avail and cannot stand. Do not fondly imagine that thy reason can grow to the knowledge of God; that God shall shine in thee divinely no natural light can help to bring about; it must be utterly extinguished and go out of itself altogether, then God can shine in with his light bringing back with him everything thou wentest out of and a thousandfold more, besides the new form containing it all.

Meister Eckhart (1260–1327),
Sermons and Collations, IV

3. Observe, grace effects nothing by itself. Moreover it exalts the soul above activity. Grace is bestowed in the essence of the soul and is received into her powers; for if the soul is to effect anything in this matter, she must needs have grace by virtue of which to transcend her own activities such as knowing and loving. Whilst the soul is in process of taking this transcendental flight out of herself into the nothingness of herself and her own activity, she is "by grace"; she is grace when she has accomplished this transcendental passage and has overcome herself and now stands in her pure virginity alone, conscious of nothing but of behaving after the manner of God.

Meister Eckhart (1260–1327),
Tractates, XIX

4. In all such matters we must not seek to know how things happened: our understanding could not grasp it, therefore why trouble ourselves on the subject? It is enough to know that it is he, the all-powerful God, who has performed the work. We can do nothing on our own part to gain this favour; it comes from God alone; therefore let us not strive to understand it.

Teresa of Avila (1515–82),
The Interior Castle, Fifth Mansions, Ch. I, 9

5. Whereupon I gather, that he whom God will set in His kingdom, whether he be rich, or whether he be poor, first He opens his eyes, that he may see his own impossibility, and the impossibility that all creatures have, to be able to give him that which he pretends, and would have.

Juan de Valdes (1490–1541),
The Divine Considerations, V

6. Let us then press on in prayer, looking upwards to the divine benignant rays, even as if a resplendent cord were hanging from the height of heaven unto this world below, and we, by seizing it with alternate hands in one advance, appeared to pull it down; but in very truth instead of drawing down the rope (the same being already nigh us above and below), we were ourselves being drawn upwards to the higher refulgence of the resplendent rays.

Dionysius the Areopagite (c. 500),
The Divine Names, Ch. III, 1

7. And grace worketh: raising, rewarding, endlessly overpassing that which our longing and our travail deserveth, spreading abroad and showing the high plenteous largess of God's royal lordship in his marvellous courtesy; and this is of the abundance of love.

Julian of Norwich (c. 1342–1420),
Revelations of Divine Love, Ch. XLVIII

8. The designs of God, the good pleasure of God, the will of God, the operation of God and the gift of his grace are all one and the same thing in the spiritual life. It is God working in the soul to make it like unto himself.

Jean-Pierre de Caussade (1675–1751),
Abandonment to Divine Providence,
Book I, Ch. I, Sec. IV

9. Make no effort to free yourselves from these divine terrors, these heavenly troubles, but open your hearts to receive these little streams from that immense sea of sorrows which God bore in his most holy soul. Sow in sorrow for as long as grace requires, and that same grace will gradually dry your tears. Darkness will disappear before the radiance of the sun, springtime will come with its flowers, and the result of your abandonment will be seen in the admirable diversity of the divine action. Indeed it is quite useless for man to trouble himself; all that takes place in him is like a dream.

Jean-Pierre de Caussade (1675–1751),
Abandonment to Divine Providence,
Book II, Ch. IV, Sec. II

10. For that which a man, however full of knowledge he may be, cannot know (for his mind fails him when it turns to and fro on itself), God shows by his grace, and makes the simple learned.

Elizabeth of Schonau (1138–65),
Visions, "Poem on the Assumption"

11. Then, next after this we must keep a firm grasp of this same humility towards God: which we must so secure as not only to acknowledge that we cannot possibly perform anything connected with the attainment of perfect virtue without his assistance and grace, but also truly to believe that this very fact that we can understand this, is his own gift.

John Cassian (c. 360–434),
The Institutes, Book XII, Ch. XXXIII

12. That I dare to say I love God, is a gift of his pure grace. For it is when my sins and sufferings are before my eyes that my soul begins to burn in the fire of the true love of God, and the sweetness is so surpassing, that even my

body shares in the divine blessedness. I write this as it were by compulsion, for I would rather hold my peace, because I live in fear and dread of a secret tendency to vainglory. Yet I am more afraid, when God has been so gracious to me, that I, poor and empty as I am, have kept silence too often and too long.

Mechthild of Magdeburg (1217–82),
The Flowing Forth of the Light of the Godhead, p. 129

13. That good and sweet affection which thou sometimes feelest is the effect of grace present, and a foretaste of thy heavenly home. But thou must not lean thereon too much, for it comes and goes.

Thomas à Kempis (c. 1379–1471),
Of the Imitation of Christ, Book IV, Ch. VI

14. Nature regards the outward things of a man: grace turns itself to the inward.

Thomas à Kempis (c. 1379–1471),
Of the Imitation of Christ, Book IV, Ch. XXXI

15. You are bound by a great debt, my soul; you have received much, and you have had none of it from yourself. And for all these things you can make no return, except only to love; for what was given to you for love cannot be repaid better or more fitly than by love.

Hugh of St Victor (c. 1096–1141),
The Soul's Betrothal Gift, p. 22

16. First, consider, my soul, that once you were not; and that you received of him as a gift that you began to be. Therefore it was his gift that you were made.

Hugh of St Victor (c. 1096–1141),
The Soul's Betrothal Gift, p. 21

17. The promises concerning eternal life are wholly free.

Grace is never our right, otherwise it would be no longer grace. Strictly speaking, God oweth us neither the grace of final perseverance, nor eternal life after the death of the body. He doth not even owe to the soul the debt of immortality. He is free to allow it to fall back into nothingness, as it were by its own dead weight.

> François Fenelon (1651–1715),
> *Maxims of the Mystics*, Article X

18. And I say also that no creature can ever do this, since there is not a creature in the world that is able to unite itself to God by all its own efforts; it must be God that must unite it to himself. If therefore one cannot be united to God by oneself, it is to cry out against a chimera, to cry out against those who put themselves into this union of themselves.

> Madame Guyon (1648–1717),
> *A Method of Prayer*, Ch. XXIV

19. The water we see before us, which looks like another starry sky, partly helps us to understand what grace is. For as the image of the heavens, mirrored in the water, makes the lake look like the sky itself, so grace, when it comes to the soul and is enthroned in it, does not merely give it the semblance, but truly brings to it a likeness of God and his qualities, and transforms it into a very heaven as far as a creature can be so transformed without losing its substance.

> Luis de Leon (1528–91),
> *The Names of Christ*, 96

20. That the greater perfection a soul aspires after, the more dependent it is upon divine grace.

> Brother Lawrence (c. 1605–91),
> *Conversations*, IV, 25 November 1667

21. But since some are unbelieving, and some are dis-
    putatious, all do not attain to the perfection of the good.
    For neither is it possible to attain it without the exercise
    of free choice; nor does the whole depend on our own
    purpose; as, for example, what is destined to happen.
    "For by grace we are saved": not, indeed, without good
    works; but we must, by being formed for what is good,
    acquire an inclination for it.

    Clement of Alexandria (c. 150–215),
    The Miscellanies, Book V, Ch. I

22. Free-will is the king of the soul. It is free by nature and
    still more free by grace. It shall be crowned with a crown
    that is called charity.

    John of Ruysbroeck (1293–1381),
    Adornment of the Spiritual Marriage, Ch. XXIV

23. The prevenient grace of God touches a man from with-
    out and from within. From without through sickness; or
    through the loss of external goods, of kinsmen, and of
    friends; or through public disgrace. Or he may be stirred
    by a sermon, or by the examples of the saints or of good
    men, their words, or their deeds; so that he learns to
    recognize himself as he is. This is how God touches a
    man from without.

    John of Ruysbroeck (1293–1381),
    Adornment of the Spiritual Marriage, Ch. I

24. This grace pours into us in the unity of our higher
    powers and of our spirit; wherefrom, through the power
    of the grace received, the higher powers flow out to
    become active in all virtues, and whereto, because of the
    bond of love, they ever return again.

    John of Ruysbroeck (1293–1381),
    Adornment of the Spiritual Marriage, Ch. III

25. I have always thought, with him, that no one ought to meddle with the prayer of recollection unless he be called to it, and also that this grace cannot be merited by good works, nor can anyone succeed in it by any effort of his own. I have only added, with Father Surin and other authors, that one can, indirectly and beforehand, dispose oneself to receive this great gift of heaven by removing obstacles, first by a great purity of conscience, secondly by purity of heart, thirdly of spirit, and fourthly of intention which will carry a soul very far on the road to it; and that having so far disposed oneself, one ought by short and frequent pauses, as if waiting to listen, to give free course to the interior spirit.

Jean-Pierre de Caussade (1675–1751),
Spiritual Counsels, Second Book, Letter IX

26. The one and infallible influence of the divine action is invariably applied to the submissive soul at an opportune moment, and this soul corresponds in everything to its interior direction. It is pleased with everything that has taken place, with everything that is happening, and with all that effects it, with the exception of sin. Sometimes the soul acts with full consciousness, sometimes unknowingly, being led only by obscure instincts to say, to do, or to leave certain things, without being able to give a reason for its action.

Jean-Pierre de Caussade (1675–1751),
Abandonment to Divine Providence, Ch. IV, Sec. V

27. And so the grace of God always co-operates with our will for its advantage, and in all things assists, protects and defends it, in such a way as sometimes even to require and look for some efforts of good will from it that it may not appear to confer its gifts on one who is asleep or relaxed in sluggish ease, as it seeks opportunities to show that as the torpor of man's

sluggishness is shaken off its bounty is not unreasonable, when it bestows it on account of some desire and efforts to gain it.

John Cassian (c. 360–434),
Third Conference of Abbot Chaeremon, Ch. XIII

28. For grace is as it were a ring or a circle, not having beginning nor end; for it operateth and proceedeth forth from God unto all creatures, and from creatures again without intermission it tendeth back to its origin.

Gerlac Petersen (1378–1411),
The Fiery Soliloquy with God, Ch. XXVI

29. Grace is not blind to what is contemptible, but bears with it nevertheless, in order to enter into the secret designs of God. She neither abandons herself to a disdainful temper, nor to an impatient disposition. No corruptions astonish her, no infirmities surprise her, because she has no dependence but on God, and sees clearly that, without him, all is nothing but sin.

François Fenelon (1651–1715),
Pious Reflections, The Twelfth Day

30. And thus by their own perverseness they stop the light of grace from their own soul that it may not rest therein; the which grace, as much as in it is, shineth to all spiritual creatures, ready to enter in where it is received as the sun shineth over all bodily creatures where it is not hindered.

Walter Hilton (1300–96),
The Scale of Perfection, Book II, Ch. XVI

31. Grace is moreover a spiritual dress and ornament for the soul, made up by the hands of the Holy Ghost, which renders her so acceptable to God that he adopts her for his daughter, and takes her for his bride. . . . This is the garment of divers colours with which the king's daughter

seated at the right hand of her bride-groom was gloriously arrayed. For, from grace come the colours of the different virtues and divine habits, wherein their beauty consists.

Luis de Granada (1504–88),
The Sinners Guide, Book I, Part II, Ch. III

32. But I know that Thy glance is that supreme Goodness which cannot fail to communicate itself to all able to receive it. Thou, therefore, canst never let me go so long as I am able to receive Thee. Wherefore it behoveth me to make myself, in so far as I can, ever more able to receive Thee. But I know that the capacity which maketh union possible is naught else save likeness. And incapacity springeth from lack of likeness. If, therefore, I have rendered myself by all possible means like unto Thy goodness, then, according to the degree of that likeness, I shall be capable of the truth.

Nicholas of Cusa (1401–64),
The Vision of God, Ch. IV

v *Prayer and Virtue*

One main consequence of the doctrine of grace is practical: true wisdom, the mystics tell us, proves itself in good works (12). The more privileged our knowledge of God's secrets, as Thomas à Kempis says (14), the harder will be the judgement against us unless we live a holy life. Indeed, the mystics do not only advise us to conduct our relations with others in light of the good we experience in contemplation; they also warn us that claims to contemplative vision are likely to be false if they do not bear fruit in our moral lives (1–22).

Prayer therefore returns us to the world of ordinary relationships, and in so doing it should enhance our sense of the spiritual integrity of each person we encounter. The mystical teaching on prayer consequently entails a further, basic warning against judging others. Knowledge of a person's heart is God's privilege which we are in no position to usurp, whether by censure, calumny or judgemental opinion. Such knowledge is not our business, and, as with non-violence, the first sign of wisdom here is restraint (23–37).

This does not mean that we are not to judge crime or suffering; as we have seen, hating the crime is different from hating the criminal (III, i), and is certainly different from judging that he is damned or saved, worthy or unworthy of God. We can never give full sentence, as Vives says (37). The sublimest elevation to God in contemplation therefore entails a particular respect for the most unregenerate humanity, in which our spirit is proved by a certain eloquence of behaviour even on usually unnoticed matters: the refusal of a hasty opinion, or a casual detraction, or what the world might see as indifferent gossip. As the mystic knows, the small is significant, and in our littlest gestures of restraint or self-indulgence lie the seeds of compassion or cruelty, light or darkness, heaven or hell.

1. I insist again: your foundation must not consist of prayer and contemplation alone: unless you acquire the virtues and practise them, you will always be dwarfs; and please God no worse may befall you than making no progress, for you know that to *stop* is to go *back* – if you love, you will never be content to come to a standstill.

   Teresa of Avila (1515–82),
   The Interior Castle, Seventh Mansions, Ch. IV, 13

2. Truth in practice proves goodness.

   Benjamin Whichcote (1609–83),
   Select Aphorisms, 64

3. What is perfected hereafter, must be begun here.

   Benjamin Whichcote (1609–83),
   Select Aphorisms, 4

4. Religion is a good mind, and a good life.

> Benjamin Whichcote (1609–83),
> *Select Aphorisms*, 92

5. All are not admitted to that mystical and surpassing
    union with God, to which no one can attain by his own
    labour and endeavours, unless he be assisted by the
    special grace of God. But those who are admitted to it
    ought to resume their own action, and holy images, and
    good works and exercises, as soon as that glorious
    operation of God in them ceases; they must remain
    humble, and persevere in their desire of progress, and so
    conduct themselves as if they were now first beginning to
    lead a good life.

> Louis de Blois (1506–65),
> *The Spiritual Mirror*, Ch. XI

6. There are some who foolishly imagine perfection to con-
    sist in this, that they being quiet and free, can dismiss
    images from their intellect, and with mere idle sensuality
    can retire into themselves; neglecting meanwhile the love
    of God, and all pious works and exercises. They indeed
    are miserable slaves of the devil, following after false
    quiet, while they from impure motives seek themselves,
    and delight in themselves rather than in God. But
    legitimate cultivators of contemplation and supernatural
    quiet, so seek after a denuded mind, and holy inactivity,
    that yet they do not abandon good works and exercises.
    For they give themselves to virtue according to their
    strength.

> Louis de Blois (1506–65),
> *The Spiritual Mirror*, Ch. XI

7. He, therefore, who wishes truly to please God, and to
    receive from him the heavenly grace, and to increase and
    be made perfect in the spirit, ought first of all to force

himself to cultivate all the virtues which are commanded, even against the will of his heart.

Macarius (c. 300–90),
Institutes of Christian Perfection, Book I, Ch. XVIII

8. Did they [preachers] but give them at first the key to the inward life, reformation of the outward actions would naturally follow.

Madame Guyon (1648–1717),
A Method of Prayer, Ch. XXIII

9. And I was to bring people off from all the world's religions, which are vain, that they might know the pure religion, and might visit the fatherless, the widows and the strangers, and keep themselves from the spots of the world. And then there would not be so many beggars, the sight of whom often grieved my heart, to see so much hard-heartedness amongst them that professed the name of Christ.

George Fox (1624–91),
Journal, 1648

10. For surely they mistake the whole nature of religion, who can think any part of their life is made more easy, for being free from it. They may well be said to mistake the whole nature of wisdom, who do not think it desirable to be always wise. He has not learnt the nature of piety, who thinks it too much to be pious in all his actions. He does not sufficiently understand what reason is, who does not earnestly desire to live in every thing according to it.

William Law (1686–1761),
A Serious Call, Ch. V

11. And note, that when I say one must not look on the will of God but on the work, my meaning is (as I have said)

that he ought not to look or behold the will apart, as it is not; but as one and the self same thing with the work, as it is; nor that he should turn his spirit and affection from the work, but contrariwise fix it still in the same, yet always, as in his will.

> Benet of Canfield (1562–1610),
> *The Rule of Perfection*, Part I, Ch. X

12. It is an indelible principle of eternal truth, that practice and exercise is the life of all. Should God give you worlds, and laws, and treasures, and worlds upon worlds and himself also in the divinest manner, if you will be lazy, and not meditate, you lose all. The soul is made for action, and cannot rest, till it be employed. Idleness is its rust. Unless it will up and think and taste and see, all is in vain.

> Thomas Traherne (c. 1636–74),
> *Centuries of Meditation*, IV, 95

13. Were I to define divinity, I should rather call it a divine life, than a divine science. Religion consists, not so much in words, as in things. He therefore who is most practical in divine things, has the purest and the most perfect knowledge of them; and not he who is most dogmatical. Knowledge puffeth up, but it is love that edifieth.

> John Smith (1618–52),
> *Select Discourses*, I

14. The more and the better thou knowest, the more severely shalt thou therefore be judged unless thy life be also more holy. Be not therefore vain of any art or science, but rather fear for the knowledge that is given thee.

> Thomas à Kempis (c. 1379–1471),
> *Of the Imitation of Christ*, Book I, Ch. II

15. Those that be perfect carry always this mind, that when

they perceive their labour to be fruitless in one place, to remove straight to another, where more good may be done.

> Gregory the Great (c. 540–604),
> *Dialogues*, Book II, Ch. III

16. Rather with fear and trembling work out your own salvation. Consider not what other men are, but, so far as in you lieth, what through you they may become; not those only that live now but also those who hereafter shall be born and whom ye shall have for followers in your holy intent.

> William of St Thierry (c. 1085–1148),
> *The Golden Epistle*, Ch. 3, 7

17. The soul that wishes to feel Me interiorly in the recesses of a secluded life, and sweetly to enjoy Me, must, first of all, be cleansed from sin, must be adorned with virtue, encircled with self-denial, decked out with the red roses of ardent love, strewn over with the fair violets of humble submission, and the white lilies of perfect purity.

> Henry Suso (c. 1295–1366),
> *The Little Book of Eternal Wisdom*, Ch. XXIII

18. The other sorrow is more one of compassion, and ariseth from the love of man; Jesus had this, and also all the pious. This sorrow can well subsist with divine joy, and he who loveth his neighbour most, and hath compassion with him, in him ariseth the greatest divine joy.

> John Tauler (c. 1300–61),
> *The Following of Christ*, Part II, 73

19. And the soul said: "What wilt thou receive in return for having been fastened to the cross by thy hands?" He

answered: "That he should exercise himself in all good
works, and avoid all evil works for My sake."

Mechthild of Hackborn (1240–98),
Select Revelations, Book I, Ch. IX

20. If he setteth his own convenience before his neighbours'
need; if in these and like things he fainteth and hath no
power over himself, but is held fast under the power of
others, then indeed an exceeding thick veil is hung up between him and God.

Gerlac Petersen (1378–1411),
The Fiery Soliloquy with God, Ch. XI

21. Here we are distinctly taught, that if we would find God
it is not enough to pray with the heart and the tongue, or
to have recourse to the help of others; we must work
ourselves, according to our power.

John of the Cross (1542–91),
A Spiritual Canticle Between the Soul and Christ, St. III

22. True wisdom, then, consists in works, not in great
talents which the world admires; for the wise in the
world's estimation – those who follow its maxims – are
the foolish who set at naught the will of God, and know
not how to control their passions.

Bridget of Sweden (1303–73),
Select Revelations, Ch. VII

23. Charity does not go so far as to require of us never to see
the defects of others. We must be blind not to see them:
but it requires of us not to fix our attention on them
voluntarily, nor without necessity, and that we should
not close our eyes to their good qualities.

François Fenelon (1651–1715),
Pious Reflections, The Twelfth Day

24. The veriest no-bodies in the world are the greatest busy-bodies.

> Benjamin Whichcote (1609–83),
> *Select Aphorisms*, 150

25. Thou shouldst never judge the will of man in anything that thou mayest see done or said by any creature whatsoever, either to thyself or to others.

> Catherine of Siena (1347–80),
> *The Dialogue*, Ch. C

26. And let all the brothers take care not to calumniate anyone, nor to contend in words; let them indeed study to maintain silence as far as God gives them grace.

> Francis of Assisi (1182–1226),
> *Rules*, 11

27. I never spoke ill in the slightest degree whatever of any one, and my ordinary practice was to avoid all detraction; for I used to keep most carefully in mind that I ought not to assent to, nor say of another, anything I should not like to have said of myself. I was extremely careful to keep this resolution on all occasions; though not so perfectly, upon some great occasions that presented themselves, as not to break it sometimes. But my ordinary practice was this: and thus those who were about me, and those with whom I conversed, became so convinced that it was right that they adopted it as a habit. It came to be understood that where I was, absent persons were safe; so they were also with my friends and kindred, and with those whom I instructed. Still, for all this, I have a strict account to give unto God for the bad example I gave in other respects.

> Teresa of Avila (1515–82),
> *Life*, Ch. VI, 4

28. Friends, keep to patience: this is the counsel of the Lord to you. Do not judge one another behind one another's backs, nor speak evil one of another, for that is that which soweth the enmity among brethren. Nor judge one another before the world, for that is that which is in the extremes, passion, and hastiness; and there ye let in the world's spirit to rejoice over you, and that is out of the patience, and love, and wisdom, and fear of God and his truth.

George Fox (1624–91),
Epistles, CIX

29. And thus puffed up with pride, they become judges of others, and there is left no means of their conversion, but by the extraordinary goodness and help of God; for it is more easy to reduce to well doing an open and public sinner, than one that sins secretly, and is covered with the cloak of apparent virtue.

Lorenzo Scupoli (1530–1610),
The Spiritual Conflict, Ch. I

30. Whatever we may see our neighbour do, we must always interpret his conduct in the best manner possible. In doubtful matters, we must persuade ourselves that what we noticed was not wrong, but that it was our own imperfection which made us think it was, in order to avoid rash judgements of the actions of others, which is a most dangerous evil, and one which we ought to have in the highest aversion. As regards things which are undoubtedly wrong, we must be full of compassion, and humble ourselves for our neighbours' faults as for our own, praying to God for their amendment with the same fervour as we should use if we were subject to the same faults.

François de Sales (1567–1622),
The Spiritual Conferences, Book IV

31. Now what is this that a man knows not at all? Surely, the heart; the secret thoughts of his neighbour. And yet how eager is he to dip the fingers of his curiosity in this covered dish reserved for the Great Master. And what is it that a man knows best of all, or at least ought to know? Surely, his own heart; his own secret thoughts. Nevertheless, he fears to enter into himself, and to stand in his own presence as a criminal before his judge. He dreads above aught besides the implacable tribunal of his own conscience, itself alone more surely convicting than a thousand witnesses.

Jean-Pierre Camus (1584–1652),
The Spirit of St Francis de Sales, pp. 86–7

32. And therefore beware: judge thyself as thou wilt, betwixt thee and thy God or thy ghostly father, and let other men alone.

The Cloud of Unknowing (late 14th Century), Ch. 30

33. Look that thou neither judge nor discuss in the deeds of God nor of man further than only thyself. As, for instance, whom he stirreth and calleth to perfection and whom he calleth not; or of the shortness of time; or why he calleth him rather than him. If thou wilt not err, look that thou judge not; but once hear and understand.

Epistle of Privy Counsel (late 14th Century), Ch. 10

34. Mortify thyself in not judging ill of any body at any time; because the evil suspicion of thy neighbour troubles the purity of the heart, disquiets it, brings the soul out of herself, and takes away her repose.

Miguel de Molinos (1640–97),
A Spiritual Guide Which Disentangles the Soul,
Ch. VIII

35. No man can justly censure or condemn another, because

indeed no man truly knows another. This I perceive in my self, for I am in the dark to all the world, and my nearest friends behold me but in a cloud; those that know me but superficially, think less of me than I do of my self; those of my near acquaintance think more; God, who truly knows me, knows that I am nothing.

Thomas Browne (1605–82),
Religio Medici, Part II, 4

36. Further, no man can judge another, because no man knows himself; for we censure others but as they disagree from that humour which we fancy laudable in our selves, and commend others but for that wherein they seem to quadrate and consent with us. So that in conclusion, all is but that we all condemn, self-love.

Thomas Browne (1605–82),
Religio Medici, Part II, 4

37. Life is no life, to such as live in suspicion or fear, but rather such life is a continual death. Be not inquisitive how other men live: for they that pass too much of other men's affairs, oft times look upon their own business but slenderly. It is a point of great folly, well to know other men and not to know thyself.

Juan Luis Vives (1492–1540),
Introduction to Wisdom, I, II

38. Wherefore it is not lawful to give full sentence of any man's virtue, vice, or disposition, because you have twice or thrice been in his company. You can give no sentence of him, though you have been with him a hundred times. No, though you have been of longest familiarity together.

Juan Luis Vives (1492–1540),
Introduction to Wisdom, H, v

Chapter VI

Personal Progress

Progress in prayer calls for a kind of artistic subtlety in assessing how an individual's needs are best served in approaching a personal God. The practices of mortification, the gifts of discernment, the function of spiritual direction, and the occurrence of special states of consciousness all bear upon this demanding process. Still, as the following excerpts suggest, there is an ease and graciousness in these matters: the task is to find it.

✠

i *Persons in God*

Christianity places high value on personality, and ventures even to describe the creator in terms of personal relationship: according to the orthodox formula, God is three persons in one divine nature. My title for this section consequently has a twofold aspect: it directs us both to what the mystics say about God as Trinity, and also to how human beings may experience their personal lives as the image of God, on a threefold model.

As we have seen, God is transcendent, but not indifferent to his creation. He is immanent, but not entirely so, for that would encourage us to worship the God within, which, as

G. K. Chesterton points out, amounts quite soon to worshipping ourselves. God allows us to be free agents, but we are not so free as to be able to achieve union with him by our own efforts. He comes down to us in an endless variety of free acts of self-disclosure, but he does not compel us to come up to him. What sort of definition, then, sustains such various experiential truths adequately? Christianity's answer is the Trinitarian formula.

We ought not to imagine, however, the persons of the Trinity in a modern, psychological sense, and the ancient definition of person as *the individual substance of a rational nature* is a more adequate initial conception. Admittedly, this philosophical definition is not entirely divorced from personhood as we know it among our human selves, but still we should be cautious not to imagine the Trinity, somehow, as three human beings. God, we recall, is at once the ineffable, hidden source of all things (Father), the means of revelation in history (Son), and our illuminator by grace, disclosing to us the relationship between historical means and originating principle (Spirit). Like most others who discuss this subject, the mystics frequently grasp for similitudes – for instance, that the Trinity is as one source producing light, brightness and heat. Though useful to counteract crude anthropomorphism, such comparisons remain limited, and the mystery preserves its deep but dazzling darkness (1–15).

We can now turn to the idea of the human soul as threefold, in God's image. Something of this teaching is already contained in the division of prayer into meditation and contemplation, with an elusive third, mediating stage, for this scheme corresponds to a widely accepted division of the soul's powers into memory, understanding and will. Meditative prayer corresponds to memory, which is chiefly deployed to compose the subject for meditation. The middle stage corresponds to understanding, whereby intellect examines and seeks to discover the truth offered by memory's images. Finally, contemplation corresponds to will, which is a movement of love and enjoyment, wherein the dialogue between memory and understanding is synthesized and transformed. Although distinct, these three processes are also single, and in its threefold oneness the soul at prayer is held to participate in God's triune activity (16–23).

Admittedly, such threefold schemes – and the literature of mysticism is ingenious in multiplying them – are more or less arbitrary, but, like the similitudes describing the Trinity itself, they provide hints at a deeper, unexpressed truth. Suffice it to say that Western mystics especially bear witness to God's dialogue with his rational creation; to a God, that is, whose perfectly enigmatic reality is partly revealed in the declaration that his nature is at least personal, and involves relationship.

1. And these are the realities which, in order to be understood by men, must be offered to them clothed with the name of Trinity or of three persons or of mutual relationships with one another, in order that men might in some way understand what is almost ineffably preached about God. Indeed, the understanding of divine realities, of which these names are seen to be signs, is not so much given to us through these names, as rather we are informed and nourished by this form of words, sound in faith, in order to understand what we desire about God.

   William of St Thierry (c. 1085–1148),
   The Enigma of Faith, 62

2. The Godhead is a spiritual substance, so impenetrable that none can say what manner of thing it is. They say: God in the Trinity is the living light in its visible radiance. In other words, the three Persons are but one in nature though distinct in Person in the same sense that the source of light is not the light nor is the source its shine. Applying this to the three Persons, the source is the Father, the Son is the light and the Holy Ghost is the

shine. The Father is the living source in whom all things
have lived eternally without themselves as in their cause.
The light is the Son in whom all things appear eternally
as in their idea. The shine is the Holy Ghost in whom all
things are one eternally as in their naught. Not that one
Person is the life and another the light: the three Persons
are one life, one light.

Meister Eckhart (1260–1327),
Tractates, XIII

3. In all love there is some producer, some means, and
   some end, all these being internal in the thing itself.
   Love loving is the producer, and that is the Father; love
   produced is the means, and that is the Son: for love is
   the means by which a lover loveth. The end of these
   means is love: for it is love, by loving: and that is the
   Holy Ghost.

Thomas Traherne (c. 1636–74),
Centuries of Meditation, II, 46

4. For that which is said, "This is my Son", shows a diversity of persons; for one and the same person cannot
   be both Father and Son to Himself. But who grasps the
   meaning, how one is in relation to the other: different in
   person, the same in essence? If you seek an example you
   can discover nothing among creatures that can satisfy
   you; if you consult reason all human reason cries out.
   For this assertion is above all human assessment and
   against all human reason to such an extent that reason
   would never have given assent to it unless faith had lifted
   it up to the certitude of these things. Therefore the hearer
   deservedly falls down in the showing of this mystery;
   sense fails; human reason succumbs.

Richard of St Victor (c. 1123–75),
The Twelve Patriarchs, Ch. LXXXII

5. By some mysterious manifestation of the truth, the three Persons of the most Blessed Trinity reveal themselves, preceded by an illumination which shines on the spirit like a most dazzling cloud of light. The three Persons are distinct from one another; a sublime knowledge is infused into the soul, imbuing it with a certainty of the truth that the Three are of one substance, power and knowledge, and are one God. Thus that which we hold as a doctrine of faith, the soul now, so to speak, understands by sight, though it beholds the Blessed Trinity neither by the eyes of the body nor of the soul, this being no imaginary vision.

Teresa of Avila (1515–82),
The Interior Castle, Seventh Mansions, Ch. I, 9

6. For the first, I understood that the high might of the Trinity is our Father, and the deep wisdom of the Trinity is our Mother, and the great love of the Trinity is our Lord: and all this have we in nature and in the making of our substance.

Julian of Norwich (c. 1342–1420),
Revelations of Divine Love, Ch. LVIII

7. Truth seeth God, and wisdom beholdeth God, and of these two cometh the third: that is, a holy marvellous delight in God; which is love. Where truth and wisdom are verily, there is love verily, coming of them both. And all of God's making: for he is endless sovereign truth, endless sovereign wisdom, endless sovereign love, unmade; and man's soul is a creature in God which hath the same properties made, and evermore it doeth that it was made for: it seeth God, it beholdeth God, and it loveth God. Whereof God enjoyeth in the creature; and the creature in God, endlessly marvelling.

Julian of Norwich (c. 1342–1420),
Revelations of Divine Love, Ch. XLIV

8. Now in the whole deep of the Father, externally without the Son, there is nothing but the manifold and unmeasurable or unsearchable power of the Father. And the unsearchable power and light of the Son is in the deep of the Father, a living, all-powerful, all-knowing, all-hearing, all-seeing, all-smelling, all-tasting, all-feeling spirit, wherein is all power, splendour and wisdom, as in the Father and the Son. And as in the four elements, there is the power and splendour of the sun and all the stars, so it is in the whole deep of the Father, and that is, and is rightly called, the Holy Ghost, which is the third self-subsisting Person in the Deity.

Jacob Boehme (1575–1624), *Aurora*, Ch. 3

9. Now when we speak or write of the three persons in the Deity, you must not conceive that therefore there are three Gods, each reigning and ruling by himself, like temporal kings on the earth. No: such a substance and being is not in God; for the Divine Being consists in power, and not in body or flesh.

Jacob Boehme (1575–1624), *Aurora*, Ch. 3

10. For there is no exact similitude between the creatures and the Creative Originals; for the creatures possess only such images of the Creative Originals as are possible to them, while the Originals themselves transcend and exceed the creatures by the very nature of their own Originality.

Dionysius the Areopagite (c. 500),
The Divine Names, Ch. II, 8

11. Light, as the parent, generates brightness. Brightness and light produce heat, so that the heat proceeds from both, although not in the manner of an offspring. Thus, if God truly is Inaccessible Light in whom Brightness and Heat are substance, but also hypostasis, in God there are truly

Father, Son and Holy Spirit; which are the proper names of the divine Persons.

Bonaventure (1221–74),
The Triple Way, Ch. III, 11

12. You should know that the heavenly Father, as a living ground, with all that lives in him, is actively turned towards his Son, as to his own Eternal Wisdom. And that same Wisdom, with all that lives in it, is actively turned back towards the Father, that is, towards that very ground from which it comes forth. And in this meeting, there comes forth the third Person, between the Father and the Son; that is the Holy Ghost, their mutual Love, who is one with them both in the same nature. And he enfolds and drenches through both in action and fruition the Father and the Son, and all that lives in both, with such great riches and such joy that as to this all creatures must eternally be silent; for the incomprehensible wonder of this love eternally transcends the understanding of all creatures.

John of Ruysbroeck (1293–1381),
Adornment of the Spiritual Marriage, Ch. IV

13. O most wondrous God, thou art neither of singular number nor yet of plural, but art above all plurality or singularity, One in Three and Three in One! I perceive, then, that in the wall of paradise, where thou, my God, dwellest, plurality is one with singularity, and that thine abode is very far removed beyond them. Teach me, Lord, how I can conceive that to be possible which I perceive to be necessary.

Nicholas of Cusa (1401–64),
The Vision of God, Ch. XVII

14. 'Tis the same, one I who am lover, and who am lovable, and who am the bond arising from the love wherewith I

love myself: I am one, and not three. Suppose, then, that my love were my essence, as 'tis in my God – then in the unity of my essence there would exist the unity of the three constituents aforesaid, and in their trinity, the unity of my essence: all would exist in limitation in my essence, after the manner in which I perceive them to exist truly and absolutely in Thee.

Nicholas of Cusa (1401–64),
The Vision of God, Ch. XVII

15. When the thought of the Holy Trinity enters into thy mind, thou shalt not fabricate for thyself any absurd idols; thou shalt not imagine the Father, Son and Holy Ghost to be as it were three men or three gods; but confess the unity of the Godhead in the Trinity of Persons. The Father is God, the Son is God, and the Holy Ghost is God; and yet the Father, the Son and the Holy Ghost are not three gods, but one God. There are three Persons, but the substance of the Persons is one. This mystery is believed by faith, but is not within the ken of human reason.

Louis de Blois (1506–65),
The Rule of the Spiritual Life, Ch. XXI

16. For the soul of every man is the breath and life of the Triune God, and as such, a partaker of the Divine Nature; but all this divinity is unfelt, because over-powered by the workings of flesh and blood, till such time as distress, or grace, or both, give flesh and blood a shock, open the long shut-up eyes, and force a man to find something in himself, that sense and reason, whilst at quiet, were not aware of.

William Law (1686–1761),
The Way to Divine Knowledge,
First Dialogue

17. First, he must turn away from all transitory things, and gather up the powers of his mind, and commune with himself, and pass over out of self into God, who is present within him, in the innermost parts of his spirit, wherein are the three highest powers of the soul, that there he may be united with and become one spirit with God; and there God will work in him. His memory will be made fruitful, his understanding will be transfigured, his will inflamed and inebriated with divine love. God himself becomes the food of his spirit, the life of his soul, and the preserver and guardian of his body. Therefore at all times we ought to commune with the image or the ground of our souls, where the three powers of our souls are one with God, that we may be united with God, poor in spirit, soul and body, fervent, and communing with God with all our powers.

John Tauler (c. 1300–61),
The Inner Way, Sermon IX

18. The image of the Holy Trinity shines forth beautifully in the soul of man. For, like the angelic spirits, the rational soul has three very excellent natural powers, namely, memory, intellect and will; which God bestowed upon it, that it might with the memory remember him, with the intellect know him, and with the will choose and love him, and enjoy him. Now, as the Father, the Son and the Holy Ghost are One God, or One Divine Substance; so those three superior and spiritual powers of the soul are one mind, or one essence of the soul.

Louis de Blois (1506–65),
The Spiritual Mirror, Ch. X

19. And thus the soul becometh conformed to the Holy Trinity, in its own measure, by the three powers which it possesseth. First, it is like unto the eternal Father, who is without beginning and from none by its memory, which

in a certain way containeth and retaineth all things, and from it all things proceed. And by it the soul becometh so conformed, if it be naked and free from all strange forms that can transform it, as never to suffer in any wise from fantasies, but powerfully to operate in all things, and wholly to disdain that its own nobleness should be busied about what is exceeding vile. Secondly, it is like unto the Son, who is truth itself, and eternal wisdom, by its reason, through which it becometh conformed, if in all things it shall walk in the sight of truth, and if all things temporal or eternal, inward or outward, equal or unequal, and all things that are made or done taste unto it as they are: and if this be so, then not in anything can it be straitened. Thirdly, it is like unto the Holy Ghost, by its will, through which it becometh conformed to him, if when the memory receiveth nothing strange or useless, the reason or the understanding receiveth nothing save what is good, true and just. By the will is it moved with its whole affection, and vehemently desireth what the memory and reason judge ought to be willed and loved.

Gerlac Petersen (1378–1411),
The Fiery Soliloquy with God, Ch. XIX

20. Nor is it to be thought impossible that the soul should be capable of so great a thing, that it should breathe in God as God in it, in the way of participation. For, granting that God has bestowed upon it so great a favour as to unite it to the most Holy Trinity, whereby it becomes like unto God, and God by participation, is it altogether incredible that it should exercise the faculties of its intellect, perform its acts of knowledge and of love, or to speak more accurately, should have it all done in the Holy Trinity together with It, as the Holy Trinity Itself? This however takes place by communication and participation, God himself effecting it in the soul, for this is to be transformed in the Three Persons in power,

wisdom and love, and herein it is that the soul becomes like unto God, who, that it might come to this, created it in his own image and likeness.

John of the Cross (1542–91),
A Spiritual Canticle Between the Soul and Christ,
St. XXXIX

21. Two lovers met: the one revealed his Beloved, and the other learned of Him. And it was disputed which of these two was nearer to his Beloved; and in the solution the Lover took knowledge of the demonstration of the Trinity.

Ramon Lull (c. 1232–1315),
The Book of the Lover and the Beloved, 361

22. It is a common observation, that the heart of man is triangular, which therefore cannot be filled with the round world, but only with the Trinity. This heart, of which we speak, is properly triangular, consisting, like the angels, of these three, Essence, Understanding and Will, the proper and immediate type of the Trinity.

Peter Sterry (c. 1614–72),
*The Rise, Race, and Royalty of the Kingdom of God
in the Soul of Man*, p. 194

23. Every act of divine life is composed of a blessed and beautiful trinity of divine loves. 1. There is the Lord Jesus, that spirit which is the supreme love, the essential image, the eternal Son of that God which is love; the bridegroom and beloved of a holy soul. 2. There is the spirit of a saint, the sister, the spouse, the love of this love, this bridegroom; spirit of the same spirit, love of the same love; sprung from the same root, formed into the same image and tree, bearing the same fruits of divine love. 3. There is the Holy Spirit, the marriage-dove, the marriage-knot, the love-union between these

two divine loves. Thus every act, every moment of a saint's life is a divine Trinity of heavenly, eternal loves coming forth in a new dress suitable to each new moment.

Peter Sterry (c. 1614–72),
*The Rise, Race, and Royalty of the Kingdom of God
in the Soul of Man*, p. 412

ii *Beginners, Proficients, Perfect*

A further threefold scheme widespread in the literature of Western mysticism describes our development in prayer by distinguishing between the conditions of *beginners*, *proficients* and *perfect*. Beginners are said to be on the *purgative* way; proficients the *illuminative*; and perfect the *unitive* (1–11).

The beginning (purgative) stage consists mainly of moral purification, and, as with meditative prayer, we must be active here on our own behalf. The proficient (illuminative) stage is like prayer between meditation and contemplation – the state, that is, of analysis or understanding – and is marked by increasing love of virtue. We not only refrain from vice at this stage, but also pursue virtue with deeper appreciation of its beauty and desirability. Moreover, we are irradiated by a variety of impulses and insights from above and below, as our reason comes to grasp the wisdom of purgation while sensing its own incapacity to arrive unaided at contemplative vision. The perfect (unitive) stage is the end to which prayer tends. It is marked by a sense of peace, assurance and fulfilment. The perfect do not display themselves as somehow dramatically, turbulently ravished into ecstasy. Even if such a thing has occurred, the mystics in general regard "spiritual phenomena" as highly suspect (see VI, v).

Clearly, the notion of a series of steps or stages suggested by the terms "beginner", "proficient" and "perfect" is convenient, but ought not to obscure the fact that spiritual development is organic. The mystics do not so much lay down hard and fast rules, as provide general directions calling for adaptation to the personal circumstances of each (12–22).

1. Now in this manner, even as one star differeth from another in brightness, so one cell differeth from another in conversation, that is to say conversation of those beginning, of those advancing, and of those that are perfect. The state of beginners may be called animal; of those advancing, rational; of the perfect, spiritual. Some things may be pardoned in those that are yet animal, which ought not to be pardoned in those that are now held to be in a manner rational; and again some things are pardoned in those that are rational which may not be pardoned in those that are spiritual, in whom all things ought to be perfect, and worthy not of blame but of praise and of imitation.

William of St Thierry (c. 1085–1148),
The Golden Epistle, Ch. 5, 12

2. Now from all of you perfection is required, albeit not all of one kind. But if thou be a beginner, begin perfectly; if thou hast begun to advance, do this also perfectly; if thou hast attained somewhat of perfection, measure thyself within thyself, and say with the Apostle: "Not that I have already attained or am perfect; but I follow after, if perchance I may comprehend Him in whom I am also comprehended."

William of St Thierry (c. 1085–1148),
The Golden Epistle, Ch. 4, 11

3. Thus there are three stages: first, the purification; secondly, the enlightening; thirdly, the union. The purification concerneth those who are beginning or repenting, and is brought to pass in a threefold wise: by contrition and sorrow for sin, by full confession, by hearty amendment. The enlightening belongeth to such as are growing, and also taketh place in three ways: to wit, by the eschewal of sin, by the practice of virtue and good works, and by the willing endurance of all manner of temptation and trials. The union belongeth to such as are perfect.

Theologia Germanica (c. 1350), Ch. XIV

4. Since every science, and particularly the science contained in Holy Scriptures, is concerned with the Trinity before all else, every science as such must perforce present some trace of this same Trinity. Hence the Wise Man says of this sacred doctrine that he has described it in three manner of ways: by a threefold spiritual interpretation, that is, moral, allegorical, and mystical. Now, this threefold interpretation corresponds to a threefold hierarchical action: purgation, illumination and perfective union. Purgation leads to peace, illumination to truth, and perfective union to love. As soon as the soul has mastered these three, it becomes holy, and its merits increase in the measure of its completion of them, for upon the proper understanding of these three states are founded both the understanding of all Scriptures and the right to eternal life.

Bonaventure (1221–74),
The Triple Way, Prologue

5. These stanzas describe the career of the soul from its first entrance on the service of God till it comes to the final state of perfection – the spiritual marriage. They refer to the three conditions of the spiritual life – the Purgative,

Illuminative and Unitive ways, some properties or effects of which they explain. The first part relates to beginners – to the purgative way. The second to the advanced – to the state of spiritual espousal, that is, the illuminative way. The next part relates to the unitive way – that of the perfect, where the spiritual marriage is brought to pass. The unitive way, or that of the perfect, follows the illuminative, which is that of the advanced. The last stanzas treat of the beatific state, which only the already perfect soul aims at.

John of the Cross (1542–91),
A Spiritual Canticle Between the Soul and Christ,
"Argument"

6. But this may I tell thee: these three be so coupled together, that unto them that be beginners and proficients – but not unto them that be perfect, as men may be here – thinking may not well be gotten, without reading or hearing coming before.

The Cloud of Unknowing (late 14th Century), Ch. 35

7. A good thing, however, is this carnal love of Christ, enabling us, as it does, to live, not a carnal, but a spiritual life, and to conquer and condemn the world. As it progresses it will become rational, and will have reached its perfection when it changes to spiritual.

Bernard of Clairvaux (1090–1153), *Sermons*, XX

8. For all our life is in *three*: in the first we have our Being, in the second we have our Increasing, and in the third we have our Fulfilling: the first is Nature, the second is Mercy, and the third is Grace.

Julian of Norwich (c. 1342–1420),
Revelations of Divine Love, Ch. LVIII

9. In these three steps you will recognize three states of the

soul, which I will explain to thee below. The feet of the soul, signifying her affection, are the first step, for the feet carry the body as the affection carries the soul. Wherefore these pierced feet are steps by which thou canst arrive at his side, which manifests to thee the secret of his heart, because the soul, rising on the steps of her affection, commences to taste the love of his heart, gazing into the open heart of my Son, with the eye of the intellect, and finds it consumed with ineffable love. . . . Having passed the second step, the soul reaches out to the third – that is – to the mouth, where she finds peace from the terrible war she has been waging with her sin. On the first step, then, lifting her feet from the affections of the earth, the soul strips herself of vice; on the second she fills herself with love and virtue; and on the third she tastes peace.

Catherine of Siena (1347–80),
The Dialogue, Ch. XXVI

10. Every state hath its beginning, its progress and its end. He would be very wrong who should resolve not to go further than the beginning. There is no art which hath not its progress. At the beginning there must be labouring with toil, but then there follows an enjoyment of the fruit of one's labour.

Madame Guyon (1648–1717),
A Method of Prayer, Ch. XXII

11. The beginning or entering into our union, is an impulse of the soul towards God. When the soul is introverted or turned inwards, in the manner aforesaid, it is in a tendency to its centre, and hath a strong propension to union. In this propension is the union begun. Afterwards it adhereth, which makes it approach nearer to God; then it is united with him, and thenceforward it comes into union, that is, it becomes of the same spirit with him.

Then it is that this spirit which went forth from God, returns back unto God; this being its sole end.

Madame Guyon (1648–1717),
A Method of Prayer, Ch. XXI

12. Perfection is neither more nor less than the faithful co-operation of the soul with this work of God, and is begun, grows, and is consummated in the soul unperceived and in secret. The science of theology is full of theories and explanations of the wonders of this state in each soul according to its capacity. One may be conversant with all these speculations, speak and write about them admirably, instruct others and guide souls; yet, if these theories are only in the mind, one is, compared with those who, without any knowledge of these theories, receive the meaning of the designs of God and do his holy will, like a sick physician compared to simple people in perfect health.

Jean-Pierre de Caussade (1675–1751),
Abandonment to Divine Providence,
Book I, Ch. I, Sec. IV

13. Perfection consists in doing the will of God, not in understanding his designs.

Jean-Pierre de Caussade (1675–1751),
Abandonment to Divine Providence,
Book I, Ch. I, Sec. IV

14. Herein there is nothing to be afraid of, but everything to hope for. Granting that such a one does not advance, nor make an effort to become perfect, so as to merit the joys and consolations which the perfect receive from God, yet he will by little and little attain to a knowledge of the road which leads to heaven.

Teresa of Avila (1515–82),
Life, Ch. VIII, 7

15. A man might live a thousand years and go on growing all the time in love, just as fire will burn so long as there is wood. The bigger the fire and the stronger the wind, the more fiercely it burns. Now put love for the fire and the Holy Ghost for the wind: the greater the love and the stronger the inspiration of the Holy Ghost in grace, the quicker the work of perfection is achieved. Yet not suddenly, but by the gradual growth of the soul. It would not be well for the whole man to be consumed at once.

> Meister Eckhart (1260–1327),
> *Sermons and Collations*, XII

16. The centre of the soul is God. When the soul shall have reached him, according to its essence, and according to the power of its operations, it will then have attained to its ultimate and deepest centre in God. This will be when the soul shall love him, comprehend him, and enjoy him with all its strength. When, however, the soul has not attained to this state, though it be in God, who is the centre of it by grace and communion with him, still if it can move further and is not satisfied, though in the centre, it is not in the deepest centre, because there is still room for it to advance. Love unites the soul with God, and the greater its love the deeper does it enter into God, and the more is it centred in him. According to this way of speaking we may say, that as the degrees of love, so are the centres, which the soul finds in God. There are many mansions in the Father's house.

> John of the Cross (1542–91),
> *The Living Flame of Love*, St. I

17. A good man's life is all of a piece.

> Benjamin Whichcote (1609–83),
> *Select Aphorisms*, 233

18. "Wherein lies the greatness of thy love, O Lover?" "My love is great in that I have no art therein."

> Ramon Lull (c. 1232–1315),
> *The Tree of Love*, Part III, Ch. I, 19

19. Up then and be doing; set yourselves earnestly about the work, and for your encouragement remember that religion is not an austere, sour and horrible thing of which you need to be afraid. Those who know it, know that it is "altogether lovely"; their great delight is in the increase and cultivation of it. It is not, like the prophet's roll, sweet as honey in the mouth, but bitter as gall in the belly. It does not consist in dejected looks, or depressions of the mind. It is liberty, love, peace, life and power; the more it is digested into our lives, the more sweet and lovely do we find it.

> John Smith (1618–52),
> *Select Discourses*, VII

20. I do not act thus to these most perfect ones who have arrived at the great perfection, and are entirely dead to their own will, but I remain continually both by grace and feeling in their souls, so that at any time that they wish they can unite their minds to Me, through love. They can in no way be separated from My love, for, by love, they have arrived at so close a union. Every place is to them an oratory, every moment a time of prayer.

> Catherine of Siena (1347–80),
> *The Dialogue*, Ch. LXXVIII

21. But, again I say, does the embryo in the mother become at once a perfect man? Has he who has laid one stone for a foundation, already finished his building? Does the seed cast into the ground become at once an ear of corn?

> Macarius (c. 300–90),
> *Institutes of Christian Perfection*, Ch. XIV

22. I begin hungry, let me not end empty.

Dame Gertrude More (1606–33),
The Holy Practices of a Divine Lover, 15

iii *Health in the Balance*

As we have seen repeatedly, mystics describe spiritual health as a harmony of various human energies and aspirations, each maintained at a maximum intensity without invalidating the others. This general attitude bears repetition especially with respect to the advice mystics give on mortification, a frequently misunderstood subject.

Mortification is most commonly associated with the purgative way, the "beginner" stage of spiritual progress. Although, indeed, there is much unlovely and excessive rigour on this subject among spiritual writers, the basic teaching considers mortification as a kind of pruning to produce better fruit. Emphatically, it ought not to be pursued to the point where energy for growth is diminished. Far from suggesting that severe physical mortification somehow frees spirit from body, the mystics insist quite to the contrary that physical self-abuse makes us less able to pray well. We are, as St Basil says (25), to avoid any kind of immoderation, for obesity and sickliness both cause inefficiency and disorder.

None of this means that mortification does not entail a certain amount of pain, for it is a kind of training which, as with any progress towards excellence, must be endured patiently and consistently. Analogies with athletic or musical performances suggest themselves, and these are, indeed, true natural symbols of a discipline required also by the life of prayer. Mystics, however, place no great value on bodily mortification for its own sake. As a natural symbol of a supernatural reality, bodily discipline ought not to assume priority, for the cart would then lead the horse. It is more desirable for spiritual mortification to stand as the main example, imitated by our bodily exercises. Basically, mortification therefore means a dying to whatever hinders enjoyment; especially enjoyment of the divine light, before which we are mortified in the very striving to make ourselves transparent (1–27).

1. Jesus Christ is health.

Luis de Leon (1528–91),
The Names of Christ, 177

2. When an apprentice gets hurt, or complains of being tired, the workmen and peasants have this fine expression: "It is the trade entering his body." Each time that we have some pain to go through, we can say to ourselves quite truly that it is the universe, the order and beauty of the world and the obedience of creation to God that are entering our body. After that how can we fail to bless with tenderest gratitude the Love that sends us this gift?

Simone Weil (1909–43),
Waiting on God, "The Love of God and Affliction"

3. They who mortify themselves by their proper industry, do principally attend unto the mortification of the flesh, they that be such having no intent to mortify the mind, not knowing, that from thence ariseth all the evil. And they, who are mortified by the holy Spirit, attend principally unto the mortification of the mind, knowing that from thence comes all the evil; and knowing that the mind being mortified, the flesh remains mortified.

Juan de Valdes (1490–1541),
The Divine Considerations, LVIII

4. I do not by this mean that we ought not at all to mortify ourselves; no! for mortification must always accompany

prayer, according to the measure of every one's strength and circumstances, and in our duty of obedience. But I say, that none ought to make mortification their chief exercise, nor absolutely to tie themselves to such and such austerities.

> Madame Guyon (1648–1717),
> *A Method of Prayer*, Ch. X

5. The deeper the knife of the surgeon penetrates to the quick, the keener is the pain; and the greater the vitality one has, the stronger is the resistance to this death. The soul, therefore, cannot arrive at this happy death and perfect detachment except by way of privations and interior renunciation. It requires a proved and heroic virtue to acquire a stripping of the heart in the midst of abundance: and renunciation in the midst of pleasures.

> Jean-Pierre de Caussade (1675–1751),
> *Spiritual Counsels*, Seventh Book, Letter XV

6. They, then, that perfectly desire the mortification of themselves, seek it as they that dig for hid treasures, for the nearer they are brought to their object, the more ardent they show themselves in the work. Therefore they never flag in their labour, but increase the more in the exercise thereof; for that in the degree that they reckon on their reward as now nearer at hand, they spend themselves the more gladly in the work.

> Gregory the Great (c. 540–604),
> *Morals on the Book of Job*, Part I, Book V, 7

7. Since he that macerates the flesh, but pants after honours, has inflicted the Cross on his flesh, but from concupiscence lives the worse to the world, in that it often happens that in the semblance of holiness, he unworthily obtains the post of rule, which except he displayed some-

thing of merit in himself, he would never attain to receive by any pains whatever.

Gregory the Great (c. 540–604),
Morals on the Book of Job, Part II, Book VIII, 73

8. There are many who while still living in this body are dead, and lying in the grave cannot praise God; and on the contrary there are many who though they are dead in the body yet bless God in the spirit.

John Cassian (c. 360–434),
First Conference of Abbot Moses, Ch. XIV

9. Therefore fastings, vigils, meditation on the Scriptures, self-denial and the abnegation of all possessions are not perfection, but aids to perfection: because the end of that science does not lie in these, but by means of these we arrive at the end.

John Cassian (c. 360–434),
First Conference of Abbot Moses, Ch. VII

10. For the struggle in each case is caused by the devices of the enemy: and excessive abstinence is still more injurious to us than careless satiety: for from this latter the intervention of a healthy compunction will raise us to the right measure of strictness, and not from the former.

John Cassian (c. 360–434),
Second Conference of Abbot Moses, Ch. XVII

11. For how can we show how absurd it is that we see that some men after their first enthusiasm of renunciation in which they forsook their estates and vast wealth and the service of the world, and betook themselves to the monasteries, are still earnestly devoted to those things which cannot altogether be cut off, and which we cannot do without in this state of life, even though they are small and trifling things; so that in their case the anxiety

about these trifles is greater than their love of all their property. And it certainly will not profit them much that they have disregarded greater riches and property, if they have only transferred their affections (on account of which they were to make light of them) to small and trifling things.

John Cassian (c. 360–434),
Conference of Abbot Daniel, Ch. XXI

12. Therefore it behoves him that will sing in God's love, and in singing will rejoice and burn, to be in the wilderness, and not to live in too much abstinence; nor to be given in any wise to superfluity or waste. Nevertheless it were better for him in little things to pass measure unknowingly, whiles he does it with good intent to sustain nature, than if for too much fasting he began to fail, and for feebleness of body he could not sing.

Richard Rolle (1300–49),
The Fire of Love, Ch. XI

13. And as I praised, there shone a great light into my soul, and in the light, God showed himself to me in great majesty, and in unspeakable glory. And it was as if he held up in his hands two golden chalices, and both were full of living wine. In the left hand was the red wine, the wine of sorrow, and in the right hand the most holy consolation. Then did the Lord say, "There are some who drink of this wine alone, although I pour out both in my divine love. Yet the golden wine is in itself the noblest, and most noble are those who drink of both, the red wine and the golden."

Mechthild of Magdeburg (1217–82),
*The Flowing Forth of the Light
of the Godhead*, pp. 8–9

14. Because in order to arrive from all to the All, thou hast to deny thyself wholly in all.

> John of the Cross (1542–91),
> *The Ascent of Mount Carmel*, Book I, Ch. XIII

15. This flame, when the soul was in the state of spiritual purgation, that is, when it was entering that of contemplation, was not so peaceful and sweet as it is now in the state of union. For before the divine fire enters into the soul and unites itself to it in its inmost depth by the perfect purgation and purity thereof, the flame wounds it, destroys and consumes the imperfections of its evil habits. This is the work of the Holy Ghost, who thereby disposes the soul for its divine union and transformation in God by love. For the flame which afterwards unites itself to the soul in the glory of love, is the very same which before enveloped and purified it; just as the fire which ultimately penetrates the substance of the fuel, is the very same which in the beginning darted its flames around it, playing about it and depriving it of its coldness until it prepared it with its heat for its own entrance into it, and transformation of it into itself.

> John of the Cross (1542–91),
> *The Living Flame of Love*, St. I

16. And therefore for God's love beware of sickness as much as thou well mayest, so that thou be not the cause of thy feebleness, as far as thou mayest. For I tell thee truly, that this work asketh a full great restfulness, and a full whole and clean disposition, as well in body as in soul.

> *The Cloud of Unknowing* (late 14th Century), Ch. 41

17. It is far better to mortify the body through the spirit than the spirit through the body. To deaden and beat down the body instead of trying to reduce the swelling of an

inflated spirit is like pulling back a horse by its tail.

Jean-Pierre Camus (1584–1652),
The Spirit of St Francis de Sales, p. 207

18. Observe, in this respect, the bounds of wise abstinence, which does not exceed the strength of your temperament, for all abstinence which is not proportioned to the natural powers displeases.

Bridget of Sweden (1303–73),
Select Revelations, Ch. XV

19. It is only true religion that teaches men to die to the world, and to rise above the clouds and vapours that darken the mind, and hinder it from enjoying the brightness of divine light.

John Smith (1618–52), *Select Discourses*, VII

20. Fasts, vigils and exterior works are, indeed, pleasing to God, when they are undertaken with discretion for the sake of God himself; yet purity of heart is far more pleasing to him, humility and charity far more acceptable.

Louis de Blois (1506–65),
The Rule of the Spiritual Life, Ch. XXIV

21. Evil passions must be mortified, but the weak body must not be oppressed, nor must nature be destroyed. The crosses and afflictions which God lays upon a man are much more safely borne than those which a man takes upon himself by his own will.

Louis de Blois (1506–65),
The Spiritual Mirror, Ch. V

22. But I ask for a disciplined mortification, which must be proportioned to the strength and the condition of each soul, giving you this piece of advice among others, that

faithful contemplation, aided by the grace of God, will have more power to mortify you and strip you of yourself, than all the rules you could ever observe.

François Malaval (1627–1719),
A Simple Method of Raising the Soul to Contemplation, First Treatise

23. It is certainly easier to mortify the body through the spirit than the spirit through the body.

François Malaval (1627–1719),
A Simple Method of Raising the Soul to Contemplation, Second Treatise, Dialogue VII

24. And for as much as, in this our pilgrimage, we bear a soul enclosed within our body, great treasures in brittle vessels, we may not utterly refuse and cast away all regard and respect of the body.

Juan Luis Vives (1492–1540),
Introduction to Wisdom, C v

25. The best rule and standard for a well-disciplined life is this: to be indifferent to the pleasure or pain of the flesh, but to avoid immoderation in either direction, so that the body may neither be disordered by obesity nor yet rendered sickly and so unable to execute commands.

Basil the Great (c. 329–79),
An Ascetical Discourse

26. In administering correction he [the Abbot] should act prudently and not go to excess, lest in seeking too eagerly to scrape off the rust he break the vessel. Let him keep his own frailty ever before his eyes and remember that the bruised reed must not be broken. By this we do not mean that he should allow vices to grow; on the contrary, as we have already said, he should eradicate them prudently and with charity, in the way which may

seem best in each case. Let him study rather to be loved than to be feared.

> Benedict of Nursia (c. 480–c. 547),
> *Rule for Monasteries*, Ch. 64

27. That all bodily mortifications, and other exercises, are useless, but as they serve to arrive at union with God by love; that he had well considered this, and found it the shortest way to go straight to him by a continual exercise of love, and doing all things for his sake.

> Brother Lawrence (c. 1605–91),
> *Conversations*, II, 28 September 1666

iv *Discernment and Direction*

Just as mortification is an art of removing impediments to maximum energy, so the whole progress of our lives in prayer needs careful monitoring to promote our best interests. Nothing along the way, in short, is secure, and discernment is the art of perpetual judgement and vigilance to sustain a healthy spiritual development (1–20). Understood in an interior sense, discernment is called discretion; in an external sense, it is spiritual direction.

As Angela of Foligno tells us, without discretion love becomes unseemly (4). Discretion consists, that is, in a kind of spiritual tact, finding a way diplomatically, neither giving offence nor surrendering integrity. The discreet person is sensitive to details of tone, circumstance, inclination, and willingly interprets the behaviour of others in the best sense. Just as humility is self-forgetful, so discretion likewise must avoid excessive introspection, for the mystics describe how this virtue is threatened especially by the neuroses of scrupulosity (10, 15) and excessive remorse (16).

The institutional aspect of discernment is spiritual direction (21–35). Here the mystics are both deferential and cautious. Directors can clarify and help us to understand; they can provide solace, comfort and confidence; they can enable us to make corrective judgements; they are a means by which corporate wisdom is brought to bear on our particular experiences and difficulties. Directors combine something of the functions of rule makers and experienced referees, for just as the potential for high performance in a game or sport degenerates into chaos and bickering without such expertise, so mysticism without a sound tradition of rule and direction easily becomes licentious and egotistical.

Mystics are also well aware that spiritual directors can be unskilled, tactless and a hindrance, not to say a danger. It follows that the choice of a director is of real consequence for spiritual development. It may even be prudent to take advice from more than one source (24), and we can seek for direction among the dead, through books. Still, not every book is appropriate for every temperament and circumstance, and there is a danger of aspiring for too much too hastily if we do not judge the difficulties of converting literature into life.

The question of spiritual direction thus throws us back once more upon the inner teacher, the spirit working within us as conscience, and calling for discretion. Our progress remains, as ever, tentative. But although the adventure remains by way of an essential solitude, it remains none the less within the web of humanity's history, where we do not find ourselves altogether without guidance.

1. But who is there that watches so vigilantly and constantly over his interior feelings, whether only in him, or also from him, that in every illicit emotion of the heart he clearly distinguishes between the natural corruption of his own mind and the bite of the serpent? In my opinion, no mortal man is capable of this, unless he who, enlightened by the Paraclete, has received that special grace

which the Apostle mentions amongst the gifts of the
Holy Ghost, and names the discernment of spirits.

Bernard of Clairvaux (1090–1153),
Sermons, XXXII

2. Take the third article of faith, that is, knowledge of God. I
    say, no man knows God who knows not himself first.
    Mark how to know yourselves. To know himself a man
    must be for ever on the watch over himself, holding his
    outer faculties, breaking them in by vigorous training to
    obey the higher powers of his soul. This discipline must be
    continued till he reach a state of consciousness so pure
    that nothing short of God can form in it. Then thou dost
    come acquainted with thyself and God.

Meister Eckhart (1260–1327), *Tractates*, VI

3. Mark well, however, that self-knowledge is indis-
    pensable, even for those whom God takes to dwell in the
    same mansion with himself. Nothing else, however
    elevated, perfects the soul which must never seek to
    forget its own nothingness. Let humility be always at
    work, like the bee at the honeycomb, or all will be lost.
    But remember, the bee leaves its hive to fly in search of
    flowers, and the soul should sometimes cease thinking of
    itself to rise in meditation on the grandeur and majesty
    of its God. It will learn its own baseness better thus than
    by self-contemplation, and will be freer from the reptiles
    which enter the first room where self-knowledge is
    acquired. Although it is a great grace from God to
    practise self-examination, yet "too much is as bad as too
    little", as they say.

Teresa of Avila (1515–82),
The Interior Castle, First Mansions, Ch. II, 9

4. That this is true is plainly proved. For if the love which
    the soul beareth unto God be not armed with great

wisdom and discretion, but moveth with undue fervour, then doth it either presently cease, or it is deceived, or it tendeth unto some unseemly end. For things wherein is no order are neither good nor healthful; and for this reason are there many persons who believe they are filled with the love of God, whereas they are filled with hatred of him and do love instead the world, the flesh and the devil.

Angela of Foligno (c. 1248–1309),
The Divine Consolation, Ch. XXVII

5. Behold, then knowledge and discernment come to be more loved than that which is discerned, for the false natural light loveth its knowledge and powers, which are itself, more than that which is known.

Theologia Germanica (c. 1350), Ch. XLII

6. And by this it is clearly shown that no virtue can possibly be perfectly acquired or continue without the grace of discretion. . . . For discretion is the mother of all virtues, as well as their guardian and regulator.

John Cassian (c. 360–434),
Second Conference of Abbot Moses, Ch. IV

7. For this is discretion, which is termed in the gospel the "eye", and "light of the body", according to the Saviour's saying: "The light of thy body is thine eye: but if thine eye be single, thy whole body will be full of light, but if thine eye be evil, thy whole body will be full of darkness": because as it discerns all the thoughts and actions of men it sees and overlooks all things which should be done. But if in any man this is "evil", i.e., not fortified by sound judgement and knowledge, or deceived by some error and presumption, it will make our whole body "full of darkness", i.e., it will darken all our mental vision and our

actions, and they will be involved in the darkness of vices
and the gloom of disturbances.

> John Cassian (c. 360–434),
> *Second Conference of Abbot Moses*, Ch. II

8. Above all things there are necessary for us a simple eye
   and a pure intention: a simple eye to examine maturely
   what each thing is according to the right truth, which
   discerneth the precious from the vile; a pure intention, to
   follow after the simple eye, and to see the truth in all
   things, and this causeth us to be wholly empty of every
   thing belonging to self, and to be comforted in every
   thing that can come upon us.

> Gerlac Petersen (1378–1411),
> *The Fiery Soliloquy with God*, Ch. XXXI

9. For out of this original sin will every day spring new and
   fresh stirrings of sin: the which thou must every day
   smite down, and be busy to shear away with a sharp
   double-edged dreadful sword of discretion. And hereby
   mayest thou see and learn that there is no certain
   security, nor yet no true rest in this life.

> *The Cloud of Unknowing* (late 14th Century), Ch. 33

10. The great imperfection of most of us proceeds from want
    of reflection, but, on the other hand, there are many who
    think overmuch, who fall into the mistake of too close
    self-inspection, and who are perpetually fretting over
    their failings and weaknesses.

> Jean-Pierre Camus (1584–1652),
> *The Spirit of St Francis de Sales*, p. 373

11. Holy discretion is a prudence which cannot be cheated, a
    fortitude which cannot be beaten, a perseverance from
    end to end, stretching from heaven to earth, that is, from

knowledge of Me to knowledge of self, and from love of Me to love of others. And the soul escapes dangers by her true humility, and, by her prudence, flies all the nets of the world and its creatures, and, with unarmed hands, that is through much endurance, discomfits the devil and the flesh with this sweet and glorious light.

Catherine of Siena (1347–80),
The Dialogue, Ch. XI

12. But in this discretion is to be used, and liberty of spirit, sometimes to use fewer, sometimes more, as may be expedient for our soul's good. For it may so happen that one or two acts of an exercise may serve with great profit for one whole time of prayer, and sometimes again twenty or forty may not serve, and in this, as I have said, and now I say it again (as a principal point to be observed), discreet liberty is to be used.

Dame Gertrude More (1606–33),
The Holy Practices of a Divine Lover,
"The Directions", 5

13. Observe in all things a holy discretion; for it is not expedient that, without regard to thy infirmity, thou shouldst at once attempt to do whatever good thou readest of, or hearest that others have done. Learn to follow humbly the grace given thee, and not impatiently to forestall it.

Louis de Blois (1506–65),
The Rule of the Spiritual Life, Ch. XXIII

14. "He that willeth to ascend ought not to rest, but ever exercise himself in God, in thoughts, words and deeds"; yet with discretion, in order that when our adversary, like a wicked traitor, assails us from behind, we may defend ourselves. He assails us from behind when, under the appearance of good, he wills to slay thee; for there is

danger in too much even as in too little.

Catherine of Bologna (1413–63),
The Spiritual Armour, 2

15. Scruples, too, for the same reason, hinder devotion; for they are like thorns which prick the conscience and disquiet it, and will not allow it to find repose and comfort in God.

Peter of Alcantara (1499–1562),
A Golden Treatise of Mental Prayer, Part II, Ch. III

16. Remorse of conscience, also, coming from those sins, will hinder devotion when it is exaggerated.

Peter of Alcantara (1499–1562),
A Golden Treatise of Mental Prayer, Part II, Ch. III

17. Having proposed in this rule so many different virtues, and given so many instructions on the regulating of our lives, our next advice is, to endeavour to procure one general virtue, which may comprehend, and as far as possible to supply, the want of the rest; this is the rather advisable, because our understanding is such that it cannot conceive many things at once. This virtue is a perpetual solicitude and vigilance, with a continual attention to whatsoever we do or say, that so every thing may be brought to the rule and moderation of reason. We are to behave ourselves in this point like an ambassador that is to speak to a sovereign prince. He has his attention fixed on the matter he is to discourse of, he weighs every word he speaks, he manages the tone of his voice, and considers every posture and motion of his body, and this all at the same time. Thus he that serves God should use his utmost endeavours to be always watchful and attentive upon himself, to consider himself and all he does, so that whether he speaks or holds his tongue, whether he asks a question or gives an answer,

whether at table, in the street, or in the church, at home or abroad, he is to have his rule and compass always with him, to measure every action, every word, nay, every thought, that so all may exact to the law of God, to the judgement of reason and decency.

Luis de Granada (1504–88),
The Sinners Guide, Part II, Ch. IX

18. The sorest afflictions never appear intolerable, but when we see them in a wrong light.

Brother Lawrence (c. 1605–91),
Letters, V

19. There is a certain mean, which neither loses its own dignity, nor takes away another man's.

Juan Luis Vives (1492–1540),
Introduction to Wisdom, I viii

20. They who are desirous to live a Christian life perfectly, ought, with the utmost providence and care, to cultivate the reasoning, discriminating and governing faculty of their souls; that exercising themselves to an accurate discernment of good and evil, and distinguishing between the passions which have invaded our nature and the original purity of our nature, they may lead their lives altogether without offence, and so use the eye of their discernment as to be able to preserve themselves uninfluenced by the impulses of evil.

Macarius (c. 300–90),
Institutes of Christian Perfection, Book V, Ch. III

21. There is nothing, therefore, that a good Christian ought to be more suspicious of, or more constantly guard against, than the authority of the Christian world.

William Law (1686–1761),
A Serious Call, Ch. XVII

22. Some confessors and spiritual directors, because they have no perception or experience of these ways, are a hindrance and an evil, rather than a help to such souls: they are like the builders of Babel; who, when required to furnish certain materials, furnished others of a very different sort, because they knew not the language of those around them, and thus the building was stopped.

John of the Cross (1542–91),
The Ascent of Mount Carmel, Prologue, 2

23. If the director, though given to prayer, has not been led by God in this way, he will at once take fright and condemn it. Therefore I advise you to choose a qualified theologian and if possible, one who is also spiritual. The Prioress ought to allow you this, for although she may feel sure that you are safe from delusion because you lead a good life, yet she is bound to permit you to consult some one for your mutual security.

Teresa of Avila (1515–82),
The Interior Castle, Sixth Mansions, Ch. VIII, 11

24. God forbid that the religious should be directed entirely by one priest if he is ill instructed, however saintly his spirit may appear, and perhaps may be in reality. Learning gives great light on all points; it is combined with holiness in some men. The greater favours our Lord shows you in prayer, the more need is there that you should be well informed about your devotions, prayer, and all your other duties.

Teresa of Avila (1515–82),
The Way of Perfection, Ch. V, 1

25. In difficult questions, although I think I understand them and am speaking the truth, I always say "it appears to me"; for, in case my opinion is wrong, I am most willing to submit to the judgement of theologians. Although

they may not have had personal experience in such matters, yet in some way I do not understand, God who sets them to give light to his Church enables them to recognize the truth when it is put before them. If they are not thoughtless and indevout, but servants of God, they are never dismayed at his mighty works, knowing perfectly well that it is in his power to perform far greater wonders. If some of the marvels told are new to them, yet they have read of others of the same kind, showing the former to be possible. I have had great experience as to this and have also met with timid, half-instructed people whose ignorance has cost me very dear.

Teresa of Avila (1515–82),
The Interior Castle, Ch. I, 7

26. The usual custom of virtuous men is, that none should take upon him to rule, who first hath not learned to obey: nor to command that obedience to his subjects, which before he hath not given to his own superiors. Yet some there be which are so inwardly taught by the doctrine of God's holy spirit, that although they have no man to instruct them outwardly, yet do they not want the direction of an inward teacher.

Gregory the Great (c. 540–604),
The Dialogues, Book I

27. I asked him if we must then run uncertainly and pursue our way without guidance. He answered: "We must seek it among the dead; among those who are no longer subject to passion or change, and who have ceased to be swayed by human interests. As an Emperor of old said that his most faithful counsellors were the dead, meaning books, so we may say that our safest spiritual directors are books of piety."

Jean-Pierre Camus (1584–1652),
The Spirit of St Francis de Sales, p. 402

28. During the time of privation also, they meet from time to time persons in whom they feel they can repose a confidence inspired by God, although they know nothing about them. This is a sign that he makes use of them to communicate certain lights, even if these are only temporary. These souls ask advice, therefore, and when it is given they follow it with the greatest docility. In default of such assistance, however, they have recourse to the maxims supplied to them by their first directors. Thus they are always very well directed, either by the old principles formerly received, or by the advice of those directors they encounter, and they make use of all until God sends them persons in whom they can confide, and who will show them his will.

Jean-Pierre de Caussade (1675–1751),
Abandonment to Divine Providence, Ch. III, Sec. I

29. The voice of books is one but informs not all alike; for I within am the teacher of the truth, the searcher of the heart, the discerner of thoughts, the prompter of actions, distributing to every man as I judge meet.

Thomas à Kempis (c. 1379–1471),
Of the Imitation of Christ, Book IV, Ch. XLIII

30. Though it be said that we may with the Lord's help set ourselves to acquire contemplation, yet no man ought to be so bold as to pass to it from the state of meditation, without the counsel of an expert director, who shall clearly know whether the soul be called by God to this inward way; or if there be no director, the soul herself shall know it by some book, treating of these matters, sent to her by divine providence, by which that shall be discovered which without knowing it she had already experienced. But though by means of the light which that book gives, the soul may venture to abandon meditation for the quiet of con-

templation, yet she will still retain an ardent desire for more perfect instruction.

Miguel de Molinos (1640–97),
A Spiritual Guide Which Disentangles the Soul,
Third Admonition, 20

31. And so he instructs the spirit fully in all that even the great doctors of mysticism would not know how to instruct it on this matter, being at once the bridegroom and the master of such chosen souls. I have known some who, after having faithfully abandoned themselves to the spirit of God, received so many graces and lights that they hardly ever read spiritual books or consulted masters of the spiritual life again except to confirm them in their way; they did not learn anything new from such books or teachers, but only assured themselves that they were not being led astray when they followed their inspirations.

François Malaval (1627–1719),
A Simple Method of Raising the Soul
to Contemplation, First Treatise

32. If a soul that is fearful and scrupulous be to choose a director, she ought to avoid one of the like temper, for passion which blinds the seeker will also blind the director, and so the blind will lead the blind.

Augustine Baker (1575–1641),
Sancta Sophia, Treat. 1, Sec. 2, Ch. 2, Part 13

33. It is a miserable thing to see how this employment of directing souls (which above all other is most difficult and exceedeth even the ability of an angel) yet out of an ambitious humour is invaded by persons wholly unfitted for it, and that without any vocation from God voluntarily undertake it.

Augustine Baker (1575–1641),
Sancta Sophia, Treat. 1, Sec. 2, Ch. 2, Part 11

34. A virtuous humble-minded director, who though he have but a very small proportion either of experience or learning, yet out of humility will not assume unto himself authority to judge of things above his reach, but will encourage the soul either to seek out one more intelligent, or to follow the directions of her own spirit illuminated by grace.

Augustine Baker (1575–1641),
Sancta Sophia, Treat. 1, Sec. 2, Ch. 2, Part 6

35. But as for spiritual books, the intention of an internal liver ought not to be such as is that of those who live extroverted lives, who read them out of a vain curiosity, or to be thereby enabled to discourse of such sublime matters, without any particular choice or consideration whether they be suitable to their spirit for practice, or no. A contemplative soul in reading such books must not say, "This is a good book or passage", but moreover, "This is useful and proper for me, and by God's grace I will endeavour to put in execution in due time and place the good instructions contained in it, as far as they are good for me."

Augustine Baker (1575–1641),
Sancta Sophia, Treat. 1, Sec. 2, Ch. 3, Part 3

v *Spiritual Phenomena*

The word "mysticism" is often loosely associated with such special effects as visions, raptures, locutions, levitation and the like. The best mystics, however, are little interested in such spiritual phenomena, and even warn us against them.

Still, mystics do sometimes experience special states, which they attempt to describe (1–7), even though the eyes of the soul, as St Teresa says, behold in a spiritual rather than in a bodily manner, and we therefore cannot imagine what mystical visions are really like. Moreover, special favours granted in prayer are not necessarily signs of unusual holiness. God in his wisdom might indeed provide them to privileged individuals, but it is unwise to seek after such consolations, and false mysticism often consists precisely in a search after special states, a sure sign of pride (8–17).

The mystics even remain cautious about spiritual phenomena which seem valid. They advise us not to be hasty in judging unusual experiences, but to be patient in testing them by results. If such experiences cultivate peace, forgiveness and steadiness of character manifested in personal relations, we should cautiously affirm them. Otherwise there is much to fear, for too much love of spiritual favours can lead to a kind of licentiousness which decays into vanity and hysteria, or just into vacancy. Besides, we are constantly reminded that the devil can visit us disguised as an angel of light, and that his deceptions are manifold (18–30).

1. We are well advised to be silent as to the favours and gifts and graces which our Lord may bestow, except it be to our spiritual director only. "Therefore," says St Bernard, "the truly devout man should have written upon the walls of his chamber these words, 'My secret to myself, my secret to myself'."

    Peter of Alcantara (1499–1562),
    A Golden Treatise of Mental Prayer,
    Part II, Ch. V

2. And when I looked, I beheld God who spake with me. But if thou seekest to know that which I beheld, I can tell thee nothing, save that I beheld a fulness and a clearness, and felt them within me so abundantly that I can in no wise describe it, nor give any likeness thereof.

For what I beheld was not corporal, but as though it were in heaven. Thus I beheld a beauty so great that I can say naught concerning it, save that I saw the Supreme Beauty which containeth within Itself all goodness.

Angela of Foligno (c. 1248–1309),
The Divine Consolation, Treatise III, Second Vision

3. For the eyes of the soul do behold a spiritual and not a bodily presence, of the which I am not able to speak because words and imagination do fail me. And in very truth the soul doth rejoice in that sight with an ineffable joy and regardeth naught else, because this it is which doth fill it with most inestimable satisfaction. This searching and beholding (whereby God is seen in such a manner that the soul can behold naught else) is so profound that much doth it grieve me that I cannot make manifest aught whatsoever of it, seeing that it is not a thing the which can be touched or imagined or judged of.

Angela of Foligno (c. 1248–1309),
The Divine Consolation, Treatise II, Ch. I

4. For example, a person who is in no way expecting such a favour nor has ever imagined herself worthy of receiving it, is conscious that Jesus Christ stands by her side although she sees him neither with the eyes of the body nor of the soul. This is called an intellectual vision; I cannot tell why.

Teresa of Avila (1515–82),
The Interior Castle, Sixth Mansions, Ch. VIII, 2

5. Yet the work of the Lord went on in some, and my sorrows and troubles began to wear off, and tears of joy dropped from me, so that I could have wept night and day with tears of joy to the Lord, in humility and

brokenness of heart. And I saw into that which was without end, and things which cannot be uttered, and of the greatness and infiniteness of the love of God, which cannot be expressed by words.

George Fox (1624–91),
Journal, 1647

6. It is called Raptus; which means, rapt away, or uplifted, or carried away. At times God grants to such men a sudden spiritual glimpse, like the lightning in the sky. It comes like a sudden glimpse of strange brightness, shining forth from the Simple Nudity. And thereby for an instant the spirit is raised above itself; but the light passes at once and the man returns to himself again. This is the work of God himself; it is something very sublime; for those to whom it happens often become illuminated men.

John of Ruysbroeck (1293–1381),
Adornment of the Spiritual Marriage, Ch. XXIV

7. If you only *say* you have a revelation from God; I must have a revelation from God too, before I can believe you.

Benjamin Whichcote (1609–83),
Select Aphorisms, 93

8. These are some of the easily recognized signs of contemplation. But each one must rather recognize it in others than in himself and act sincerely and without reflection, seeking with all his strength to love God, holding himself in his presence, and desiring to live unknown to himself.

François Malaval (1627–1719),
*A Simple Method of Raising the Soul
to Contemplation*, First Treatise

9. Don't strain after more light than you've got yet: just wait quietly. God holds you when you cannot hold Him, and when the time comes to jump He will see to it that you *do* jump – and you will find you are not frightened then. But probably all that is a long way ahead still. So just be supple in His hands and let Him mould you (as He is doing) for His own purposes, responding with very simple acts of trust and love.

Evelyn Underhill (1875–1941),
Letters, 20 July 1933, To L.K.

10. God does not bestow these favours on certain souls because they are more holy than others who do not receive them, but to manifest his greatness.

Teresa of Avila (1515–82),
The Interior Castle, Ch. I, 5

11. He who would pass out of this state, and upraise his spirit, in order to taste consolations denied him, will, in my opinion, lose both the one and the other. These consolations being supernatural, and the understanding inactive, the soul is then left desolate and in great aridity. As the foundation of the whole building is humility, the nearer we draw unto God the more this virtue should grow; if it does not, everything is lost. It seems to be a kind of pride when we seek to ascend higher, seeing that God descends so low, when he allows us, being what we are, to draw near unto him.

Teresa of Avila (1515–82),
Life, Ch. XII, 5

12. The different kinds of vice, the use of drugs, in the literal or metaphorical sense of the word, all such things constitute the search for a state where the beauty of the world will be tangible. The mistake lies precisely in the

search for a special state. False mysticism is another form
of this error.

Simone Weil (1909–43),
Waiting on God,
"Forms of the Implicit Love of God"

13. Many religious people, I'm told, have physical symptoms
like the "prickles" in the shoulder. But the best mystics
set no value on that sort of thing, and do not set much on
visions either. What they seek and get is, I believe, a kind
of direct experience of God, immediate as a taste or
colour. There is no *reasoning* in it, but many would say
that it is an experience of the intellect – the reason
resting in its enjoyment of its object. . . .

C. S. Lewis (1898–1963),
Letters, 19 April 1951, To a Lady

14. The man said: "O Beloved, tell me what kind of hook
the evil spirit used to catch these men and hold them?"
The *answer* came: "The hook is that these men want
consolation or knowledge of God more than other men
have." The man said: "Beloved, I thought such a desire
was good." The *answer* came: "You talk foolishly. What
they want is not bad, but it is not the quickest way to
their origin. You see, as soon as they desire more consolation and help from God than from other men, that is a
secret, heavenly sin whereby they wish to be like other
men and not allow God to work his works in them how,
when and with whom he will."

Rulman Merswin (c. 1307–82),
The Book of the Nine Rocks, Sixth Discourse

15. For a remedy, then, my dear child, since you have not yet
your wings for flight, and your own powerlessness puts a
bar to your efforts, do not flutter, do not make eager
attempts to fly: have patience till you get your wings, like

the doves. I greatly fear that you have a little too much ardour for the quarry, that you are over-eager, and multiply desires a little too thickly. You see the beauty of illuminations, the sweetness of resolutions, you seem almost to grasp them, and the vicinity of good excites your appetite for it, and this appetite agitates you, and makes you dart forth, but for nothing; for the master keeps you fastened on the perch, or perhaps you have not your wings as yet; and meanwhile you grow thin by this constant movement of the heart, and continually lessen your strength. You must make trials, but moderate ones, and without agitating yourself, and without putting yourself into heat.

François de Sales (1567–1622),
The Spiritual Conferences, Book VI,
Various Letters, II, To Madame de Chantal

16. Blessed are they who live a superhuman, ecstatic *life*, raised above themselves, though not ravished above themselves in prayer! Many saints are in heaven who were never in ecstasy or ravishment of contemplation; for of how many martyrs and great saints does history tell us that they have never had in prayer any other privilege than devotion and fervour!

François de Sales (1567–1622),
The Spiritual Conferences, Book VI,
Various Letters, LVII

17. Desire not inordinately visions and revelations (which are sometimes granted even to the wicked). Those who foolishly seek after them, and thoughtlessly lend faith to them, are easily deceived by Satan, who transformeth himself into an angel of light (2 Corinthians 11:14), and in order to mislead, mostly mingles truth with falsehood.

Louis de Blois (1506–65),
The Spiritual Mirror, Ch. XI, 3

18. I repeat that I know a number of people whom our Lord has raised to supernatural things, giving them the prayer of contemplation I described, and though they have other faults and imperfections, I never saw one who was unforgiving, nor do I think it possible if these favours were from God. If anyone receives signal consolations, let her notice whether these effects increase with them; if these are wanting, there is cause for great fear. Let her not believe such feelings come from God, for he always enriches the souls he visits. This is certain, for although the favour and consolation may pass away quickly, it is detected later on by the benefits it has left in the soul.

Teresa of Avila (1515–82),
The Way of Perfection, Ch. XXXVI, 11

19. Many a lofty intellect, angels not excepting (for in life and nature an angel is nothing but pure mind), has erred and lapsed eternally from the eternal truth and this may happen also to those who, like the angels, preserve their idiosyncrasy and find satisfaction in the exercise of their own intelligence. Hence the masters urge, and the saints as well, the use and the necessity of careful observation and close scrutiny to test the light which flashes in, the light of understanding and of vision which man has here in time, lest he be the subject of hallucination.

Meister Eckhart (1260–1327),
Tractates, VII

20. Behold, these men have gone astray into the vacant and blind simplicity of their own being, and they seek for blessedness in bare nature; for they are so simply and so idly united with the bare essence of their souls, and with that wherein God always is, that they have neither zeal, nor cleaving to God, neither from without, nor from within. For in the highest part into which they have entered, they feel nothing but the simplicity of their own

proper being, dependent upon the Being of God. And the onefold simplicity which they there possess, they take to be God, because they find a natural rest therein. And so they think themselves to be God in their simple ground; for they lack true faith, hope and charity.

John of Ruysbroeck (1293–1381),
The Book of Supreme Truth, Ch. IV

21. Either in sounding of ear, or savouring in the mouth, or smelling at the nose, or else any sensible heat, as it were fire glowing and warming the breast or any other part of the body, or any other thing that may be felt by bodily wit, though it be never so comfortable and liking, these are not true contemplation; nor are they aught but simple and secondary, though they be good in regard of spiritual virtues, and of this spiritual knowing and loving of God. For all such manner of feeling may be good, wrought by a good angel, or they may be deceivable, wrought by a wicked angel when he transfigureth himself into an angel of light.

Walter Hilton (1300–96),
The Scale of Perfection, Book I, Ch. X

22. But now beware of the midday fiend, that feigneth light as if it came out of Jerusalem but is not so. For the fiend seeth that our Lord Jesus showeth light to his lovers of truth; therefore in deceiving of them that are unwise he showeth a light that is not true, under colour of a true light, and deceiveth them.

Walter Hilton (1300–96),
The Scale of Perfection, Book II, Ch. XXVI

23. Why also should I speak of one (whose name we had rather not mention as he is still alive), who for a long while received a devil in the brightness of an angelic form, and was often deceived by countless revelations

from him and believed that he was a messenger of righteousness.

John Cassian (c. 360–434),
Second Conference of Abbot Moses, Ch. VII

24. There are some spiritual directors who fall at once into
error, because their instructions to those, who are liable
to visions, are such as to lead them astray or perplex
them with regard to their visions; or they do not direct
them in the way of humility. They suffer their penitents
to make much of their visions, which is the reason why
they walk not according to the pure and perfect spirit of
faith; neither do they build them up nor strengthen them
in faith, while they attach so much importance to these
visions. This kind of direction shows that they themselves consider visions matters of importance; and their
penitents, observing this, follow their example, dwelling
upon these visions, not building themselves up in faith;
neither do they withdraw, nor detach themselves from
them, so that they may take their flight upward in the
obscurity of faith.

John of the Cross (1542–91),
The Ascent of Mount Carmel, Book II, Ch. XVIII

25. One of the means by which the devil makes an easy prey
to incautious souls, and impedes their progress in true
spirituality, is the exhibition of strange and unusual
things in connection with images.

John of the Cross (1542–91),
The Ascent of Mount Carmel, Book III, Ch.XXXVI

26. These [ecstasies] arise from a sensible relish, and may be
termed a kind of spiritual sensuality, wherein the soul
letting itself go too far by reason of the sweetness it finds,
falls imperceptibly into decay. The crafty enemy presents
such sorts of interior elevations and raptures for baits to

trepan the soul – to render it sensual – to fill it with vanity and self love.

Madame Guyon (1648–1717),
The Devout Christian, "Extasies"

27. Sometimes, through such love as this, the soul receives even more damage than if her affection is altogether placed in consolations and visions which I often give to My servants, for, when she feels herself deprived of them, she falls into bitterness and tedium of mind.

Catherine of Siena (1347–80),
The Dialogue, Ch. LXX

28. Another delusion that the devil often practises upon such souls is that he transforms himself into a form of light.

Catherine of Siena (1347–80),
The Dialogue, Ch. LXXI

29. Be not curious in seeking for heavenly revelations: for those who rashly desire, and lightly give credence to them, lay themselves open to many dangers, and to many snares of the devil. For our common enemy often transforms himself into an angel of light, that he may deceive the careless. If thou dost not at once believe a vision shown to thee, but remainest humbly in doubt, till thou hast more evident and certain knowledge of it; thou offendest not God, even if it should have been sent by God himself.

Louis de Blois (1506–65),
The Rule of the Spiritual Life, Ch. XXVI

30. The appearance of objects how beautiful and celestial soever ought not suddenly to be welcomed, nor affection to be placed upon them.

Augustine Baker (1575–1641),
Sancta Sophia, Treat. 3, Sec.4, Ch. 3, Part 18

Chapter VII

The Directions of Culture

Just as biographical circumstances provide particular opportunities for prayer, so cultural history offers timely opportunities for realizing God. Through language and symbol culture provides a principal means for mystics to mediate the ultimate vision beyond time – a vision to which, for its own survival, the mystics tell us, culture must strive to remain open. No less than individuals, however, cultures can forget their highest good, becoming enchanted with false affections, distracted by acquisitiveness, neglectful of how time must either be pressed to the service of a reality in which time is fulfilled, or dissolve into meaningless oblivion.

✠

i *Wisdom and Science*

One of the glories and urgent responsibilities of Western civilization is the development of science and technology, a cultural achievement of such sophistication that it has transformed the face of the earth within a period of three hundred years. Today, mainly through nuclear weapons, that same triumphant achievement threatens with equal sophistication utterly to destroy the same earth it has transformed.

To some, the rise of science during the sixteenth and seventeenth centuries represents a great leap forward of the human mind, entailing an emancipation from religious superstition. But it is equally a fact that the world-transforming impulses of Western spirituality contributed to the historical development of modern scientific methodology. Thus, among the mystics we have already discovered a desire to redeem the material world rather than deny it; to affirm incarnational process whereby a new heaven means also a new earth; to conceive of God in terms of a dynamic relationship calling for man's co-operation in the work of changing things for the better. Such basic terms even as "nature", "object", "energy", "relation" and "science" are commonplaces of pre-scientific Western theology, and there is a particular, unique intimacy between the history and responsibilities of these two aspects of our culture.

Against the argument that modern science emancipates us from religion, the mystics reply that it is folly to think human beings can outgrow religion and stay human. Self-will, we recall, is the root of evil, and the first fruit of pride is anger. The mystics therefore point us to a clear conclusion: science unsustained by a vision of a Reality such as the mystic way describes, is bound to destroy its makers.

We must choose sides. Either science is our most powerful tool for bringing good into the world, or it is an instrument of self-assertive power and secular force. We have no alternative but to interpret science somehow in terms of value, for technology must be put to use. And on this issue, the mystics remain unhesitant: the way of material acquisitiveness and rootless secularism is, by definition, the way of self-destruction.

A spiritual combat therefore continues to be fought at the heart even of our secular culture, not just in terms of raw nuclear capability, but in terms of the ideals such capability will serve. The issues reflect all the varieties of narrow self-interest and magnanimous selflessness, luminous moral compassion and blind religious fanaticism, inspiring spirituality and consuming national pride, unholy fear and holy terror. Among such intermittences of the modern, secularized human heart, it is not easy to determine where Christ is served, though the mystics would have us see the relevance of seeking to find out, lest inadvertently we stumble in the desire to save ourselves upon the very trigger which destroys us.

The first group of excerpts (1–12) draws our attention to a basic willingness among mystics to respond with wonder and admiration to nature's intricate designs, mindful of nature's higher causes. Admittedly, this kind of wonder can deflect us from detailed investigation of the physical world by referring our attention from things to their maker. None the less, science is fundamentally nourished by such willing admiration, and, as William Law says (3), the Atonement itself should be understood basically as setting nature right; production of good by harnessing nature's energies confirms the idea of a God who has created the world for our use. But it also follows that such work divorced from God's service is vain and dangerous. Science is the world's best treasure, Jacob Boehme says, and it must be rightly used; otherwise it cannot but contribute to unhappiness (13–18).

We are asked, then, either to acknowledge the irreducible mystery of man's relation to nature, a mystery not subject to quantification and which we call spiritual, or to treat this relation as a puzzle, another problem to be made objective and solved. The belief implicit in this second option is that our so-called spiritual reality is in fact material because quantifiable; yet for the mystics such quantification abolishes man by reducing him to a thing manipulated by power expressed merely as force. Assuredly, there is a long road ahead through the life of prayer for a person preferring the first option; the mystics, however, suggest at least that in such a choice lies the beginning of wisdom.

1. The ancients counted only a thousand and twenty-two stars, but today no one dares to count them. God indeed has told us that no man can ever number them! The invention of telescopes compels us, however, to recognize that the catalogues which we have of them are very imperfect. They contain only those which can be discovered by the naked eye, that is, of course, the smallest number. I believe that there are more than one will ever be able to render visible even by the aid of the best telescopes, and meanwhile there is good ground for believing that a very large proportion of these stars yield neither in grandeur nor majesty to the vast body which to us on earth appears the most luminous and most beautiful. How great then God is in the heavens, how sublime in their depths, how magnificent in their brilliance, how wise and powerful in the regulation of their movements!

Nicolas Malebranche (1638–1715),
Dialogues on Metaphysics and on Religion,
Tenth Dialogue, I

2. We are lost, Aristes, in the realm of the small, just as we are in that of the great. There is no one who can claim to have discovered the smallest animal. At one time this was taken to be the midge, but today the little midge has become prodigious in its size. The more our microscopes are perfected, the more convinced do we become that the smallness of matter imposes no limit upon the wisdom of the Creator, that out of nothing, so to speak, out of an atom which is not accessible to our senses, He produces works which transcend our imagination, and which are beyond even the vastest intellect.

Nicolas Malebranche (1638–1715),
Dialogues on Metaphysics and on Religion,
Tenth Dialogue, II

3. And the Atonement of Christ to be nothing else in itself, but the highest, most natural, and efficacious means, through all the possibility of things, that the infinite love and wisdom of God could use, to put an end to sin, and death, and hell, and restore to man his first divine state or life. I say, the most natural, efficacious means through all the possibilities of nature; for there is nothing that is supernatural, however mysterious, in the whole system of our redemption; every part of it has its ground in the workings and powers of nature, and all our redemption is only nature set right, or made to be that which it ought to be.

> William Law (1686–1761),
> *The Spirit of Love*, Second Dialogue

4. This may sound like a tall proposition, but is in fact no taller than the paradoxical phenomena on which it is based. We live submerged in a universe of "undulating quantum foam" which ceaselessly creates weird phenomena by means transcending the classical concepts of physical causation. The purpose and design of this acausal agency is unknown, and perhaps unknowable to us; but intuitively we feel it somehow to be related to that striving towards higher forms of order and unity-in-variety which we observe in the evolution of the universe at large, of life on earth, human consciousness, and lastly science and art. One ultimate mystery is easier to accept than a litter-basket of unrelated puzzles.

> Arthur Koestler (1905–83),
> *Bricks to Babel*, Part 6, Ch. 52, "Beyond Materialism"

5. Now iron, which by nature falls, will rise, against its nature, and hang suspended to a loadstone in virtue of the master-force the stone receives from heaven. Wherever the stone turns there the iron goes with it. Even so the mind, unsatisfied with this infernal light, will scale the

firmament and search the heavens to find the breath that spins them, the heavens by their revolution causing all things on earth to grow and flourish. Its spirit never rests content until it pierces to the coil, into the primal origin where the breath has its source. This spirit knows no time nor number: number does not exist apart from the malady of time.

Meister Eckhart (1260–1327),
Sermons and Collations, LXXIV

6. This desire, this longing, we believe to be unquestionably implanted within us by God; and as the eye naturally seeks the light and vision, and our body naturally desires food and drink, so our mind is possessed with a becoming and natural desire to become acquainted with the truth of God and the causes of things. Now we have received this desire from God, not in order that it should never be gratified or be *capable* of gratification; otherwise the love of truth would appear to have been implanted by God into our minds to no purpose, if it were never to have an opportunity of satisfaction.

Origen (c. 185–253),
On First Principles, Book II, Ch. XI

7. For he teaches, as I think, that true instruction is desire for knowledge; and the practical exercise of instruction produces love of knowledge. And love is the keeping of the commandments which lead to knowledge. And the keeping of them is the establishment of the commandments, from which immortality results. "And immortality brings us near to God."

Clement of Alexandria (c. 150–215),
The Miscellanies, Book VI, Ch. XV

8. The more, as an irresistible effect of technical progress and reflection, mankind becomes conscious of the im-

mensity, and even more the *organicity*, of the world around it, the more the necessity for *a soul* makes itself felt: for a soul that is capable of maintaining and directing the vast process of planetization in which we are involved. The more, too, it becomes clear that the only form of spirit capable of producing this soul is that which we defined earlier as sustaining and impelling the universe in the direction of progressively better forms of arrangement: isotope 2 (the most recently discovered!) – the spirit of greater love and greater consciousness.

Pierre Teilhard de Chardin (1881–1955),
Activation of Energy, "A Clarification:
Reflections on Two Converse Forms of Spirit", VIII

9. Every day the reality of an ultra-human becomes more insistent; and there is no possible way for our generation to enter into it except with the help of a new form of psychic energy in which the personalizing depth of love is combined with the totalization of what is most essential and most universal in the heart of the stuff of the cosmos and the cosmic stream – and for this new energy we have as yet *no name*!

Pierre Teilhard de Chardin (1881–1955),
Activation of Energy, "A Clarification:
Reflections on Two Converse Forms of Spirit", VIII

10. For in fact what is man in nature? A Nothing in comparison with the Infinite, an All in comparison with the Nothing, a man between nothing and everything. Since he is infinitely removed from comprehending the extremes, the end of things and their beginning are hopelessly hidden from him in an impenetrable secret; he is equally incapable of seeing the Nothing from which he was made, and the Infinite in which he is swallowed up.

Blaise Pascal (1623–62),
Pensées, 72

11. Do you believe it to be impossible that God is infinite, without parts? – Yes. I wish therefore to show you an infinite and indivisible thing. It is a point moving everywhere with an infinite velocity; for it is one in all places, and is all totality in every place. Let this effect of nature, which previously seemed to you impossible, make you know that there may be others of which you are still ignorant. Do not draw this conclusion from your experiment, that there remains nothing for you to know; but rather that there remains an infinity for you to know.

Blaise Pascal (1623–62),
Pensées, 231

12. Those strange and mystical transmigrations that I have observed in silkworms, turned my philosophy into divinity. There is in these works of nature, which seem to puzzle reason, something divine, and hath more in it than the eye of a common spectator doth discover.

Thomas Browne (1605–82),
Religio Medici, Part I, 39

13. But when the intelligent creature turns from God to self, or nature, he acts unnaturally, he turns from all that which makes nature to be good; he finds nature only as it is in itself, and without God. And then it is, that nature, or self, has all evil in it.

William Law (1686–1761),
The Spirit of Love, Third Dialogue

14. They who work with human wisdom find content in their own works, but mingled with arrogancy, and with presumption. And they who work with the Holy Spirit find likewise content in their own works, but most different, and mingled with humility, and mortification.

Juan de Valdes (1490–1541),
The Divine Considerations, XLVIII

15. For hence it is that in books, in works of the hand and in buildings, by the exceedingly manifold inventions of men, so many manners of study have come forth, so many kinds of callings, subtleties, exquisite sciences, arts and eloquences, varieties of offices and dignities, and the inventions of this world without number, which those men also who are called the wise of this world do use together with the simple and sons of God, unto necessity and profit. But those abuse them unto curiosity, lust and pride; these use them for necessity's sake, having their joy otherwhere.

William of St Thierry (c. 1085–1148),
The Golden Epistle, Ch. 6, 15

16. The more light, science, and capacity a person has, the more he is to be feared if he does not possess a foundation of piety, which consists in being satisfied with God and His will. It is by a well-regulated heart that one is united to the divine action; without this everything is purely natural, and generally, in direct opposition to the divine order. God makes use only of the humble as His instruments. Always contradicted by the proud, He yet makes use of them, like slaves, for the accomplishment of His designs.

Jean-Pierre de Caussade (1675–1751),
Abandonment to Divine Providence,
Book II, Ch. IV, Sec. X

17. We have a clear example in Lucifer, and also in Adam the first man, of what self doth when it getteth the light of nature to be its own, and may walk with the understanding in its own dominion. We see also in men learned in arts and sciences, that when they get the light of this outward world or nature into the possession of their reason, nothing cometh of it but pride of themselves. And yet all the world so vehemently desireth and

seeketh after this light as the best treasure; and indeed it is the best treasure this world affordeth, if it be rightly used.

Jacob Boehme (1575–1624),
The Way to Christ, "Of True Resignation", 1

18. These men who measure the distances of the stars and describe them, both those of the North, always shining brilliantly in our view, and those of the southern pole visible to the inhabitants of the South, but unknown to us; who divide the Northern zone and the circle of the Zodiac into an infinity of parts, who observe with exactitude the course of the stars, their fixed places, their declensions, their return and the time that each takes to make its revolution; these men, I say, have discovered all except one thing: the fact that God is the Creator of the universe, and the just Judge who rewards all the actions of life according to their merit. They have not known how to raise themselves to the idea of the consummation of all things, the consequence of the doctrine of judgement, and to see that the world must change if souls pass from this life to a new life.

Basil the Great (c. 329–79),
Hexaemeron, Homily I, 4

19. For if the mystery is the deep ground of all things, of all nature, and all creatures, etc., then the one conclusion that infallibly flows from it, is this, that no acuteness or ability of natural reason can so much as look into it. For natural reason is no older than flesh and blood; it has no higher a nature or birth than natural doubting; it had no existence when nature began its first workings and therefore can bear no witness to them. It was not present, had no eyes, when things first came forth; it never stood in the centre, from whence the birth of everything must arise; it never saw the forming of the first seeds of

every life. And yet the mystery, you see, contains all this. And therefore the one plain and necessary conclusion is this: that natural reason is, and must be, as incapable of entering into this mystery, as flesh and blood is incapable of entering into the Kingdom of Heaven.

William Law (1686–1761),
The Way to Divine Knowledge, Second Dialogue

20. The man who has become conscious of *I*, that is, the man who says *I-It*, stands before things, but not over against them in the flow of mutual action. Now with the magnifying glass of peering observation he bends over particulars and objectifies them, or with the field glass of remote inspection he objectifies them and arranges them as scenery, he isolates them in observation without any feeling of their exclusiveness, or he knits them into a scheme of observation without any feeling of universality. The feeling of exclusiveness he would be able to find only in relation, the feeling of universality only through it. Now for the first time he experiences things as sums of qualities.

Martin Buber (1878–1965),
I and Thou, Part I

21. Should one say that knowledge is founded on demonstration by a process of reasoning, let him hear that first principles are incapable of demonstration; for they are known neither by art nor sagacity. For the latter is conversant about objects that are susceptible of change, while the former is practical solely; and not theoretical. Hence it is thought that the first cause of the universe can be apprehended by faith alone.

Clement of Alexandria (c. 150–215),
The Miscellanies, Book II, Ch. IV

22. Again, a watch keeping correct time is no guarantee that

the bearer shall not suffer pain. The owner of the watch may be soulless, without mind-fire, a mere creature. No benefit to the heart or to the body accrues from the most accurate mechanism.

Richard Jefferies (1848–87),
The Story of My Heart, Ch. II

23. As I move about in the sunshine I feel in the midst of the supernatural: in the midst of immortal things. It is impossible to wrest the mind down to the same laws that rule pieces of timber, water or earth. They do not control the soul, however rigidly they may bind matter.

Richard Jefferies (1848–87),
The Story of My Heart, Ch. III

24. When will it be possible to be certain that the capacity of a single atom has been exhausted? At any moment some fortunate incident may reveal a fresh power. One by one the powers of light have been unfolded.

Richard Jefferies (1848–87),
The Story of My Heart, Ch. XI

25. For as he is better off, who knows how to possess a tree, and returns thanks to Thee for the use thereof, although he know not how many cubits high it is, or how wide it spreads, than he that can measure it, and count all its boughs, and neither owns it, nor knows or loves its Creator: so a believer, whose all this world of wealth is, and who having nothing, yet possesseth all things, by cleaving unto Thee, whom all things serve, though he know not even the circles of the Great Bear, yet is it folly to doubt but he is in a better state than one who can measure the heavens, and number the stars, and poise the elements, yet neglecteth Thee who hast made all things in number, weight and measure.

Augustine of Hippo (345–430),
Confessions, Book V, 7

26. Nature and life are two distinct things; nature deriving its beginning from the sun of the world, and life its beginning from the Sun of heaven. The sun of the world is pure fire, and the Sun of heaven pure love; that which proceeds from the former is called nature, but that which proceeds from the latter is called life. That which proceeds from pure fire is dead, but that which proceeds from pure love is living; therefore it is evident that nature in itself is dead.

Emanuel Swedenborg (1688–1772),
God, Providence, Creation, 95

27. Science has never discovered any "God", epistemological criticism proves the impossibility of knowing God, but the psyche comes forward with the assertion of the experience of God. God is a psychic fact of immediate experience, otherwise there would never have been any talk of God. The fact is valid in itself, requiring no non-psychological proof and inaccessible to any form of non-psychological criticism. It can be the most immediate and hence the most real of experiences, which can be neither ridiculed nor disproved. Only people with a poorly developed sense of fact, or who are obstinately superstitious, could deny this truth.

C. G. Jung (1875–1961),
Spirit and Life, 625

ii *Attention*

Attention might well have been discussed in Chapter V, for it is often associated with prayer. But I have chosen to place it directly following the section on science, because cultures are largely defined by the problems and issues to which they choose to give attention. The variety of human cultures –

indeed, the variety of knowledge among individuals – is largely a result of decisions to attend to certain enquiries, each considered significant. It follows that the human capacity for attention is creative, and mystics who stress a close association between attention and prayer remind us of the spiritual significance of a fundamental aptitude perhaps too frequently taken for granted.

Attention is also closely associated with our capacity to forget, for in attending to a certain subject we not only enshrine it with significance, but, in effect, we forget about all the other paths to knowledge which we have not taken. The rise of science itself involves the isolation of a certain set of problems and of a certain methodology which the pioneers felt sufficiently significant to deserve concentrated effort. The triumph of science thus rests on a particular quality of creative attention, and one of the implicit, enduring threats to a humane science is precisely the kind of forgetfulness induced by its success: forgetfulness, that is, of the spiritual nature of the humanity it should serve.

In this context, the mystics remind us of a further close association between attention and watchfulness, and how we ought to be on guard against activities distracting us needlessly from spiritual matters (1–10). Diligent watchfulness operates as a kind of preventative measure facilitating our creative pursuit of what some mystics call the prayer of simple attention to God (11–17).

1. Attention animated by desire is the whole foundation of religious practices.

> Simone Weil (1909–43),
> *Waiting on God*,
> "Forms of the Implicit Love of God"

2. Although thou passest over many words without attention, and thou attendest to only one little word; or

even though thou canst not pronounce one word with attention, thy labour will not be lost, if thou art watchful and right at heart. Do thou ever wisely avoid interior perplexity, impetuosity, over-anxiety and vehement efforts, and beware of seeking after many various methods of keeping thyself attentive; for these things are apt to produce confusion in the mind, and to exclude the influence of divine grace.

Louis de Blois (1506–65),
The Rule of the Spiritual Life, Ch. XVII

3. But as it is necessary to come to this exercise with attention and recollectedness, so at the same time we should take care that this attention should be tempered with discretion, that it may not be hurtful to our bodily health, nor really hindering to our devotion. For while some fatigue their brains by the exaggerated violence which they use to make themselves attentive to what they are meditating upon, there are others who, to avoid this evil, become very lax and wanting in earnestness and easily carried away by every wind that blows. To avoid these extremes, we should take such middle course that we may neither fatigue the mind with over-much attention, nor through indolence or weakness allow the thoughts to go wandering whithersoever they will. Just as we should counsel one riding a restive horse, to hold the rein firmly; that is, not too tightly, nor too loosely, lest the animal should either jib backwards or bolt dangerously on; so we should endeavour to secure that our attention may be maintained in calm moderation, unforced: with care, but without any fatiguing excess.

Peter of Alcantara (1499–1562),
A Golden Treatise of Mental Prayer, Part I, Ch. V

4. Learn to abide with attention in long waiting upon God in the state of quiet; give no heed to your imagination,

nor to its operations, for now, as I have said, the powers of the soul are at rest, and are not exercised, except in the sweet and pure waiting of love.

> John of the Cross (1542–91),
> *The Ascent of Mount Carmel*, Book II, Ch. XII

5. The third sign is the most certain of the three, namely, when the soul delights to be alone, waiting lovingly on God, without any particular considerations, in interior peace, quiet and repose, when the acts and exercises of the intellect, memory, and will, at least discursively – which is the going from one subject to another – have ceased; nothing remaining except that knowledge and attention, general and loving, of which I have spoken, without the particular perception of aught else.

> John of the Cross (1542–91),
> *The Ascent of Mount Carmel*, Book II, Ch. XIII

6. My most usual method is this simple attention, and such a general passionate regard to God; to whom I find myself often attached with greater sweetness and delight than that of an infant at the mother's breast.

> Brother Lawrence (c. 1605–91), *Letters*, I

7. Whether you read or hear anything, do it with attention and effectively, let not thy mind wander, but constrain it to be there, and do that thing which is in hand, and none other.

> Juan Luis Vives (1492–1540),
> *Introduction to Wisdom*, D v

8. And he shall enter into the kingdom with gladness, and the companions of the Bridegroom shall love him, because he was to be found keeping watch in His vineyard.

> Pachomius (–c. 346),
> *The Instructions*, VI

9. He that watcheth shall hear and see it; but he that sleepeth in sin, and saith in the fat days of his belly, *All is peace and quiet, we hear no sound from the Lord,* shall be blind.

Jacob Boehme (1575–1624),
The Way to Christ, "Of True Resignation", Ch. 3

10. The sermon also might have ended here, only that I have not yet admonished each one of you, according to my custom, of the careful attention due to his own particular vineyard. Which of us, my brethren, has so completely cut away from himself every superfluity, that he can now discover nothing whereon to use the pruning-knife?

Bernard of Clairvaux (1090–1153),
Sermons, LVIII

11. According to our point of view, then, so long as that geometer or physician continues to exercise himself in the study of his art and in the practice of its principles, the knowledge of his profession abides with him; but if he withdraw from its practice, and lay aside his habits of industry, then, by his neglect, at first a few things will gradually escape him, then by and by more and more, until in course of time everything will be forgotten, and be completely effaced from the memory. It is possible, indeed, that when he has first begun to fall away, and to yield to the corrupting influence of a negligence which is small as yet, he may, if he be aroused and return speedily to his senses, repair those losses which up to that time are only recent, and recover that knowledge which hitherto had been only slightly obliterated from his mind.

Origen (c. 185–253),
On First Principles, Book I, Ch. IV

12. Love for our neighbour, being made of creative attention, is analogous to genius.

Creative attention means really giving our attention to what does not exist. Humanity does not exist in the anonymous flesh lying inert by the roadside. The Samaritan who stops and looks gives his attention all the same to this absent humanity, and the actions which follow prove that it is a question of real attention.

Simone Weil (1909–43),
Waiting on God,
"Forms of the Implicit Love of God"

13. So also one may bind oneself more surely by promises made by another on one's behalf than by one's own promises; one may practise a virtue on behalf of another more easily than for oneself. The mere attention of the mind to such a life of substitution will itself provide instances and opportunities. What is needed is precisely that attention.

Charles Williams (1886–1945),
The Image of the City, "Exchange"

14. Now whereas to all manner of prayer, as hath been said, there is necessarily required an attention of the mind, without which it is not prayer, we must know that there are several kinds or degrees of attention.

Augustine Baker (1575–1641),
Sancta Sophia, Treat. 3, Sec. 1, Ch. 2, Part 12

15. As soon as man thinks with even a little attention of the divinity, he feels a certain delightful emotion of the heart, which testifies that God is God of the human heart; and our understanding is never so filled with pleasure as in this thought of the divinity, the smallest knowledge of which, as says the prince of philosophers,

is worth more than the greatest knowledge of other things.

François de Sales (1567–1622),
Treatise on the Love of God, Book I, Ch. XV

16. I have quitted all forms of devotion and set prayers, but those to which my state obliges me. And I make it my business only to persevere in this holy presence, wherein I keep myself by a simple attention, and a general loving regard to God, which I may call an actual presence of God; or to speak better, an habitual, silent and secret conversation with God, which often causes joys and raptures inwardly, and sometimes also outwardly, so great that I am forced to use means to prevent their appearance to others.

Brother Lawrence (c. 1605–91),
Letters, I

17. "Give heed to thyself", that is, to your soul. Adorn it, care for it, to the end that, by careful attention, every defilement incurred as a result of sin may be removed and every shameful vice expelled, and that it may be embellished and made bright with every ornament of virtue. Examine closely what sort of being you are. Know your nature – that your body is mortal, but your soul, immortal; that our life has two denotations, so to speak: one relating to the flesh, and this life is quickly over, the other referring to the soul, life without limit. "Give heed to thyself" – cling not to the mortal as if it were eternal; disdain not that which is eternal as if it were temporal.

Basil the Great (c. 329–79),
Homily on the Words: "Give Heed to Thyself"

iii *Time and Eternity*

Attention aspires to the simple presence of God. That simple presence is eternity, which has neither before nor after, and so does not come into being nor pass away. It is another name for God's uncreated being: life itself without origin, as Emanuel Swedenborg says (11). But time and space are necessary conditions for human language (which is spoken discursively and articulated by physical means), and it follows that descriptions of eternity are paradoxical. None the less, the mystics tell us that contemplative vision is accompanied by a sense of timelessness which is not just vacancy, but filled with God's presence (1–12).

We can suggest a rough correspondence, therefore, between nature, body and time on the one hand, and grace, spirit and eternity on the other. Grace redeems time for eternity by using body to mediate the eternal spirit to human nature. The more fully time is irradiated and penetrated by spirit, the more God's presence fills our attention. As Thomas Browne says (23), time consumes all things in forgetfulness, in contrast to the wakeful, silent and blessed immediacy of eternal life (13–24).

Like the world itself, time remains a context within which human beings discover God, and human life is often described as a pilgrimage, a journey towards rest in a promised homeland. The Western mystics stress not so much escaping from time into eternity, as fulfilling time by dwelling in it faithfully. Time should tell the story of our individual progress towards God, just as history should issue in the second coming, or final restoration of all things. A spoken sentence, after all, does not make complete sense until the silence which ensues once it is uttered; that silence, the ingathering present in which a text is discovered meaningful, indicates something of the relationship of time (process) to eternity (the end in which process is fulfilled). By contrast, a human journey directed aimlessly through time is not a pilgrimage at all, but merely wandering, just as speech without meaning is not a sentence, but merely babble.

Analogously, culture records the material and historical conditions of a people while symbolizing that people's attitude to the eternal verities which transcend culture and give it a direction. As the mystics make clear, cultural symbols need to be transparent to transcendence, or they will fall into an oblivion which the mere passage of unredeemed time guarantees. Such transcendence is affirmed by the mystics in a twofold manner: first, by direct intuition of the eternal, for one result of contemplative prayer is a sense of God's presence outside time; second, by faith that history itself is a creature of eternal wisdom fulfilling a purpose which we can trust, however puzzling it appears to us because of a necessary, partial blindness accompanying our embodiment in time. The principal sign of our limitation both by time and space remains of course the sign of faith itself; the cross, as St François de Sales says (29), is the ladder by which we climb out of time towards eternity (25–30).

1. We feel an inkling of the perfection and stability of eternity, for there is neither time nor space, neither before nor after, but everything present in one new, fresh-springing *now* where millenniums last no longer than the twinkling of an eye.

    Meister Eckhart (1260–1327),
    Sermons and Collations, XII

2. The contemplation of eternity maketh the soul immortal, whose glory it is, that it can see before and after its existence into endless spaces. Its sight is its presence. And therefore is the presence of the understanding endless,

because its sight is so. O what glorious creatures should we be, could we be present in spirit with all eternity! How wise, would we esteem this presence of the understanding, to be more real than that of our bodies!

Thomas Traherne (c. 1636–74),
Centuries of Meditation, I, 55

3. All motions, successions, creatures and operations with their beginnings and ends were in Him from everlasting, to whom nothing can be added, because from all eternity He was, whatsoever to all eternity He can be. All things being now to be seen and contemplated in His bosom: and advanced therefore into a diviner light, being infinitely older and more precious than we were aware. Time itself being in God eternally.

Thomas Traherne (c. 1636–74),
Centuries of Meditation, III, 65

4. For I saw truly that God doeth all-thing, be it never so little. And I saw truly that nothing is done by hap nor by adventure, but all things by the foreseeing wisdom of God: if it be hap or adventure in the sight of man, our blindness and our unforesight is the cause. For the things that are in the foreseeing wisdom of God from without beginning (which rightfully and worshipfully and continually He leadeth to the best end), as they come about fall to us suddenly, ourselves unwitting; and thus by our blindness and our unforesight we say: these be haps and adventures. But to our Lord God they be not so.

Julian of Norwich (c. 1342–1420),
Revelations of Divine Love, Ch. XI

5. There is no separation – no past; eternity, the Now, is continuous. When all the stars have revolved they only produce Now again. The continuity of Now is for ever. So that it appears to me purely natural, and not super-

natural, that the soul whose temporary frame was interred in this mound should be existing as I sit on the sward. How infinitely deeper is thought than the million miles of the firmament! The wonder is here, not there; now, not to be, now always.

Richard Jefferies (1848–87),
The Story of My Heart, Ch. III

6. And I saw that all things did harmonize, not with their places only, but with their seasons. And that Thou, who only art eternal, didst not begin to work after innumerable spaces of times spent; for that all spaces of times, both which have passed, and which shall pass, neither go nor come, but through Thee, working and abiding.

Augustine of Hippo (345–430),
Confessions, Book VII, 21

7. Yet they strive to comprehend things eternal, whilst their heart fluttereth between the motions of things past and to come, and is still unstable. Who shall hold it, and fix it, that it be settled awhile, and awhile catch the glory of that ever-fixed eternity, and compare it with the times which are never fixed, and see that it cannot be compared; and that a long time cannot become long, but out of many motions passing by, which cannot be prolonged altogether; but that in the eternal nothing passeth, but the whole is present; whereas no time is all at once present: and that all time past is driven on by time to come, and all to come followeth upon the past; and all past and to come is created, and flows out of that which is ever present? Who shall hold the heart of man, that it may stand still, and see how eternity ever still-standing, neither past nor to come, uttereth the times past and to come? Can my hand do this, or the hand of my mouth by speech bring about a thing so great?

Augustine of Hippo (345–430),
Confessions, Book XI, 13

8. He who does not praise God while here on earth shall in eternity be dumb. To praise God is the dearest and most joyous work of every loving heart; and the heart which is full of praise desires that every creature should praise God. The praise of God has no end, for it is our bliss; and most justly shall we praise Him in eternity.

> John of Ruysbroeck (1293–1381),
> *Adornment of the Spiritual Marriage*, Ch. XIII

9. O if thou couldst look upon Me, and see how incommutable is My subsistence, and that in Me there is neither before nor after, but only the self-same, that I alone am: then wouldst thou too be able to be freed from all unevenness and perverse changeableness, and to be with Me in a certain sense the self-same.

> Gerlac Petersen (1378–1411),
> *The Fiery Soliloquy with God*, Ch. XI

10. At other times, also, the divine light strikes the soul with such force that the darkness is unfelt and the light unheeded; the soul seems unconscious of all it knows, and is therefore lost, as it were, in forgetfulness, knowing not where it is, nor what has happened to it, unaware of the lapse of time. It may and does occur that many hours pass while it is in this state of forgetfulness; all seem but a moment when it again returns to itself. The cause of this forgetfulness is the pureness and simplicity of this knowledge.

> John of the Cross (1542–91),
> *The Ascent of Mount Carmel*, Book II, Ch. XIV

11. Because God is uncreated, he is, also, eternal; for life itself, which is God, is life in itself, neither from itself, nor from nothing, thus it is without origin; and what is without origin is from eternity, and is eternal. But an idea of that which is without origin cannot be grasped by

the natural man, neither can the idea of God from eternity; but these things are apprehended by the spiritual man. The thought of the natural man cannot be separated and withdrawn from the idea of time, this idea inhering in it from nature in which the natural man is; neither can it be separated and withdrawn from the idea of origin, because it regards origin as implying a beginning in time.

Emanuel Swedenborg (1688–1772),
God, Providence, Creation, 32

12. Here they live in endless being:
    Passingness hath passed away:
 Here they bloom, they thrive, they flourish,
    For decayed is all decay.

Peter Damian (1007–72),
Hymn on the Glory of Paradise

13. It is said also that paradise is an outer court of heaven. Even so this world is verily an outer court of the eternal, or of eternity, and specially whatever in time, or any temporal things or creatures, manifesteth or remindeth us of God or eternity; for the creatures are a guide and a path unto God and eternity. Thus this world is an outer court of eternity, and therefore it may well be called a paradise, for it is such in truth.

Theologia Germanica (c. 1350), Ch. L

14. Eternal life, which is no other thing than the Divinity itself, in so far as it will vivify our souls with his glory and felicity; a life which is the only true life, and for which alone we ought to live in this world, since all life which has not its term in a living eternity, is rather death than life.

François de Sales (1567–1622),
The Spiritual Conferences,
Book IV, Letters to Men of the World, XII

15. For instance, when a man is overladen with time and creatures he hath also his working in time and with the creature, and he cannot be empty of them. When now he turneth himself from time and from creatures, and turneth to God and to eternity, he hath henceforth his working with God and in eternity, and no longer in time and with the creature; hence out of time he maketh eternity, and out of the creature, God. And this is what poverty seeketh, and therefore is its working pure.

John Tauler (c. 1300–61),
The Following of Christ, Part I, 45

16. The devil, however, has not the knowledge of future events; but sometimes foretells the end of things from the beginning, which he sees. When he beholds some one preparing for a journey into Italy, what wonder if, impelled by the malice of his nature, he looks forward, and announces that such a one is coming to Italy? And, when he sees that heavy rain is falling all over Ethiopia, is it a great thing that he should dare to promise that there will be an inundation of the Nile in Egypt? By these means the deceiver induces many to have faith in him. Neither the predictions of astrologers, nor the wonders of magic, nor the arts or charms of Satan can effect anything against those who trust in God, and commit themselves wholly to Him.

Louis de Blois (1506–65),
The Rule of the Spiritual Life, Ch. XII

17. Man is created for time and for eternity – for time in his body, for eternity according to his spirit. Everything strives towards its origin; as now the body is made of earth and for time, it inclineth to earthly and temporal things, and seeketh its delight in them; but the spirit has sprung from God and is created for eternity, therefore it inclineth to God and eternity.

This contradicting inclination of both formeth this opposite lusting or desire.

> John Tauler (c. 1300–61),
> *The Following of Christ*, Part I, 112

18. Grace seeks no thing temporal; nor demands any other wages than God alone for her reward; nor asks more of temporal necessaries than what may serve her for the obtaining of things eternal.

> Thomas à Kempis (c. 1379–1471),
> *Of the Imitation of Christ*, Book IV, Ch. LIV

19. Nature has an eye to the temporal, rejoices over earthly gains, sorrows for loss, is vexed by a little injurious word; but grace looks to things eternal, cleaves not to things temporal, is not disturbed at losses, nor soured by hard words, because she has placed her treasure and joy in heaven where nothing is lost.

> Thomas à Kempis (c. 1379–1471),
> *Of the Imitation of Christ*, Book IV, Ch. LIV

20. For time, place and body, these three, should be forgotten in all spiritual working. And therefore beware in this work that thou take no example from the bodily ascension of Christ for to strain thine imagination in the time of thy prayer bodily upwards, as though thou wouldst climb above the moon. For it should in no wise be so, spiritually.

> *The Cloud of Unknowing* (late 14th Century), Ch. 59

21. The Lover saw that the world was created so that eternity should be more in harmony with his Beloved, who is infinite essence of greatness and all perfection, than with the world, which is a finite quantity; and therefore the justice of his Beloved was before time and finite quantities were.

> Ramon Lull (c. 1232–1315),
> *The Book of the Lover and the Beloved*, 273

22. "Consider, ye Lovers," said the Lover, "how that my Beloved is greater than all things that are created, for all these things are begun and ended, and my Beloved is eternal and infinite. Wherefore all majority is an image and a figure signifying the infinite and eternal greatness and goodness and other dignities of my Beloved."

> Ramon Lull (c. 1232–1315),
> *The Tree of Love*, Part II, Ch. II, 16

23. There is no antidote against the opium of time, which temporally considereth all things. Our fathers find their graves in our short memories, and sadly tell us how we may be buried in our survivors. Grave-stones tell truth scarce forty years. Generations pass while some trees stand, and old families last not three oaks.

> Thomas Browne (1605–82),
> *Hydriotaphia*, Ch. 5

24. When I consider the short duration of my life, swallowed up in the eternity before and after, the little space which I fill, and even can see, engulfed in the infinite immensity of spaces of which I am ignorant, and which know me not, I am frightened, and am astonished at being here rather than there; for there is no reason why here rather than there, why now rather than then. Who has put me here? By whose order and direction have this place and time been allotted to me?

> Blaise Pascal (1623–62),
> *Pensées*, 205

25. For time is made for man, and not man for time.

> *The Cloud of Unknowing* (late 14th Century), Ch. 4

26. And for as much as this life is none other thing but a certain pilgrimage whereby we still be entering into

another life eternal . . . we need very few things for the performance of the said journey.

> Juan Luis Vives (1492–1540),
> *Introduction to Wisdom*, E viii

27. And the end of piety is eternal rest in God. And the beginning of eternity is our end.

> Clement of Alexandria (c. 150–215),
> *The Instructor*, Book I, Ch. XIII

28. Thus, when I assert the existence of an end without an end, I admit darkness to be light, ignorance to be knowledge, and the impossible to be a necessity. Since we admit the existence of an end of the finite, we needs must admit the infinite, or the ultimate end, or the end without an end. Now we cannot but admit the existence of finite beings, wherefore we cannot but admit the infinite. Thus we admit the coincidence of contradictories, above which is the infinite.

> Nicholas of Cusa (1401–64),
> *The Vision of God*, Ch. XIII

29. My desire then assures me that I can have eternity: what remains for me but to hope that I shall have it? And this is given to me by the knowledge of the infinite goodness of him who would not have created a soul capable of thinking of and tending towards eternity, unless he had intended to give the means of attaining it. Thus, my brother, we shall find ourselves at the foot of the crucifix, which is the ladder by which from these temporal years we pass to the eternal years.

> François de Sales (1567–1622),
> *The Spiritual Conferences*,
> Book VII, Letters of the Saint about Himself, XXIV

30. During this mortal life we must choose eternal love or
    eternal death, there is no middle choice.

                              François de Sales (1567–1622),
                  Treatise on the Love of God, Book XII, Ch. XIII

iv *Union*

As we have seen at the beginning of this book, culture provides stories and symbols by which we may orient ourselves
as intelligent though alienated creatures condemned to travel
in search of meaning and to die in a universe the design of
which is largely unknown to us. Mythology, however, remains timebound and imperfect, and mystics deploy it as a
means of bearing witness to a supreme Reality which they
claim to have encountered experientially. The highest state
of such experiential knowledge is the prayer of union,
whereby we may become as God is: according to the formula,
in union we are by grace as God is by nature.

Literature of mysticism offers numerous records of unitive
experience, described by a variety of metaphors. It is as a
river flowing into a sea, a flame in a fire, water poured into
wine, clouds melting into rain; it is more intensely
pleasurable than the extremest human pleasure, and it is
beyond time; it is an assimilation to God, a participation in
his very being, a living flame of love in which we are not
conscious of our own action, but of eternal bliss (1–17).

Such descriptions suggest that we become identical with
God, but Western mystics characteristically stop short of
claiming outright that this is so. The favourite figure of iron
in a fire helps to make the point (18–22): just as red-hot
metal becomes all fire and yet remains metal, so the soul in
union is penetrated throughout by God, but without losing
its created essence (18–26).

Admittedly, it is difficult to draw the line exactly between experience and interpretation, and a culturally orthodox theology will to some extent colour the written record. None the less, Western tradition tends strongly to affirm that we do not cease to be creatures while God sustains us, and therefore we know him as creatures also in the union of mystical love. Still, we stand here on the threshold of a great mystery – on the boundary, that is, between culture and a reality about which the mystics repeatedly say they can tell us nothing directly. The good which they describe consequently remains elusive until we are filled with it beyond language, time and art (27–30). Part of the task assumed by the literature of mysticism is to declare such good as real, to be its ambassador, and to state its conditions. The great body of mystical writing is therefore fulfilled, as the authors themselves assure us, only in silence following the last word; yet none should assume the last word has been spoken until the close of time itself.

1. And all those men who are raised up above their created being into a God-seeing life are one with this Divine brightness. And they are that brightness itself, and they see, feel and find, even by means of this Divine Light, that, as regards their uncreated essence, they are that same onefold ground from which the brightness without limit shines forth in the Divine way, and which, according to the simplicity of the Essence, abides eternally onefold and wayless within. And this is why inward and God-seeing men will go out in the way of contemplation, above reason and above distinction and above their created being, through an eternal intuitive gazing. By means of this inborn light they are transfigured, and made one with that same light through which they see and which they see.

John of Ruysbroeck (1293–1381),
Adornment of the Spiritual Marriage, Ch. III

2. When I behold and am in that Good, I remember
nothing of the humanity of Christ, of God inasmuch as
he was man, nor of aught else that had shape or form;
and albeit I seem to see nothing, yet do I see all things.

Angela of Foligno (c. 1248–1309),
The Divine Consolation, Treatise III, Seventh Vision

3. The man said: "Tell me, Beloved, what are these men
called who have beheld the origin?" The *answer* came:
"These men have lost their names; they are nameless, for
they have become God." The man replied: "Beloved, I
am surprised to hear that thou sayest a man can become
God!" The *answer* came: "Do not be surprised.
Whomever God permits to see the origin becomes by
grace what God is by nature." The man said: "Tell me,
Beloved, how much dost thou love these men?" The
answer came: "With all your senses and abilities you
could not comprehend how much God loves them."

Rulman Merswin (c. 1307–82),
The Book of the Nine Rocks, Last Discourse

4. I am ashes, because I am a sinner, and therefore am I
eaten by Him. I am masticated when I am reproved; I am
swallowed when I am instructed; I am undergoing de-
composition in the stomach when I begin to change my
life; I am digested when I am transformed into His
image; I am assimilated when I am conformed to His
will. "Wonder not at this", my brethren. The
Bridegroom both feeds us and is fed by us in order to
unite us the more closely to Himself. Without such re-
ciprocity of relation we should not be perfectly one with
Him. For were I to feed on Him whilst He did not feed
on me, He, just as now, would appear to be in me, yet I
should not truly be in Him.

Bernard of Clairvaux (1090–1153),
Sermons, LXXI

5. O let me so long eye Thee, till I be turned into Thee, and look upon me till Thou art formed in me, that I may be a mirror of thy brightness, an habitation of thy love and a temple of thy glory.

Thomas Traherne (c. 1636–74),
Centuries of Meditation, I, 87

6. And the more disengaged and abstracted the self-egression of such souls is, the more free will be their soaring exaltation; and the more free their exaltation, the deeper will be their penetration into the vast wilderness and unfathomable abyss of the unknown Godhead, wherein they are immersed, overflowed and blended up, so that they desire to have no other will than God's will, and that they become the very same that God is: in other words, that they be made blessed by grace as He is by nature.

Henry Suso (c. 1295–1366),
The Little Book of Eternal Wisdom, Ch. XII

7. The soul seeth itself consummated in Him who is one, and perceiveth itself one or one spirit with the Self-same, and that Self-same which is God transformed into itself.

Gerlac Petersen (1378–1411),
The Fiery Soliloquy with God, Ch. X

8. O unquenchable fire of love, thou love that ever burnest, and never canst be put out, set me also on fire, burn into my whole being, that in myself I may wholly fall away, and be wholly tranformed by thy love; melt my whole being, that I may wholly lose myself in thee. Consume me wholly, O my God, in the fire of thy burning love, that utterly forgetful of my own self and of all that is in the world, I may, with the arms of love, embrace thee, the highest and most excellent Good.

John Tauler (c. 1300–61),
Meditations on the Life and Passion, Ch. 27

9. Spiritual marriage uniteth the bride to the Bridegroom immediately, essentially, substantially, that is to say, will to will, by means of the pure love which we have so often explained. Then God and the soul are one spirit, even as in marriage bridegroom and bride are one flesh. He that is joined to God is made one spirit with him by means of the entire conformity of will which grace worketh. The soul is filled with the joy of the Holy Ghost; it hath a foretaste of the blessedness of heaven.

> François Fenelon (1651–1715),
> *Maxims of the Mystics*, Article XLI

10. As it is impossible to enjoy happiness without the fruition of God, so it is impossible to enjoy God without assimilation to his nature. For we cannot enjoy God by external contact with him, but by an internal union with the divine spirit, which diffuses the strength of a divine life through our souls, and thus communicates a holy energetical felicity to them.

> John Smith (1618–52),
> *Select Discourses*, IV

11. "And yet I tell thee, if thou shouldst ask Me, who these are, I should reply [said the sweet and amorous Word of God] they are another Myself, inasmuch as they have lost and denied their own will, and are clothed with Mine, are united to Mine, are conformed to Mine." It is therefore true, indeed, that the soul unites herself with God by the affection of love.

> Catherine of Siena (1347–80),
> *The Dialogue*, Ch. I

12. So too the soul — and this is the subject of these stanzas — when transformed and glowing interiorly in the fire of love, is not only united with the divine fire

but becomes a living flame, and itself conscious of it.

John of the Cross (1542–91),
The Living Flame of Love, Prologue

13. Feel the transcendent virtue of pure love dissolving you also into a sea of pure love, a sea of glass and fire, a sea of pure crystal, divine beauty without any spot of flesh, or earth, darkness, or death; a sea of pure crystal shining, and burning with a pure flame of heavenly joys without any smoke of lusts, or passions.

Peter Sterry (c. 1614–74),
The Rise, Race, and Royalty of the Kingdom of God in the Soul of Man, p. 396

14. At this she was wholly rapt into God, so that as a drop of water poured into wine is wholly changed into wine, even so did this blessed soul pass into God, as if she had been made one spirit with him.

Mechthild of Hackborn (1240–98),
Select Revelations, Book II, Ch. V

15. And as the ship in this river being not hindered, necessarily is transported by the stream thereof into the sea, so the soul having no impediment, is carried by the course of this will unto the naked essence of God; and as when one is so led into the main ocean, he seeth no more the river (though the same in substance) but the sea, so he which is transported into the essential will, seeth no more this (as such) but God only.

Benet of Canfield (1562–1610),
The Rule of Perfection,
Part II, A Letter

16. All that has taken place up to this point has been in the individual capacity of the creature; but here the creature is taken out of his own capacity to receive an infinite

capacity in God himself. And as the torrent, when it enters the sea, loses its own being in such a way that it retains nothing of it, and takes that of the sea, or rather is taken out of itself to be lost in the sea; so this soul loses the human in order that it may lose itself in the divine, which becomes its being and its subsistence, not essentially, but mystically. Then this torrent possesses all the treasures of the sea, and is as glorious as it was formerly poor and miserable.

Madame Guyon (1648–1717),
Spiritual Torrents, Part I, Ch. IX

17. But how does this sacred outflowing of the soul into its well-beloved take place? An extreme complacency of the lover in the thing beloved begets a certain spiritual powerlessness, which makes the soul feel herself no longer able to remain in herself. Wherefore, as melted balm, that no longer has firmness or solidity, she lets herself pass and flow into what she loves: she does not spring out of herself as by a sudden leap, nor does she cling as by a joining and union, but gently glides as a fluid and liquid thing, into the divinity whom she loves. And as we see that the clouds, thickened by the south wind, melting and turning to rain, cannot contain themselves, but fall and flow downwards, and mix themselves so entirely with the earth which they moisten that they become one thing with it, so the soul which, though loving, remained as yet in herself, goes out by this sacred outflowing and holy liquefaction, and quits herself, not only to be united to the well-beloved, but to be entirely mingled with and steeped in him.

François de Sales (1567–1622),
Treatise on the Love of God, Book VI, Ch. XII

18. However, if we may speak without offence, the metal iron is capable of cold and heat. If, then, a mass of iron

be kept constantly in the fire, receiving the heat through all its pores and veins, and the fire being continuous and the iron never removed from it, it become wholly converted into the latter; could we at all say of this, which is by nature a mass of iron, that when placed in the fire, and incessantly burning, it was at any time capable of admitting cold? On the contrary, because it is more consistent with truth, do we not rather say, what we often see happening in furnaces, that it has become wholly fire, seeing nothing but fire is visible in it? And if any one were to attempt to touch or handle it, he would experience the action not of iron, but of fire. In this way, then, that soul which, like an iron in the fire, has been perpetually placed in the Word, and perpetually in the Wisdom, and perpetually in God, is God in all that it does, feels and understands, and therefore can be called neither convertible nor mutable, inasmuch as, being incessantly heated, it possessed immutability from its union with the Word of God.

Origen (c. 185–253),
On First Principles, Book II, Ch. VI, 6

19. It is a great thing, an exceeding great thing, in the time of this exile, to be joined to God in the divine light by a mystical and denuded union. This takes place when a pure, humble and resigned soul, burning with ardent charity, is carried above itself by the grace of God, and through the brilliancy of the divine light shining on the mind, it loses all consideration and distinction of things and lays aside all, even the most excellent images; and all liquefied by love, and, as it were, reduced to nothing, it melts away into God. It is then united to God without any medium, and becomes one spirit with Him, and is transformed and changed into Him, as iron placed in the fire is changed into fire, without ceasing to be iron. It becomes one with God, yet not so as to be of the same

substance and nature as God. Here the soul reposes, and ceases from its own action; and sweetly experiencing the operation of God, it abounds with ineffable peace and joy.

Louis de Blois (1506–65),
The Spiritual Mirror, Ch. XI

20. At the wound of the heart, He said: "In this wound of love, which is of such mighty compass that it embraceth the heavens and the earth, and all that in them is, gather up all thy love into My love, that henceforth it may be perfected, and, like an iron glowing with fire, may be brought into one love with Mine."

Mechthild of Hackborn (1240–98),
Select Revelations, Book I, Ch. X

21. For as heated iron is made all fire, so the soul united with love is made all love, save only its own essential properties, which must needs be different for ever.

Gerlac Petersen (1378–1411),
The Fiery Soliloquy with God, Ch. XIX

22. Holy writers explain this to us by this familiar example: when we take a piece of iron out of the fire, it sparkles and looks red like fire itself, but continues still to be iron, retaining the same name and substance it had before, though the brightness, heat and other accidents belong to fire: so grace, which is a heavenly quality, infused by God into the soul, transforms man into God in such manner as to make him in some measure partake of the virtues and purity of God, without ceasing to be man. Thus was he transformed who said: "I live, yet not I, but Christ liveth in me" (Galatians 2:20).

Luis de Granada (1504–88),
The Sinners Guide, Book I, Part II, Ch. III

23. 'Tis not so when human nature is united unto the divine, for human nature cannot pass over into essential union with the divine, even as the finite cannot be infinitely united unto the infinite, because it would pass into identity with the infinite, and thus would cease to be finite when the infinite were verified in it. Wherefore this union, whereby human nature is united unto the divine nature, is naught else than the attraction in the highest degree of the human nature unto the divine.

Nicholas of Cusa (1401–64),
The Vision of God, Ch. XX

24. Now the soul in this profound and strong act, being wholly turned towards its God, hath not any perception of its own action because it is direct and not reflex: which is the reason that some persons not explaining themselves well, say that they do not act at all: but it is a mistake, for the soul never does anything better or more effective. Let it rather say, "I do not now distinguish any acts" and not "I do not do any acts".

Madame Guyon (1648–1717),
A Method of Prayer, Ch. XXII

25. The sun as it arises, doth gradually swallow up all the light of the stars, which were very distinct before he appeared. It is not for want of light that we cannot then distinguish the stars, but for the excess of light. The case is the same here; the creature cannot distinguish its own operation because a general and strong Light absorbeth all its little distinct lights, and by His surpassing splendour and brightness makes them entirely disappear.

Madame Guyon (1648–1717),
A Method of Prayer, Ch. XII

26. Love and loving, Lover and Beloved are so straitly united in the Beloved that they are of his essence, and are one.

And this though Lover and Beloved are entities distinct, which agree without diversity of essence. So the Beloved is to be loved above all other objects of affection.

Ramon Lull (c. 1232–1315),
The Book of the Lover and the Beloved, 205

27. In this the fourth state there is no sense of anything, only fruition, without understanding what that is the fruition of which is granted. It is understood that the fruition is of a certain good containing in itself all good together at once; but this good is not comprehended. The senses are all occupied in this fruition in such a way that not one of them is at liberty, so as to be able to attend to anything else, whether outward or inward.

Teresa of Avila (1515–82),
Life, Ch. XVIII, 2

28. And godlike minds, angelically entering (according to their powers) unto such states of union and being deified and united, through the ceasing of their natural activities, unto the light which surpasseth Deity, can find no more fitting method to celebrate its praises than to deny it every manner of attribute. For by a true and supernatural illumination from their blessed union therewith, they learn that it is the cause of all things and yet itself is nothing, because it super-essentially transcends them all.

Dionysius the Areopagite (c. 500),
The Divine Names, Ch. I, 5

29. For while thy soul is specifically spirit, she has form; the while she has form she has neither unity nor union; the while she lacks union she has never really loved God, for actual love lies in union. Wherefore let thy soul be despirited of all spirit; let it be spiritless; if thou lovest God as God, as spirit, as Person or as image, that must all go.

– "Then how shall I love him?" – Love him as he is: a not-God, a not-spirit, a not-Person, a not-image; as sheer, pure, limpid unity, alien from all duality. And in this one let us sink down eternally from nothingness to nothingness. So help us God. Amen.

Meister Eckhart (1260–1327),
Sermons and Collations, XCIX

30. The third and highest unity is above the comprehension of our reason, and yet essentially within us. We possess it in a supernatural way when in all our works of virtue we have in mind the praise and glory of God, and above all aims, above ourselves, and above all things would rest only in him. This is that unity wherefrom we have come forth as creatures, and wherein, according to our being, we are at home.

John of Ruysbroeck (1293–1381),
Adornment of the Spiritual Marriage, Ch. II

Bibliographical Guide
to the Excerpts

(Numbers refer to chapters, sections and excerpts within the anthology)

Aelred of Rievaulx (c. 1110–67)
Spiritual Friendship, trans. Mary Eugenia Laker (Washington: Cistercian Publications, 1974). III, iv, 26; IV, iv, 20

Angela of Foligno (c. 1248–1309)
The Book of Divine Consolation, trans. Mary G. Steegman (London: New Mediaeval Library, 1908). I, ii, 3; I, iv, 35; I, iv, 36; II, iii, 9; III, ii, 9; III, iii, 9; III, iii, 10; III, iv, 5; III, iv, 25; IV, iv, 16; V, iii, 20; VI, iv, 4; VI, v, 2; VI, v, 3; VII, iv, 2

Anselm (1033–1109)
Anselm's Incentive to Holy Love, or Meditations upon the Passion of Our Lord (London: 1751). I, i, 41; III, i, 9

Augustine of Hippo (345–430)
Confessions, trans. E.B. Pusey (London: J.M. Dent, 1907). I, i, 10; I, iv, 15; II, iv, 4; III, iv, 14; V, iii, 6; VII, i, 25; VII, iii, 6; VII, iii, 7
Christian Doctrine, trans. J.F. Shaw, A Select Library of the Nicene and Post-Nicene Fathers, vol. II (Buffalo: The Christian Literature Company, 1887). III, iv, 3

Baker, Augustine (1575–1641)
Sancta Sophia (Douay: 1657). I, iii, 8; I, iii, 9; II, i,1; II, i, 10; III, i, 37; III, ii, 28; III, iii, 29; IV, i, 7; IV, i, 8; IV, iii, 5; V, i, 27; V, iii, 15; V, iii, 16; VI, iv, 32; VI, iv, 33; VI, iv, 34; VI, iv, 35; VI, v, 30; VII, ii, 14

Basil the Great (c. 329–79)
An Ascetical Discourse, trans. Sister M. Monica Wagner, *St Basil. Ascetical Works*, The Fathers of the Church, vol. 9 (Washington: Catholic University of America Press, 1950). VI, iii, 25

Homily on the Words: "Give Heed to Thyself", trans. Sr. M. Monica Wagner, *St Basil. Ascetical Works*. VII, ii, 17

The Hexaemeron, trans. Blomfield Jackson, *St Basil. Select Works*, A Select Library of the Nicene and Post-Nicene Fathers of the Christian Church, second series, vol. VIII (New York: The Christian Literature Company, 1895). VII, i, 18

Benedict of Nursia (c. 480–c. 547)

Rule for Monasteries, trans. Leonard J. Doyle (Collegeville, Minnesota: Liturgical Press, 1948). III, v, 10; VI, iii, 26

Benet of Canfield (William Fitch) (1562–1610)

The Rule of Perfection (Roan: 1609). II, iii, 36; V, i, 3; V, v, 11; VII, iv, 15

Bernard of Clairvaux (1090–1153)

St Bernard's Sermons on the Canticle of Canticles, trans. by a priest of Mount Mellary, 2 vols. (Dublin: Browne and Nolan, 1920). I, i, 30; I, iii, 29; II, i, 28; II, ii, 39; II, iii, 14; II, iii, 37; II, iv, 32; III, iii, 30; III, iv, 21; III, iv, 22; IV, ii, 6; VI, ii, 7; VI, iv, 1; VII, ii, 10; VII, iv, 4

Boehme, Jacob (1575–1624)

Quotations are from *The Works of Jacob Behmen*, 4 vols. (London: M. Richardson, 1764).

Aurora, Works, vol. I. I, i, 11; I, ii, 21; I, iii, 6; I, iii, 11; I, iii, 23; I, iii, 24; II, ii, 11; II, iii, 15; II, iv, 33; VI, i, 8; VI, i, 9

The Way to Christ, Works, vol. IV. I, i, 35; I, ii, 22; I, ii, 23; III, iii, 16; VII, i, 17; VII, ii, 9

Bonaventure (1221–74)

Quotations are from *The Works of St. Bonaventure*, trans. Jośe de Vinck, 3 vols. (New Jersey: St Anthony Guild Press, 1960–66).

The Breviloquium, Works, vol. II. I, ii, 11; IV, iv, 12

The Triple Way, Works, vol. I. I, iii, 4; VI, i, 11; VI, ii, 4

On the Perfection of Life, Works, vol. I. II, i, 16

Bridget of Sweden (1303–73)

Select Revelations of St Bridget, Princess of Sweden (London: Art and Book Co., 1892). I, ii, 30; I, iii, 16; III, i, 33; IV, iv, 8; V, v, 22; VI, iii, 18

Browne, Thomas (1605–82)

Quotations are from *The Prose Works of Sir Thomas Browne*, ed. Norman Endicott (London: University of London Press, 1968).

Religio Medici. V, v, 35; V, v, 36; VII, i, 12

Hydriotaphia. VII, iii, 23

Buber, Martin (1878–1965)

I and Thou, trans. Ronald Gregor Smith (New York: Charles Scribner's Sons, 2nd ed. 1958). VII, i, 20

Camus, Jean-Pierre (1584–1652)

The Spirit of St Francis de Sales, trans. J.S. (London: Burns and Oates, 1910). III, i, 8; III, iii, 33; IV, i, 20; IV, iv, 24; V, v, 31; VI, iii, 17; VI, iv, 10; VI, iv, 27

Cassian, John (c. 360–434)

Quotations are from *The Works of John Cassian*, trans. Edgar C.S. Gibson, A Select Library of Nicene and Post-Nicene Fathers of the Christian Church, second series, vol. XI (Oxford: James Parker, 1834).

The Institutes. III, i, 20; III, ii, 3; III, ii, 4; V, iv, 11

Conferences. I, i, 36; I, iii, 1; II, i, 14; III, iii, 4; IV, iii, 7; V, i, 9; V, i, 18; V, iv, 27; VI, iii, 8; VI, iii, 9; VI, iii, 10; VI, iii,11; VI, iv, 6; VI, iv, 7; VI, v, 23

Catherine of Bologna (1413–63)

The Spiritual Armour, trans. Alan G. McDougall (London: Burns, Oates and Washbourne, 1926). III, ii, 5; VI, iv, 14

Catherine of Genoa (1447–1510)

The Treatise on Purgatory, trans. H.E. Manning (London: Burns and Lambert, 1858). I, iv, 6; I, iv, 34

Catherine of Siena (1347–80)

The Dialogue, trans. Algar Thorvold (London: Kegan Paul, Trench, Trubner, 1896). I, iv, 27; I, iv, 28; I, iv, 33; III, i, 34; III, i, 35; III, i, 36; V, v, 25; VI, ii, 9; VI, ii, 20; VI, iv, 11; VI, v, 27; VI, v, 28; VII, iv, 11

Caussade, Jean-Pierre de (1675–1751)

Abandonment to Divine Providence, ed. J. Ramière, 2nd English edition, including the *Spiritual Counsels* (Exeter: Catholic Records Press, 1925). II, iv, 2; II, iv, 3; III, ii, 18; III, ii, 19; III, v, 2; III, v, 3; III, v, 4; IV, i, 19; IV, ii, 14; IV, iii, 22; V, iv, 8; V, iv, 9; V, iv, 26; VI, ii, 12; VI, ii, 13; VI, iv, 28; VII, i, 16

Spiritual Counsels. I, iv, 26; I, iv, 32; II, ii, 12; IV, iii, 1; V, i, 15; V, iii, 22; V, iv, 25; VI, iii, 5

Clement of Alexandria (c. 150–215)

Quotations are from *Fathers of the Second Century*, trans. Mr

Wilson, *The Ante-Nicene Fathers*, vol. II (Buffalo: The Christian Literature Publishing Company, 1885).

Exhortation to the Heathen. II, ii, 9

The Stromata, or Miscellanies. II, iv, 15; V, iv, 21; VII, i, 7; VII, i, 21

The Instructor. VII, iii, 27

Cloud of Unknowing anon. (late 14th Century)

The Cloud of Unknowing and other Treatises by an English Mystic of the Fourteenth Century, with a Commentary on the Cloud by Father Augustine Baker, trans. Justin McCann (London: Burns, Oates and Washbourne, 1924). II, ii, 6; III, iii, 1; IV, iii, 12; IV, iii, 13; i, 33; V, i, 34; V, iii, 14; V, iii, 23; V, v, 32; VI, ii, 6; VI, iii, 16; VI, iv, 9; VII, iii, 20; VII, iii, 25

Damian, Peter (1007–72)

Hymn on the Glory of Paradise, trans. J.M. Neale (London: H.R. Allenson, 1908). VII, iii, 12

Denis Hid Divinity, anon. (late 14th Century)

The Cloud of Unknowing and other Treatises by an English Mystic of the Fourteenth Century, with a Commentary on the Cloud by Father Augustine Baker, trans. Justin McCann (London: Burns, Oates and Washbourne, 1924). I, i, 2; I, i, 25; II, iii, 25

Dionysius the Areopagite (c. 500)

Quotations are from *Dionysius the Areopagite on the Divine Names and the Mystical Theology*, trans. G.E. Rolt (London: SPCK, 1920).

The Divine Names. I, ii, 12; I, iii, 13; II, iii, 29; III, v, 5; IV, ii, 1; IV, ii, 2; IV, iv, 17; V, i, 8; V, iv, 6; VI, i, 10; VII, iv, 28

The Mystical Theology. II, ii, 10; V, iii, 18; V, iii, 19

The Celestial Hierarchy, by John Colet, trans. J.H. Lupton, *Two Treatises on the Hierarchies of Dionysius* (London: Bell and Daldy, 1869). I, i, 28; I, iii, 3; I, iii, 10; I, iii, 12; I, iii, 27

Eckhart, Meister (1260–1327)

Quotations are from *Meister Eckhart*, ed. Franz Pfeiffer, trans. C. de B. Evans, 2 vols. (London: John Watkins, 1924).

Sermons and Collations, in *Meister Eckhart*, vol. I. I, i, 3; I, i, 9; I, i, 29; I, iii, 14; I, iii, 15; I, iv, 18; I, iv, 19; II, ii, 14; III, iii, 8; IV, ii, 10; V, i, 1; V, iv, 2; VI, ii, 15; VII, i, 5; VII, iii, 1; VII, iv, 29

Sayings, in *Meister Eckhart*, vol. I. I, i, 8; III, ii, 1

Tractates, in *Meister Eckhart*, vol. I. I, iv, 17; V, iv, 3; VI, i, 2; VI, iv, 2; VI, v, 19

In Collationibus, in *Meister Eckhart*, vol. II. II, i, 19; V, i, 2

Epistle of Privy Counsel, anon. (late 14th Century)

The Cloud of Unknowing and other Treatises by an English Mystic of the Fourteenth Century, with a Commentary on the Cloud by Father Augustine Baker, ed. Justin McCann (London: Burns, Oates and Washbourne, 1924). I, iv, 5; V, ii, 24; V, v, 33

Erasmus, Desiderius (1466?–1536)

Extracts from Erasmus on the Subject of War: taken from a publication under the title of "Antipolemus", trans. V. Knox (London: 1814). II, ii, 2; III, i, 10; III, i, 12; III, i, 13; III, i, 14

Fenelon, François (1651–1715)

Maxims of the Mystics, trans. Watkin W. Williams (London: A.R. Mowbray, 1909). III, iv, 1; III, iv, 4; IV, ii, 16; IV, iii, 8; IV, iii, 9; IV, iii, 11; IV, iv, 14; V, i, 10; V, iii, 25; V, iv, 17; VII, iv, 9

Pious Reflections, trans. William Coppinger, *True Piety* (Cork: J. Geary, 1813). I, iv, 4; II, ii, 4; III, ii, 24; III, ii, 25; III, iii, 27; IV, iii, 10; V, iv, 29; V, v, 23

On Faithfulness in Little Things, in The Agate, "A Selection of Pieces Calculated to Promote Piety and Happiness" (New York: W. Alexander, 1833). II, iv, 5; III, v, 15; III, v, 16

Fox, George (1624–91)

Epistles, 2 vols. (New York: Isaac T. Hopper, 1831). II, ii, 8; III, i, 5; V, v, 28

The Journal, ed. Norman Penney, 2 vols. (Cambridge: Cambridge University Press, 1911). III, i, 6; III, i, 26; V, v, 9; VI, v, 5

Francis of Assisi (1182–1226)

Quotations are from *The Writings of Saint Francis of Assisi*, trans. Paschal Robinson (London: J.M. Dent, 1906).

Admonitions. I, ii, 8; V, ii, 13

Rules of the Friars Minor. III, i, 24; V, v, 26

Letter to All the Faithful. III, i, 30

The Canticle of the Sun. III, i, 29; III, v, 22

François de Sales (1567–1622)

Quotations are from the *Library of St Francis de Sales*, trans. H.B. Mackey, 7 vols. (London: Burns and Oates, 1883).

The Spiritual Conferences. III, ii, 15; III, ii, 16; III, iii, 12; III, v, 12; IV, iii, 19; V, ii, 2; V, v, 30; VI, v, 15; VI, v, 16; VII, iii, 14; VII, iii, 29

The Mystical Explanation of the Canticle of Canticles. I, i, 20; II, i, 26

Treatise on the Love of God. IV, iii, 3; IV, iii, 4; V, i, 38; V, ii, 4; V, iii, 2; VII, ii, 15; VII, iii, 30; VII, iv, 17

Gertrude the Great (1256–1301)

Stations of the Passion, and Select Devotions on the Passion from the Prayers of St Gertrude, trans. Henry Collins (London: Thomas Richardson, 1879). I, i, 31; IV, iii, 21

Gregory the Great (c. 540–604)

The Dialogues of St Gregory the Great, trans. G.F. Hill (London: Philip Lee Warner, 1911). II, iv, 14; V, v, 15; VI, iv, 26

Morals on the Book of Job, trans. James Bliss, A Library of the Fathers, 3 vols. (Oxford: John Henry Parker, 1844–50). IV, iv, 9; VI, iii, 6; VI, iii, 7

Guyon, Madame (1648–1717)

A Method of Prayer, trans. Dugald MacFadyen (London: James Clarke, 1902). I, iv, 24; I, iv, 25; II, i, 21; II, iv, 7; IV, i, 5; IV, iii, 2; IV, iii, 23; IV, iii, 24; V, i, 11; V, i, 16; V, i, 29; V, ii, 25; V, iv, 18; V, v, 8; VI, ii, 10; VI, ii, 11; VI, iii, 4; VII, iv, 24; VII, iv, 25

Spiritual Torrents, trans. A.W. Marston (London: H.R. Allenson, 1908). II, ii, 21; II, iii, 3; IV, i, 22; V, ii, 3; V, iii, 7; VII, iv, 16

The Devout Christian, trans. Clericus (Brighton: 1847). I, iv, 3; VI, v, 26

Hilton, Walter (1300–96)

The Scale of Perfection, trans. by an Oblate of Solesmes (London: Burns, Oates and Washbourne, 1927). I, ii, 18; I, iii, 17; II, iii, 5; II, iii, 22; III, ii, 26; III, iv, 9; V, i, 7; V, iii, 8; V, iv, 30; VI, v, 21; VI, v, 22

Hugh of St Victor (c. 1096–1141)

The Soul's Betrothal Gift, trans. F. Sherwood Taylor (Westminster: Dacre Press, 1945). III, iv, 19; III, iv, 30; IV, iii, 20; IV, iv, 26; V, iv, 15; V, iv, 16

Hume, Basil (1923–)

To Be a Pilgrim. A Spiritual Notebook (Slough: St Paul Publications, 1984). II, ii, 1; V, i, 6

Jefferies, Richard (1848–87)

The Story of My Heart (London: Longmans, Green, 1907). I, i, 38; I, i, 51; I, iii, 5; I, iv, 16; II, i, 24; II, iv, 12; III, v, 24; V, iii, 5; VII, i, 22; VII, i, 23; VII, i, 24; VII, iii, 5

John of the Cross (1542–91)

Quotations are from *The Complete Works of Saint John of the Cross*, trans. David Lewis, 2 vols. (London: Longman, Green, Longman, Roberts, and Green, 1864).

The Ascent of Mount Carmel, in *Works*, vol. I. II, iii, 32; II, iv, 1; II, iv, 8; V, iii, 12; VI, iii, 14; VI, iv, 22; VI, v, 24; VI, v, 25; VII, ii, 4; VII, ii, 5; VII, iii, 10

The Obscure Night of the Soul, in *Works*, vol. I. III, iii, 24; V, i, 36; V, iii, 10; V, iii, 11

A Spiritual Canticle Between the Soul and Christ, in *Works*, vol. II. II, i, 6; II, ii, 15; II, ii, 16; II, iii, 19; III, iv, 29; V, v, 21; VI, i, 20; VI, ii, 5

The Living Flame of Love, in *Works*, vol. II. IV, i, 10; VI, ii, 16; VI, iii, 15; VII, iv, 12

Spiritual Maxims, in *Works*, vol. II. I, iii, 19; I, iii, 25; II, i, 22; II, i, 27; III, iii, 5; III, iv, 18; IV, iii, 16; V, i, 35; V, ii, 9

John of Ruysbroeck, (1293–1381)

Quotations are from *The Adornment of the Spiritual Marriage. The Sparkling Stone. The Book of Supreme Truth*, trans. C.A. Wynschenk (London: J.M. Dent, 1916).

Adornment of the Spiritual Marriage. II, ii, 17; II, ii, 18; II, ii, 35; II, iii, 7; II, iii, 16; III, ii, 10; III, iii, 20; III, iv, 16; III, iv, 17; III, v, 11; IV, i, 2; IV, i, 12; IV, ii, 11; IV, ii, 12; IV, iii, 6; IV, iii, 25; V, iii, 1; V, iv, 22; V, iv, 23; V, iv, 24; VI, i, 12; VI, v, 6; VII, iii, 8; VII, iv, 1; VII, iv, 30

The Sparkling Stone. I, i, 16; I, iv, 13; I, iv, 14; I, iv, 23; IV, i, 11; V, ii, 21

The Book of Supreme Truth. VI, v, 20

Julian of Norwich (c. 1342–1420)

Revelations of Divine Love, ed. Grace Warrack (London: Methuen, 1914). I, i, 6; I, i, 7; I, iii, 7; II, iii, 11; II, iii, 12; II, iii, 17; II, iv, 16; III, i, 16; III, i, 17; III, i, 18; III, v, 21; IV, iv, 1; V, i, 4; V, i, 5; V, ii, 15; V, ii, 20; V, iii, 3; V, iv, 7; VI, i, 6; VI, i, 7; VI, ii, 8; VII, iii, 4

Jung, Carl Gustav (1875–1961)

Spirit and Life, trans. R.F.C. Hull, in *The Structure and Dynamics of the Psyche*, Bollingen Series XX (New York: Pantheon, 1960). VII, i, 27

Koestler, Arthur (1905–83)

Bricks to Babel (London: Hutchinson, 1980). VII, i, 4

Law, William (1686–1761)

Quotations are from *The Works of William Law*, 9 vols. (London: J. Richardson, 1762).

The Spirit of Love, in *Works*, vol. VIII. I, i, 39; I, ii, 5; I, ii, 24; I, ii, 25; II, iii, 20; III, i, 15; V, ii, 17; V, iv, 1; VII, i, 3; VII, i, 13

A Serious Call to a Devout and Holy Life, in *Works*, vol. IV. I, ii, 2; II, iii, 8; III, i, 19; III, ii, 2; III, iii, 2; III, iii, 3; III, iv, 2; III, v, 9; IV, iv, 18; V, ii, 1; V, v, 10; VI, iv, 21

The Way to Divine Knowledge, in *Works*, vol. VII. I, ii, 13; VI, i, 16; VII, i, 19

Address to the Clergy, in *Works*, vol. IX. I, ii, 20; I, iv, 20; III, i, 1; III, i, 2

Lawrence, Brother (c. 1605–91)

Quotations are from *Letters of Brother Lawrence*, ed. John Wesley, *A Christian Library*, vol. XXIII (London: 1825).

Letters. VI, iv, 18; VII, ii, 6; VII, ii, 16

Conversations. III, v, 17; III, v, 18; V, iv, 20; VI, iii, 27

Lead, Jane (1623–1704)

The Ascent to the Mount of Vision (1699). I, ii, 9; II, i, 20; II, ii, 24; III, ii, 27

Lewis, C.S. (1898–1963)

Letters of C.S. Lewis, ed. W.H. Lewis (London: Geoffrey Bles, 1966). IV, iv, 19; V, i, 14; VI, v, 13

Louis de Blois (1506–65)

Quotations are from *The Spiritual Works of Louis of Blois*, trans. John Edward Bowden (London: R. Washbourne, 1871).

The Rule of the Spiritual Life. I, i, 13; I, i, 18; I, i, 37; III, v, 26; IV, i, 18; V, i, 19; VI, i, 15; VI, iii, 20; VI, iv, 13; VI, v, 29; VII, ii, 2; VII, iii, 16

The Spiritual Mirror. III, iii, 14; V, i, 17; V, ii, 8; V, v, 5; V, v, 6; VI, i, 18; VI, iii, 21; VI, v, 17; VII, iv, 19

Luis de Granada (1504–88)

The Sinners Guide (Dublin: P. Wogan, 1803). I, i, 12; III, i, 2; III, i, 21; V, iv, 31; VI, iv, 17; VII, iv, 22

Luis de Leon (1528–91)

The Names of Christ, trans. by a Benedictine of Stanbrook (London: Burns, Oates and Washbourne, 1926). II, ii, 25; II, ii, 26; III, iv, 31; IV, i, 16; IV, i, 17; V, iv, 19; VI, iii, 1

Lull, Ramon (c. 1232–1315)

The Book of the Lover and the Beloved, trans. E. Allison Peers (London: SPCK, 1923). II, i, 11; II, i, 12; II, ii, 5; II, ii, 30; II, iii, 2; III, iv, 8; IV, iv, 25; VI, i, 21; VII, iii, 21; VII, iv, 26

The Tree of Love, trans. E. Allison Peers (London: SPCK, 1926). I, i, 14; II, iv, 25; III, ii, 23; III, iii, 13; III, v, 14; IV, i, 27; VI, ii, 18; VII, iii, 22

Macarius (c. 300–90)

Quotations are from *Institutes of Christian Perfection*, trans. Granville Penn (London: J. Nisbet, 1828).

Institutes of Christian Perfection. II, ii, 22; II, iii, 23; III, ii, 29; III, ii, 30; III, iv, 20; IV, ii, 22; V, i, 21; V, ii, 14; V, v, 7; VI, ii, 21; VI, iv, 20

Sayings. IV, i, 24; V, i, 22

Malaval, François (1627–1719)

A Simple Method of Raising the Soul to Contemplation, trans. Lucy Menzies (London: J.M. Dent, 1931). I, iv, 2; I, iv, 29; II, ii, 23; II, iii, 24; II, iii, 38; II, iv, 9; II, iv, 23; III, iv, 10; III, v, 23; IV, i, 9; IV, i, 15; IV, i, 21; IV, ii, 19; IV, ii, 20; IV, ii, 21; V, i, 24; V, i, 25; V, i, 26; V, i, 37; VI, iii, 22; VI, iii, 23; VI, iv, 31; VI, v, 8

Malebranche, Nicolas (1638–1715)

Dialogues on Metaphysics and on Religion, trans. Morris Ginsberg (London: George Allen and Unwin, 1923). VII, i, 1; VII, i, 2

Mechthild of Hackborn (1240–98)

Select Revelations of St Mechtild, trans. by a secular priest (London: Thomas Richardson, 1875). III, i, 32; III, iv, 7; IV, i, 4; IV, iv, 7; V, ii, 5; V, v, 19; VII, iv, 14; VII, iv, 20

Mechthild of Magdeburg (1217–82)

Matilda and the Cloister of Hellfde. Extracts from the Book of Matilda of Magdeburg, trans. Frances Bevan (London: James Nisbet, 1896). II, iii, 26; IV, ii, 5; V, iv, 12; VI, iii, 13

Merswin, Rulman (c. 1307–82)

Mystical Writings of Rulman Merswin, trans. Thomas S. Kepler (Philadelphia: Westminster Press, 1960). I, ii, 19; II, iii, 34; III, i, 7; IV, iv, 21; V, ii, 16; VI, v, 14; VII, iv, 3

Merton, Thomas (1915–68)

New Seeds of Contemplation (New York: New Directions, 1972; first published, 1962). II, i, 17; II, i, 18; II, iv, 13; III, i, 25

The Silent Life (London: Burns, Oates and Washbourne, 1957). III, ii, 6; IV, i, 13

Molinos, Miguel de (1640–97)

A Spiritual Guide Which Disentangles the Soul, trans. Kathleen Lyttleton (London: Methuen, 1907). II, i, 3; II, i, 4; II, iv, 6; III, iii, 28; III, iii, 32; IV, i, 25; IV, i, 26; IV, ii, 17; V, i, 30; V, i, 31; V, i, 32; V, iii, 24; V, v, 34; VI, iv, 30

More, Dame Gertrude (1606–33)

The Holy Practices of a Divine Lover, ed. H. Lane Fox (London: Sands & Co., 1909). VI, ii, 22; VI, iv, 12

Nicholas of Cusa (1401–64)

The Vision of God, trans. Emma Gurney Salter (London: J.M. Dent, 1928). I, iv, 12; II, iii, 6; II, iii, 28; II, iv, 10; III, iv, 6; IV, ii, 3; V, iii, 21; V, iv, 32; VI, i, 13; VI, i, 14; VII, iii, 28; VII, iv, 23

Nun Gertrude (Abbess, 1251–91)

Insinuationes divinae pietatis, trans. Frances Bevan, in *Matilda and the Cloister of Hellfde* (London: James Nisbet, 1896). I, i, 5

Origen (c. 185–253)

On First Principles, trans. Frederick Crombie, The Ante-Nicene Fathers, vol. IV (Buffalo: The Christian Literature Publishing Co., 1885). I, iii, 22; II, iii, 10; VII, i, 6; VII, ii, 11; VII, iv, 18

The Song of Songs. Commentary and Homilies, trans. R.P. Lawson (London: Longmans, Green, 1957). I, iii, 28

Pachomius (–c. 346)

The Instructions of Apa Pachomius, trans. E.A. Wallis Budge, *Coptic Apocrypha in the Dialect of Upper Egypt* (Printed by the order of the Trustees, the British Museum, and Longmans, 1913). III, i, 28; III, iii, 15; VII, ii, 8

Pascal, Blaise (1623–62)

Pensées, trans. W.F. Trotter (New York: P.F. Collier, 1910). VII, i, 10; VII, i, 11; VII, iii, 24

Peter of Alcantara (1499–1562)

A Golden Treatise of Mental Prayer, trans. George Seymour Hollings (London: A.R. Mowbray, 1905). II, i, 5; IV, i, 6; V, i, 20; V, i, 28; VI, iv, 15; VI, iv, 16; VI, v, 1; VII, ii, 3

Petersen, Gerlac (1378–1411)

The Fiery Soliloquy with God, trans. by a secular priest (London: Thomas Richardson, 1872). I, i, 22; II, iii, 4; II, iii, 33; III, i, 31; III, iii, 23; III, iv, 27; III, v, 1; IV, iii, 15; V, iii, 9; V, iv, 28; V, v, 20; VI, i, 19; VI, iv, 8; VII, iii, 9; VII, iv, 7; VII, iv, 21

Richard of St Victor (c. 1123–75)

Quotations are from *Richard of St Victor. The Twelve Patriarchs, The Mystical Ark, Book Three of the Trinity*, trans. Grover A. Zinn (New York: Paulist Press, 1979).

The Mystical Ark. II, i, 25; IV, ii, 7

The Twelve Patriarchs. II, iv, 18; VI, i, 4

Rolle, Richard (1300–49)

The Fire of Love, or the Melody of Love and the Mending of Life, trans. Frances M.M. Comper (London: Methuen, 1914). I, iii, 20; I, iii, 21; II, i, 23; II, iv, 19; III, iii, 22; IV, ii, 13; IV, iv, 13; VI, iii, 12

Smith, John (1618–52)

Select Discourses (London: 1820). I, i, 21; I, i, 23; I, i, 24; I, ii, 1; I, ii, 10; I, ii, 15; II, ii, 3; II, ii, 29; II, iv, 24; V, v, 13; VI, ii, 19; VI, iii, 19; VII, iv, 10

Sterry, Peter (1614–72)

The Rise, Race, and Royalty of the Kingdom of God in the Soul of Man (London: 1683). II, ii, 20; II, ii, 27; II, ii, 28; IV, ii, 18; VI, i, 22; VI, i, 23; VII, iv, 13

Suso, Henry (c. 1295–1366)

Little Book of Eternal Wisdom (London: R. and T. Washbourne, 1910). I, i, 32; I, iv, 10; I, iv, 11; II, iii, 1; II, iii, 39; II, iii, 40; III, ii, 14; IV, ii, 23; V, i, 23; V, ii, 22; V, ii, 23; V, iii, 17; V, v, 17; VII, iv, 6

Swedenborg, Emanuel (1688–1772)

God, Providence, Creation, trans. Isaiah Tansley (London: The Swedenborg Society, 1902). VII, i, 26; VII, iii, 11

Tauler, John (c. 1300–61)

Meditations on the Life and Passion of Our Lord Jesus Christ,

trans. by a secular priest (London: Thomas Richardson, 1875).
I, iv, 9; II, ii, 33; II, ii, 34; III, iv, 28; IV, iv, 5; IV, iv, 6; VII, iv, 8

The Inner Way, trans. Arthur Wollaston (London: Methuen, 1901). I, i, 27; I, iii, 2; III, ii, 17; IV, iii, 14; IV, iv, 22; V, ii, 6; VI, i, 17

The Following of Christ, trans. J.R. Morell (London: Burns and Oates, 1886). I, iii, 26; II, ii, 13; II, iii, 27; IV, ii, 4; IV, iv, 23; V, ii, 7; V, v, 18; VII, iii, 15; VII, iii, 17

Teilhard de Chardin, Pierre (1881–1955)

Hymn of the Universe, trans. Simon Bartholomew (London: William Collins, 1965). I, ii, 14; I, iv, 31; II, iii, 21; III, v, 25

Activation of Energy, trans. René Hague (London: Collins, 1970). II, ii, 36; II, iv, 30; IV, iv, 3; IV, iv, 10; VII, i, 8; VII, i, 9

Teresa of Avila (1515–82)

The Interior Castle, trans. by a Benedictine of Stanbrook (London: Thomas Baker, 1930). I, i, 17; II, ii, 19; III, iii, 6; III, iii, 17; III, iv, 23; III, v, 8; IV, i, 3; IV, i, 23; IV, ii, 8; V, ii, 18; V, iii, 4; V, iv, 4; V, v, 1; VI, i, 5; VI, iv, 3; VI, iv, 23; VI, iv, 24; VI, iv, 25; VI, v, 4; VI, v, 10

The Way of Perfection, trans. by a Benedictine of Stanbrook (London: Thomas Baker, 1911). II, i, 9; III, iii, 7; III, iii, 31; III, v, 7; IV, i, 14; V, i, 13; V, i, 39; VI, v, 18

The Life of St Teresa of Jesus, trans. David Lewis (London: Thomas Baker, 1916). II, ii, 37; II, iii, 30; II, iii, 31; III, iv, 24; V, ii, 26; V, v, 27; VI, ii, 14; VI, v, 11; VII, iv, 27

Theologia Germanica, anon. (c. 1350)

Theologia Germanica, trans. Susanna Winkworth (London: Longman, Brown, Green and Longmans, 1854). I, i, 4; I, i, 33; I, i, 34; I, ii, 4; I, ii, 26; I, ii, 27; I, iv, 22; II, iii, 13; III, i, 23; III, ii, 7; VI, ii, 3; VI, iv, 5; VII, iii, 13

Thomas à Kempis (c. 1379–1471)

Of the Imitation of Christ, trans. C. Bigg (London: Methuen, 1905). I, i, 19; I, i, 26; I, ii, 17; I, iv, 7; II, i, 13; II, ii, 7; II, ii, 31; II, iv, 21; III, ii, 21; III, ii, 22; III, v, 13; IV, i, 28; IV, i, 29; IV, i, 30; IV, iii, 17; IV, iii, 18; V, ii, 10; V, ii, 11; V, ii, 12; V, iii, 13; V, iv, 13; V, iv, 14; V, v, 14; VI, iv, 29; VII, iii, 18; VII, iii, 19

Traherne, Thomas (c. 1636–74)

Centuries, Poems, and Thanksgivings, ed. H.M. Margoliouth, 2 vols. (Oxford: Clarendon Press, 1958). I, ii, 7; I, ii, 28; II, i, 8; II,

ii, 38; III, i, 4; III, ii, 20; III, iv, 11; III, v, 19; III, v, 20; IV, ii, 9;
IV, iv, 2; V, ii, 19; V, v, 12; VI, i, 3; VII, iii, 2; VII, iii, 3; VII, iv, 5

Underhill, Evelyn (1875–1941)

The Letters of Evelyn Underhill, ed. Charles Williams (London:
Longmans, Green, 1943). III, i, 22; III, v, 6; V, i, 12; VI, v, 9

Valdes, Juan de (1490–1541)

Divine Considerations, trans. Nicholas Ferrar (London: John
Lane, 1905). I, ii, 6; II, iv, 17; II, iv, 31; III, i, 3; V, iv, 5; VI, iii, 3;
VII, i, 14

Vives, Juan Luis (1492–1540)

Introduction to Wisedom, trans. Sir R. Morison (London: 1540).
I, iv, 1; I, iv, 30; II, iv, 20; III, i, 38; III, i, 39; IV, iv, 15; V, v, 37;
V, v, 38; VI, iii, 24; VI, iv, 19; VII, ii, 7; VII, iii, 26

Weil, Simone (1909–43)

Waiting on God (USA: *Waiting for God*), trans. Emma Craufurd
(London: Routledge and Kegan Paul Ltd, 1951 *and* Fount
Paperbacks; New York: Harper and Row, 1973). I, ii, 29; II, iii,
18; VI, iii, 2; VI, v, 12; VII, ii, 1; VII, ii, 12

Whichcote, Benjamin (1609–83)

Select Aphorisms, Christian Tract Society, XXVIII (London: G.
Smallfield, 1822). I, i, 1; I, i, 15; I, ii, 16; I, iii, 18; I, iv, 8; I, iv,
21; II, i, 2; II, ii, 32; II, iv, 26; II, iv, 27; II, iv, 28; II, iv, 29; III, ii,
8; III, iii, 25; III, iii, 26; V, v, 2; V, v, 3; V, v, 4; V, v, 24; VI, ii,
17; VI, v, 7

William of St Thierry (c. 1085–1148)

The Golden Epistle, trans. Walter Shewring (London: Sheed and
Ward, 1930). II, i, 7; II, i, 15; III, iii, 11; III, iii, 19; III, iv, 15; IV,
i, 1; V, v, 16; VI, ii, 1; VI, ii, 2; VII, i, 15

The Enigma of Faith, trans. John D. Anderson (Washington:
Cistercian Publications, 1974). I, i, 40; II, iv, 22; VI, i, 1

Exposition on the Song of Songs, trans. Mother Columba Hart
(Shannon, Ireland: Irish University Press, 1970). III, iii, 18

Williams, Charles (1886–1945)

The Image of the City and Other Essays, ed. Ann Ridler
(London: Oxford University Press, 1958). I, ii, 31; II, iii, 35; II,
iv, 11; III, v, 27; IV, iv, 4; IV, iv, 11; VII, ii, 13

Religion and Love in Dante (Westminster: Dacre Press, 1941).
III, iv, 12; III, iv, 13

Recommended Books

The following list of fifty titles is meant to suggest various points of entry into the vast subject of Western mysticism. Many of the works cited contain excellent bibliographies through which particular tastes, preferences and lines of enquiry may be developed.

Auden, W.H. "The Protestant Mystics", ed. Edward Mendelson, in *Forewords and Afterwords* (New York: Vintage Books, 1974). An outstanding essay by the famous poet and man of letters, proclaiming, among other things, that "in relation to each other we are protestants; in relation to the truth we are catholics".

Berger, Peter L. *A Rumor of Angels. Modern Society and the Rediscovery of the Supernatural* (New York: Doubleday, 1970). A renowned sociologist assesses the experience of transcendence in our times.

Bohm, David. *Wholeness and the Implicate Order* (London: Ark Paperbacks, 1983. First published, 1980). A searching study of how modern scientific advances may open up to spiritual wholeness.

Bowker, John. *The Religious Imagination and the Sense of God* (Oxford: Clarendon Press, 1978). Learned analysis of the process of vital transformation and traditional dogma in Judaism, Christianity, Islam and Buddhism.

Bucke, Richard M. *Cosmic Consciousness* (New York: E.P. Dutton, 1956). An influential and provocative account of the attainability of higher consciousness.

Butler, Cuthbert. *Western Mysticism. With Afterthoughts* (London: Grey Arrow Books, 1960. First published, 1922). Ground-breaking study outlining the basis of Western mysticism in contemplative prayer during the "Benedictine centuries" (550–1150).

Chitty, Derwas J. *The Desert a City* (Oxford: Basil Blackwell,

1966). Excellent general account of the desert fathers and the foundations of monasticism.

D'Arcy, Martin C. *The Meeting of Love and Knowledge: Perennial Wisdom* (New York: Harper and Row, 1957). Distinguishes Eastern and Western mysticism in terms of the Christian stress on personal relationship to a personal God.

Eaton, Gai. *The Richest Vein. Eastern Tradition and Modern Thought* (London: Faber and Faber, 1949). Excellent study of relationships between East and West in some early twentieth-century authors. Should be better known.

Ferguson, John. *An Illustrated Encyclopaedia of Mysticism and the Mystery Religions* (London: Thames and Hudson, 1976). A useful and interesting reference work in a popular format.

Ferguson, John. *The Politics of Love. The New Testament and Non-Violent Revolution* (Cambridge: James Clarke, 1973). Discusses the New Testament basis of Christian pacifism and non-violence.

Fremantle, Anne. *The Protestant Mystics* (Boston: Little, Brown, 1964). A fine anthology illustrating the Protestant contribution to Western mysticism.

Fry, Timothy, ed. *R.B. 1980. The Rule of St Benedict in Latin and English, with Notes* (Collegeville, Minnesota: Liturgical Press, 1981). This magnificent edition, with extensive introduction, commentary and indices is an invaluable tool for the study of early Western spirituality in relation to our times.

Graef, Hilda. *The Story of Mysticism* (New York: Doubleday, 1965). Well-written, informative historical outline of Western mysticism.

Gilson, Etienne. *The Mystical Theology of St Bernard*, trans. A.H.C. Downes (London: Sheed and Ward, 1940. Reprinted, 1955). A basic study of mediaeval mystical sensibility by a leading scholar.

Guénon, René. *The Reign of Quantity and the Signs of the Times*, trans. Lord Northbourne (Harmondsworth: Penguin Books, 1972. First published, 1945). Elegant and powerful denunciation of the West's loss of traditional metaphysical knowledge since the scientific revolution.

Happold, F.C. *Mysticism. A Study and an Anthology* (Harmondsworth: Penguin Books, 1963). Well-chosen anthology with informative commentary.

Hardy, Alister. *The Spiritual Nature of Man* (Oxford: Clarendon Press, 1979). Fascinating collection, statistically analysed, of unusual spiritual experiences reported by ordinary people.

Hastings, James, ed. *Encyclopaedia of Religion and Ethics* (New York: Charles Scribner's Sons, 1910–34). Sometimes dated, but still invaluable and respected reference work with many entries pertinent to mysticism.

Hick, John, ed. *The Existence of God* (London: Collier Macmillan, 1974). Wide-ranging, valuable collection of essays by various hands.

Huxley, Aldous. *The Perennial Philosophy* (New York: Harper, 1945). Outstanding, wittily written attempt to describe and anthologize the common factors in the world's religions.

Inge, W.R. *Mysticism in Religion* (London: Hutchinson's University Library, 1947). Lively discussion by the brilliant, iconoclastic former Dean of St Paul's, calling for a mysticism transcending narrow ecclesiastical considerations.

James, William. *The Varieties of Religious Experience. A Study in Human Nature* (London: Collier, 1960; and Fount Paperbacks. First published, 1901–2). Famous study of a wide range of religious experiences from a rationalist, tolerant perspective.

Jung, C.G. *Memories, Dreams and Reflections* (New York: Random House, 1961; London: Fontana, 1967). Autobiography of unusual interest for students of mysticism, by one of the founders of modern psychology.

Katz, Steven, ed. *Mysticism and Philosophical Analysis* (London: Sheldon Press, 1978). Excellent collection of learned essays by various hands.

Knowles, David. *The English Mystical Tradition* (London: Burns and Oates, 1961). Scholarly account of the fourteenth-century English mystics by an influential author.

Leclerq, Jean. *Bernard of Clairvaux and the Cistercian Spirit*, trans. Claire Lavoie (Kalamazoo: Cistercian Publications, 1976). Learned study of the ideals transforming mediaeval Christian spirituality.

Maritain, Jacques. "Natural Mystical Experience and the Void", in *Ransoming the Time* (New York: Scribners, 1941). Interpretation of differences between natural mysticism of absorption and supernatural mysticism of grace by a leading Neo-Thomist philosopher.

Martz, Louis. *The Poetry of Meditation* (New Haven: Yale University Press, 1962). Deals with English devotional poetry of the Renaissance in light of the literature of mysticism. A groundbreaking book for English literary scholarship.

Merton, Thomas. *The Seven Storey Mountain* (New York: Harcourt, Brace, Jovanovich, 1948; London: SPCK). Autobiography by a major figure in twentieth-century mysticism.

O'Donoghue, Noel. *Heaven in Ordinarie* (Edinburgh: T. & T. Clark, 1979). A deeply considered, striking series of essays on mysticism.

Otto, Rudolf. *The Idea of the Holy*, trans. John W. Harvey (New York: Oxford University Press, 1958). Celebrated account of the *mysterium tremendum et fascinans* in which Otto discovers the ground of holiness.

Panikkar, Raimundo. *The Trinity and the Religious Experience of Man* (London: Darton, Longman and Todd, 1973). An accomplished, thought-provoking synthesis by a comparatist.

Poulain, A. *The Graces of Interior Prayer. A Treatise on Mystical Theology*, trans. Leonora L. Yorke Smith (London: Routledge and Kegan Paul, 1910). Technical, theological descriptions and assessments of the terms and concepts of Western mysticism.

Pourrat, Pierre. *Christian Spirituality in the Middle Ages*, trans. S.P. Jacques (Westminster, Maryland: Newman Press, 1953). A scholarly and influential study of Western spiritual tradition.

Rahner, Karl, et al. *Sacramentum Mundi* (New York: Herder, 1968–70). Sophisticated reference work, with many entries pertinent to mysticism.

Rahner, Karl. *Spirit in the World*, trans. William Dych (New York: Herder, 1968). A searching, technical appraisal of human transcendence towards God from the point of view of Thomist metaphysics.

Scholem, G.G. *Major Trends in Jewish Mysticism* (New York: Schocken Books, 1961). A standard work on this subject.

Smith, Huston. *Forgotten Truth. The Primordial Tradition* (New York: Harper and Row, 1976). A challenging assessment of the limitations of Western science in explaining the religious nature of man.

Staal, Frits. *Exploring Mysticism. A Methodological Essay* (Berkeley: University of California Press, 1975). Cautionary study of linguistic and methodological difficulties of comparative mysticism.

Steiner, Rudolf. *Mysticism and Modern Thought*, trans. George Metaxa (London: Anthroposophical Publishing Co., 1928). Challenging assessment of Western mysticism in context of the rise of science, by the founder of Anthroposophy.

Stoner, Carol, and Jo Ann Parke. *All God's Children* (Harmondsworth: Penguin Books, 1979). Popular, disturbing account of contemporary religious cults and their disastrous effects on some young people. A timely warning against spurious mysticism.

Tournier, Paul. *The Meaning of Persons*, trans. Edwin Hudson (New York: Harper and Row, 1973. First published, 1957). Penetrating but accessible reflections on the spiritual nature of personhood in light of modern science and medicine.

Underhill, Evelyn. *Mysticism. A Study in the Nature and Development of Man's Spiritual Consciousness* (New York: E.P. Dutton, 1961. First published, 1911). Ground-breaking study of the Western mystics by a highly influential and prolific author.

Von Hugel, Baron Friedrich. *The Mystical Element of Religion as Studied in Saint Catherine of Genoa and her Friends* (London: Dent, 1923). A basic study of the interdependence of mystical experience and the Church.

Wainwright, William J. *Mysticism. A Study of its Nature, Cognitive Value and Moral Implications* (Brighton: Harvester Press, 1981). Clear, densely argued philosophical assessment of some major modern descriptions of mysticism.

Watts, Alan. *Behold the Spirit. A Study in the Necessity of Mystical Religion* (New York: Pantheon Books, 1950). A plea for spiritual awareness in the modern age by a popular and prolific author.

Williams, Rowan. *The Wound of Knowledge. Christian Spirituality from the New Testament to St John of the Cross* (London: Darton, Longman and Todd, 1981. First published, 1979). Excellent, learned and readable study of the demanding, transformative nature of Western spirituality.

Wilson, Colin. *Religion and the Rebel* (Boston: Houghton Mifflin, 1957). Pungent, racy account of the mystic as outsider in society.

Zaehner, R.C. *Mysticism Sacred and Profane. An Inquiry into Some Varieties of Praeternatural Experience* (London: Oxford University Press, 1961. First published, 1957). Provocative attempt to distinguish Christian, "theistic" mysticism from varieties of "monism".

Acknowledgements

Permissions to reproduce excerpts have been received from The Catholic University of America Press for Basil the Great, *St Basil. Ascetical Works*, trans. Sister M. Monica Wagner, Fathers of the Church, vol. 9; from Oxford University Press for Charles Williams, *The Image of the City and other Essays*, ed. Anne Ridler; from the Longman Group, Ltd for Origen, *The Song of Songs. Commentary and Homilies*, trans. R.P. Lawson, and for *The Letters of Evelyn Underhill*; from A.D. Peters and Co., Ltd and Random House, Inc. for Arthur Koestler, *Bricks to Babel*; from Adam and Charles Black for Hugh of St Victor, *The Soul's Betrothal Gift*, trans. F. Sherwood Taylor, and for Charles Williams, *Religion and Love in Dante*; from Harper and Row, Inc. and St Paul Publications for Basil Hume, *To Be a Pilgrim. A Spiritual Notebook*; from the Putnam Publishing Group and Routledge and Kegan Paul for Simone Weil, *Waiting on God*, trans. Emma Craufurd, © 1951, renewed 1979 by G.P. Putnam's Sons; from the Franciscan Herald Press for *The Works of St Bonaventure*, trans. José de Vinck; from Cistercian Publications for William of St Thierry, *Exposition on the Song of Songs*, Cistercian Fathers Series, 6, trans. Mother Columba Hart, © 1970; *The Enigma of Faith*, Cistercian Fathers Series, 9, trans. John D. Anderson, © 1974; Aelred of Rievaulx, *Spiritual Friendship*, trans. M. Eugenia Laker, Cistercian Fathers Series, 5, © 1974; from Princeton University Press and Routledge and Kegan Paul for *The Collected Works of C.G. Jung*, trans. R.F.C. Hull, Bollingen Series XX, vol. 8: *The Structure and Dynamics of the Psyche*, copyright © 1960, 1969, by Princeton University Press. Excerpts from *The Silent Life* by Thomas Merton, copyright © 1957 by The Abbey of Our Lady of Gethsemani are reprinted by permission of Ferrar, Straus and Giroux, Inc. Excerpts from Thomas Merton, *New Seeds of Contemplation*, copyright © 1961 by the Abbey of Gethsemani, Inc. are reprinted by permission of New Directions, and Anthony Clarke Books, whose edition is entitled *Seeds of Contemplation*. Excerpts from *Mystical Writings of Rulman Merswin*, edited and interpreted by Thomas S. Kepler, © W.L. Jenkins MCMLX, are used by permission of The Westminster Press, Philadelphia, PA, USA. Excerpts from St Benedict, *Rule for Monasteries*, trans. L. Doyle, copyright © 1948 by The Order of St Benedict, Inc., published by the Liturgical Press, Collegeville, Minnesota, are used with permission. Excerpt from Martin

Buber, *I and Thou*, translated by Walter Kaufmann, translation copyright © 1970 Charles Scribner's Sons; introduction copyright © 1970 Walter Kaufmann is reprinted by permission of Charles Scribner's Sons, and T. and T. Clark. Excerpts from *Richard of St Victor. The Twelve Patriarchs, The Mystical Ark, Book Three of the Trinity*, from the Classics of Western Spirituality Series, trans. Grover A. Zinn, © 1979 by the Missionary Society of St Paul the Apostle in the State of New York are used by permission of the Paulist Press, and The Society for Promoting Christian Knowledge. Excerpts from Pierre Teilhard de Chardin, *Activation of Energy*, trans. René Hague, and *Hymn of the Universe*, trans. Simon Bartholomew, and from C.S. Lewis, *Letters*, are reproduced by permission of William Collins.

I, i, 30 LOVE
pg 43 #28

ECKHART
   pg 204 #2
   pg 270 #15
   pg 323 #1
   pg 342 #29

pg 97 #19